A SYSTEM OF
THE SCIENCE OF MUSIC
AND PRACTICAL COMPOSITION

Da Capo Press Music Reprint Series

GENERAL EDITOR

FRANK D'ACCONE
University of California at Los Angeles

A SYSTEM OF
THE SCIENCE OF MUSIC
AND PRACTICAL COMPOSITION

Incidentally Comprising What is Usually Understood by the Term Thorough Bass

BY

J. B. LOGIER

DA CAPO PRESS • NEW YORK • 1976

Library of Congress Cataloging in Publication Data

Logier, Johann Bernhard, d. 1846.
   A system of the science of music and practical
composition, incidentally comprising what is usually
understood by the term thorough bass.

   Reprint of the 1st ed., 1827, published by J. Green,
London.
   1. Composition (Music) 2. Harmony. I. Title.
MT24.L83 1976b   781.3   76-20715
ISBN 0-306-70793-4

This Da Capo Press edition of *A System of the Science of Music and Practical Composition*
is a republication of the first edition published in London in 1897.
The text incorporates the corrections from the Errata Sheet on page xx.
It is reproduced from an original in the collections of the UCLA Music Library.

Published by Da Capo Press, Inc.
A Subsidiary of Plenum Publishing Corporation
227 West 17th Street, New York, N.Y. 10011

J.R. Maguire, Delt.   *B. Moore, Sculp.*

To the Pupils of Mr. Logier, and to the Professors of The Logierian System of Musical Education, this Print is respectfully inscribed by their &c. &c.

J.R. Maguire

of Dublin.

A

SYSTEM

OF

THE SCIENCE OF MUSIC

AND

PRACTICAL COMPOSITION;

INCIDENTALLY COMPRISING WHAT IS USUALLY UNDERSTOOD BY
THE TERM THOROUGH BASS.

BY

J. B. LOGIER.

LONDON:
PUBLISHED BY J. GREEN, 33, SOHO-SQUARE.
PUBLISHER OF ALL Mr. LOGIER'S WORKS,
MANUFACTURER OF THE PATENT CHIROPLAST OR HAND-DIRECTOR, &c., &c.

THIS WORK IS ALSO PUBLISHED IN THE FRENCH AND GERMAN LANGUAGES:
At *Paris*, by MAURICE SCHLESSINGER, and at *Berlin*, by W. LOGIER.

MDCCCXXVII.

LONDON:
Printed by W. CLOWES,
Stamford-street.

DEDICATED,

(BY PERMISSION,)

TO HIS MOST GRACIOUS MAJESTY,

KING GEORGE THE IV.ᵀᴴ,

BY

THE AUTHOR.

INTRODUCTION.

IT is a duty incumbent on every member of a community to contribute, according to the best of his abilities, to the advancement of that Art or Science which he himself professes; and though he may meet with obstacles and opposition, which those who deviate from the beaten path most frequently experience, this should not deter him from steadily pursuing his object, and following the impulse of his honest inclination.

It has often been lamented, that Books of Instruction on scientific subjects have been written in terms not sufficiently intelligible to the uninitiated. Should the Author be fortunate enough, by the present work, to render less abstruse the interesting subject of the Science of Music, he will feel himself amply repaid for any trouble which may have been bestowed upon it. One difficulty must ever be experienced by writers on such subjects:—in oral instruction, the Teacher is enabled to vary his mode of expression, and suit his examples in illustration of his subject, to the different capacities of his pupils: in a written work he is deprived of this advantage, and must in the same terms address all his readers; thus, it may be found that, even after the utmost care, he will be censured by one as having been prolix, whilst another complains of his brevity.

The Author's system of Musical Education comprises three distinct branches :—the art of playing on the Pianoforte (in the elementary part of which is employed the chiroplast);—Harmony and Composition;—and the peculiar method by which the instruction is conveyed to pupils.

b 2

The first part has been long before the Public, under the title of " The First and Second Companions to the Chiroplast," with their " Sequels"*.

The two other branches it was the Author's intention to have united; but, on further reflection, and at the suggestion of some friends upon whose judgment he has implicit reliance, he has detached the latter part, which is separately published, under the title of " The Manual," for the convenience of those who are disposed to make themselves acquainted with his method of giving instructions, and which will be found to approach as near as possible to the style of *viva voce* instruction adopted in Academies.

The present work, therefore, must be considered as relating solely to Music as a Science, and the application of that science to practical composition.

No previous knowledge of music is required in order to commence the study of the science from this work, except a slight acquaintance with introductory matters already explained in the First Companion to the Chiroplast, or which may be found in any common instruction-book, as the Staff, Clefs, Time-Table, &c.†: nor is it necessary that the student should be possessed of that particular talent and genius for music which is generally supposed to be requisite ; it will be seen that the rules from the commencement arise so progressively and obviously out of each other, as to be comprehensible to minds of very moderate capacity, producing of themselves effects always pleasing as well as correct.

A short summary of the plan may not be uninteresting, as it may serve to give a general idea of the work before perusal.

Instead of commencing (as has been usual) with the different intervals and their various modifications, sharp, extreme sharp, flat, and diminished, the Chords major, minor, and imperfect, &c. &c., which would rather have the effect of obscuring than elucidating the subject, the student is first made acquainted with the construction of the Diatonic Scale (page 1),

---

* *Note of the Publisher.*—The degree of approbation with which Mr. Logier's Elementary Works have been favoured may be best estimated by the simple statement, that nearly 70,000 copies have been sold in these kingdoms alone.

† A separate sheet, printed uniformly with this work, may be had of the Publisher, containing the rudiments here omitted, together with much other information useful to a young composer.

with an easy method of finding and recollecting the sharps and flats belonging to each key (p. 4).

Having constructed a common chord (11), an unerring rule is given for accompanying a simple melody with a Bass (14). By the addition of the common chord, a simple and natural harmony is produced (18), which, when heard for the first time, never fails to excite a considerable degree of interest, still further increased by the construction of Variations (24).

The simplicity of the harmony thus produced by the three Fundamental Basses, consisting only of common chords, will be found to prepare the ear for the variety of effects which immediately follow.

The prevention of Consecutive Fifths and Eighths (20) introduces a new interval, the Fundamental Seventh, producing the *chord* of the Fundamental Seventh, followed by its resolution (25 to 28). Here the harmony begins to acquire a higher degree of interest; for the fundamental seventh, which has hitherto appeared on the seventh of the scale only, is now introduced in other situations (32). Melodies are harmonized with the addition of this fundamental seventh, by which a new effect is produced (33). The simple rules by which certain intervals of the scale may be differently accompanied (35 to 41), without any addition to the number of Fundamental Basses, are calculated to afford a wider scope; and a new and extensive field is opened to the student on being made acquainted with Modulation (53). In the introduction to this important branch of harmony, he is shewn the original source from which are derived the Fundamental Basses, and the Diatonic Scale (47).

The Author has not considered it necessary to write a treatise on Acoustics, that subject having been ably treated by several celebrated authors. He has merely availed himself of as much of it as was necessary to illustrate the principles upon which his system is founded.

The student is next made acquainted with Dissonances (62). He will perceive that these give to the harmony a higher degree of light and shade, which commenced with the introduction of the Fundamental Seventh.

To this point all exercises have been written with fundamental harmonies only, but now the Bass by inversion participates in the general variety,

(73, also 99,) effects an interchange of character, and the four parts afterwards move in flowing and graceful melodies (111 and 112). Double Counterpoint in the octave is also produced, between the alto and tenor, by a simple process, and a new and striking effect is the consequence (118).

Thus far the work has advanced without deviating from the fundamental law of nature, as discovered in the vibration of a string, and the student is now prepared for the introduction of that which is more artificial. The most striking deviation from the path which he has hitherto pursued is the Minor Scale (102), from the agreeable variety produced by a mixture of major and minor chords, together with the introduction of a new chord, the Minor Ninth, with its four inversions, arises a new and striking feature in the succeeding harmony (122 to 136). The greater part of those airs which were before employed, may now be reharmonized by changing the key from major to minor; and a number of beautiful and effective modulations naturally arise out of the chord of the Minor Ninth.

Modulation by the intervals of a melody opens a most interesting field of harmony, with new combinations and effects, the rules of which may be said to contain within themselves a fund of musical beauty and variety (137 to 149). In page 150 is introduced the chord of the sharp sixth, and in page 152 the compound sharp sixth, by the addition of which, the means of producing new effects are considerably augmented, as shewn in the minor airs which immediately follow. After harmonizing airs in the alto and tenor (162), the student is made acquainted with the method of harmonizing a melody in the Bass, which will be found particularly useful to those who are desirous of playing from figured Basses.

Here is introduced another new and important branch of the subject, Passing and Auxiliary Notes, (or, in other words, notes of embellishment,) and secondary harmonies (171). These notes of embellishment, introduced among the simple notes of a melody, afford a higher degree of refinement; in exercising upon which, the former Themes may again be most effectively employed.

The student is now shown how he may employ some part of the knowledge which he has acquired in writing for the Pianoforte in the style of variations, which will be found a very fertile and agreeable subject (188). The chords of the eleventh and thirteenth are explained, both of which will be found subsequently introduced in airs arranged for the Pianoforte (196 to 203).

The variety of Cadences which follow from Example 276; the different motions in harmony (Ex. 326), and prevention of 5ths and 8ths (Ex. 327), seem to form no connecting link in this chain of instructions. They may be considered as isolated parts of the Treatise, and are referred to as occasion occurs.

Modulation, that most interesting subject, which has been already treated upon in several parts of this work, here concludes, with equivocal, deceptive, and protracted Modulations (Ex. 295 to 304).

However extraordinary it may appear, yet still it is true that all the variety of harmony which has been employed up to the present time has been derived solely from two original Fundamental Basses, the *Tonic* and the *Dominant* (Ex. 64)*. The student, however, at this point is made acquainted with Basses, by which the harmony of the scale receives a certain degree of modification; that is, Basses will now be admitted which are not to be found amongst the harmonics produced by the vibration of a string. With the assistance of the harmonies arising from these Basses, the student is enabled to modify the uniformity of effect produced, particularly by major keys (Ex. 305).

Now follow Sequences of 7ths, the grand source from which the ancient church-composers drew their themes for Fugue and imitation. The effect of these sequences is bold and majestic, and by being diametrically opposed to modulation, they are calculated to make a novel and strong impression, when judiciously interwoven with softer harmonies. Preparatory to the construction of melodies by the student, the different descriptions of Time are explained, with Rhythm, and musical Periods (Ex. 332, 360). Here a simple method of sketching the groundwork of a Melody is pointed out (Ex. 361). The specimens as far as Ex. 378 will be sufficient to show the vast resources of the science; the path which lies before the student is now indeed

---

* The Subdominant being, in point of fact, the Tonic of its own scale. (Ex. 67.)

unlimited in extent, and presents to his view an inexhaustible field of variety*.

Analyzation concludes the whole: by this he will discover the peculiar beauties and excellencies of the works of ancient and modern composers, their ingenious contrivances, and their peculiar manner of treating their subjects.

In presenting this work to the public, the Author does not arrogate to himself the discovery of new principles in harmony†,—he merely endeavours to develop a method simple and efficacious, by which the principles already established may be more easily comprehended and effectually put into practice.

The course of Lectures by which the Author has, during so many years, conveyed his instructions to his pupils, is here faithfully delineated; and as a single example is often found to be more advantageous than pages of explanation, he has not been sparing of that method of illustrating the subject.

His not having quoted the works of other writers on this subject he trusts will not be attributed to any want of respect: it will be perceived that the plan of his work did not admit of it.

In conclusion, he begs leave to observe, that it is not his desire to appear before the public as a literary character, to which he lays no claim. His only object has been to convey his ideas in simple and intelligible language, and to be useful to those who are desirous of studying the Science of Music; the public he trusts will accept his endeavours and do him justice.

---

* See concluding observation, page 320.

† As will be seen by his " Theoretical and Practical Studies," wherein the works of ancient and modern writers have been analyzed, according to the principles here assumed.

TABLE OF CONTENTS.

The Reader is requested to correct with a Pen the following Errata.

Page	Line from the top	IS	OUGHT TO BE
4,	8,	From the first and second . . .	From the first to the second.
7,	15,	From A	From A ♭.
13,	note,	See remarks on Example 69 . .	See note ‡, page 49.
17,	15,	Example 22	Example 24.
21,	note*,	Example 49	Example 327.
28,	7th staff,	Bar 5, E♯	F♯.
33,	2d ,,	,, 4, A	C.
39,	bass staff,	,, 7, ...	First E to be figured $\frac{6}{4}$.
43,	6,	Whence	Which.
44,	4th staff,	Bar 1, $\frac{6}{X}$	$\frac{5}{X}$.
,,	,,	,, 5, ...	The F♭ to be figured $^♭$5$_♭$.
49,	2, 12, 29,	Harmonies	Harmonics.
50,	1st staff,	Bar 5, 3rd chord, G♭, A, and D	G♭, A, and C.
57,	note*,	See explanation of Major and Minor half tones	{ From C to C♯ is a minor semitone. From C to D♭ is a major do.
81,		Between lines 21 and 22 insert .	And this shall be a minor chord.
,,	23,	This last chord	the present dominant which shall be minor, and
88,	2 last staffs,	Quaver rests	Crotchet rests.
89,	Staff 1,	The third D A in bar 2.	F D in alt.
,,	,, 7,	Bar 4, Semiquavers	Demisemiquavers.
,,	,, 10,	,, 4, ...	Add a crotchet rest after the last crotchet.
91,	,, 2,	,, 1, E	E♭.
,,	,, 7,	,, 2, B	B♭.
92,	,, 3,	,, 1, ...	Before the last G place a ♮.
130,	,, 4,	,, 2, ...	B♭ to be figured ✕.
136,		N.B. resumed at Ex. 207. . .	205.
138,	,, 6,	Bar 3, F	D.
140,	,, 2,	,, 3, ...	C to be figured $\frac{4}{♭}$♯.
155,	,, 4,	,, 5, ...	Two C's to be figured $\frac{6}{4}$—$\frac{5}{♮}$.
,,	,, 8,	,, 7, ...	C to be figured $\frac{7}{♮}$.
,,	,, 12,	,, 1, Omit the figuring over A♭ .	Place the same over G.
158,	,, 2,	,, 1, B, B, B.	D. D. D.
168,	,, 4,	,, 2, ...	D to be figured $\frac{7}{♯}$.
189,		Paco	Poco
217 to 222,		. . . .	To be headed, EQUIVOCAL MODULATION.
224,	Staff 8,	Treble Clef	Bass Clef.
274,	,, 2,	. . . .	Signature required ♭$^♭_♭$.
275,	,, 2,	Bar 6, The second E	D.
278,	Line 1,	" from page"	" at page"
279,	Staff 1,	Bar 8, B	B♮.
,,	,, 2,	,, 8, ...	Figuring ought to be ♮$\frac{9}{4}$♯ $\frac{8}{3}$

A

TREATISE

ON

THE SCIENCE OF MUSIC.

The Scale, or Musical Alphabet.

MUSIC may be considered as a language whose alphabet consists of only seven sounds; by the different combinations of which all musical effects are produced. When these seven sounds are arranged in the following order, they are called

A Scale.

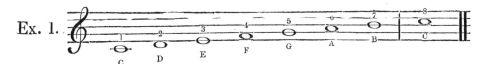

Ex. 1.

The *eighth* sound, (or octave) bears the same name as the *first*, and must be considered merely as a repetition of that sound. In the same manner, were we still further to ascend in the scale, the *9th* would be a repetition of the *2d*, the *10th* would be a repetition of the *3d*, and thus we might continue to repeat the alphabet.

This, perhaps, may be more clearly understood by reflecting, that we always consider any letter as the same in sound, whether it be written large or small A A a *or* a; thus the following example (being the notes representing the white keys of the piano-forte) is merely

B

A Continued Repetition of the First Seven Sounds.

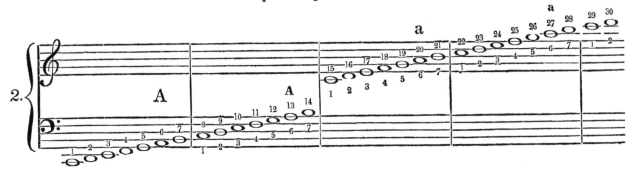

Now let us minutely examine Example 1, which is called

The Diatonic Scale.

On looking at the keys of the piano-forte, we perceive that between the first note C, and the second note D, there occurs a black key, which is called C♯.

Thus then we will say it is *a whole tone* from C to D, because there is a note half way called C♯.

From D to E is also *a whole tone*, because D♯ occurs between them.

From E to F is only *a half tone*, as there is no sound between them.

From F to G is *a whole tone:*

And so with the rest, except from B to C, which we find is only *a half tone.*

To shew this at one view, let us again write the scale, and wherever a whole tone occurs, we will insert the sound which intervenes, as in the lower staff of the following Example, which forms the *Ascending* Chromatic Scale hereafter referred to.

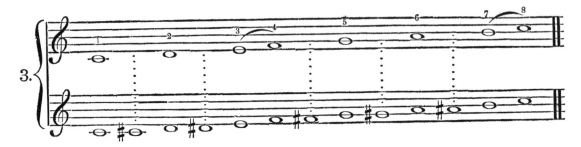

Should it be required of us to explain " What is the Diatonic Scale?" it may be thus described :—

" The Diatonic Scale consists of seven sounds, and an eighth, which is merely a repetition of the first. These sounds are disposed at intervals of whole tones and half tones, and the half tones occur between the 3d and 4th, and the 7th and 8th !"

Thus are formed all Diatonic Scales, at what note soever they may commence: Suppose we commence the scale at **D.**

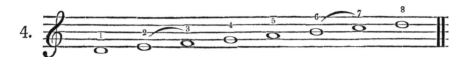

On examining the keys of the piano-forte, we shall find that in the above scale, *as it stands at present,* the half tones *do not* occur where they ought, according to our model. We find them here between the 2d and 3d, and between the 6th and 7th, as marked by the curved lines.

It is necessary, therefore, to raise the F and C a half tone, by placing a sharp before each of them, and when thus corrected, it forms

The Diatonic Scale of D.

From E to F was before (in Example 4) only a half tone.

But *between the 2d and 3d of the scale should be a whole tone,* therefore, by placing a sharp before the F, we have raised it half a tone, and from E to F♯ being now a whole tone, this part of the scale is correct.

From B to C the same circumstance again occurs, and is treated exactly in the same manner.

It will be now perceived *why* TWO sharps are used in the key of **D.**

They are necessary to *preserve the order of the Diatonic Scale.*

On the model above described, the learner should proceed to form correct scales, commencing at G, A, E, and B, each of which will require a different number of sharps.

The first sound of any Scale is called the Key-note.

Thus, in the last Example, the key-note is **D**, and all the notes in that scale are said to be in the *key of D.*

B 2

On referring to the analysis of the Diatonic Scale, Example 3, it will be perceived that the lower staff contains twelve sounds[*], (independently of the last, which is merely a repetition of the first.)

Each of these twelve sounds may be employed as a key-note for the formation of a new scale.

Let us take, for instance, F♯.

From F♯ to G is only a half tone, but, as the order of the Diatonic Scale requires that *from the first and second of the scale should be a whole tone,* we must raise the G by placing a sharp before it.

For the same reason we must place also a ♯ before the A, C, D, and E.

It will be here remarked, that by raising the E a half tone, it becomes the same sound on the piano-forte as F[†]; but in this scale the F must be sharp, which leaves the proper interval of a half tone between the 7th and 8th of the scale.

In forming the scale of C♯ a similar circumstance occurs on raising the B, which becomes the same sound, on the piano-forte, as C♮.

For exercise, we may go still further, and form scales which require double sharps; for instance, in the key of G♯, we require a double sharp to be placed before F[‡].

In the key of D♯, both F and C will require double sharps.

Method of impressing on the Memory the number of Sharps belonging to each Key.

The perfect recollection of the sharps required in any key, will be found to afford a considerable facility in our further progress.

The following method of accomplishing so desirable a purpose, it is hoped, will not be the less acceptable on account of its simplicity; it has been found by experience to remove every difficulty, although in itself it may be made a mere matter of amusement even to children.

The left hand being held open with the palm towards the face, after having given the name of C to the elbow, let us call the thumb G.

The first finger	D.
The second finger . . .	A.
The third finger	E.
The fourth finger . . .	B.

---

[*] This is called the Chromatic Scale, and proceeds by intervals of half tones only.

[†] This is called an Enharmonic Change. See Example 11.

[‡] To spare the trouble of writing two sharps, a cross (×) is used to represent a double sharp.

The fourth finger of the right hand (to complete the circle) we shall call F.

By holding up the thumb (G) alone, we are reminded that the key of G requires only *one* sharp.

The first finger (D) being held up, (without removing the thumb,) reminds us that there are *two* sharps in the key of D.

When the second finger (A) is also held up, we see *three* fingers, and the key of A has *three* sharps.

How many sharps are in the key of E ? We raise the third finger, which, with three before it, makes *four*, and we answer—Four.

How many sharps in the key of B ? Five.

The order in which the Notes requiring Sharps occur in each Key.

In the circle of fingers above described, for the *order of the sharps*, begin always with the little finger of the right hand (F), then the left elbow (C), then proceed with the thumb, first finger, second, third, and fourth—for instance :—

When *one* sharp only is required it must be F♯, (the little finger of the right hand.)

Two sharps must be F♯ and C♯.

The key of A requires *three* sharps, F♯, C♯, and G♯.

The key of F♯ has *six* sharps, F♯, C♯, G♯, D♯, A♯, E♯.

Proceeding thus round the circle.

By placing a sharp *before the key-note* of any scale, we add *seven* sharps more to the number belonging to that scale—for instance :—

The key of G has *one* sharp, the key of G♯ requires *seven more, i. e., eight sharps*[*].

By the foregoing method of recollecting the sharps belonging to each key, we are enabled more readily to form the Diatonic Scales, by adding the sharps as they present themselves on the fingers, without the necessity of examining each interval.

Examination of the Diatonic Scale, Descending.

Let us write the Descending Scale of C, and proceed to analyze it in the same manner as we have done the Ascending Scale.

---

[*] As there are only seven sounds in the Diatonic Scale, if more than seven sharps are used, some of the notes will necessarily have two sharps, or, (as it is called) a double sharp. The double sharps follow in the same order as the single sharps; for instance, in the key of D there are two sharps, F♯ and C♯; in the key of D♯ there are nine sharps, and the notes requiring double sharps are F and C.

From C to B is a half tone, from B to A is a whole tone, because a black key lies between them ; this black key being half a tone below B, is here called B flat, as we are now descending ; the same black key was called A♯ in the Ascending Scale, being half a tone above A.

From A to G is a whole tone. The black key which is found between those two notes is, of course, here called A♭, and not G♯, as formerly in the Ascending Scale ; and thus proceed with the rest.

From this examination arises a *descending* Chromatic Scale, in which *flats* are employed. On referring to Example 3, it will be perceived that SHARPS were employed in forming the same scale ASCENDING.

Each of the sounds of the above descending Chromatic Scale also may be taken as a key-note. Let us take, for instance, E flat.

What is the distance from E♭ to F? A whole tone.
Is this correct? Yes.
Why? Because *between the first and second of the scale ought to be a whole tone.*
From F to G? A whole tone.
Is this correct? Yes.
From G to A? A whole tone. This is not correct, because *between the 3d and 4th of the scale should only be a half tone.*
How shall we reduce this to a half tone? By placing a flat before the A ; from G to A♭ will be then only a half tone, which is correct, (see the following Example.)
From A♭ to B? This is a distance of *three* half tones.
What ought it to be between the 4th and 5th of the scale? It ought to be only *two* half tones, or, in other words, a whole tone.
How can we reduce it to a whole tone? By placing a flat before B. Thus from A♭ to B♭ is a whole tone, and it is now correct.

How much is it now from B♮ to C? A whole tone, and correct.

From C to D? The same.

From D to E? A whole tone. This is wrong, as *from the 7th to the 8th should be only a half tone.*

How is it corrected? By placing a flat before the E, which thus becomes the same as the first, and completes

The Scale of E♭.

As the opposite effect of a ♭ and a ♯ must now be clearly understood, as well as the principle upon which the Diatonic Scale is formed, no difficulty can possibly arise in writing a scale upon any given key-note, and it will be useful as exercise to write scales requiring double flats.—For instance :—

Why is a double flat placed before the B? Because it was necessary to lower it two half tones, from A♭ to B♮ being three half tones, and *between the 3d and 4th of the scale ought only to be one.*

Method of recollecting the Flats belonging to each Key, and the order in which they occur,—by means of the Fingers.

The order of the flats will be found to be merely the reverse of that of the sharps.

In the circle of fingers, we before set out from C, (which we call the natural key, requiring neither sharp nor flat,) and proceeded first to the thumb G, requiring *one* sharp, then to the first finger D with *two,* &c. &c.

For the flat keys we now pursue the contrary direction ; setting out as before from C, we proceed first to the fourth finger of the right hand, and say, F requires *one flat.* Then to the fourth finger of the left hand (B), which, with all that follow, must be flatted. Thus we say, the key of B♭ has *two flats,* E♭ has *three flats,* A♭ has *four,* D♭ *five,* G♭ *six,* and C♭ *seven.*

We have found by the circle of fingers that the *first* note made sharp is **F**, the fourth finger of the right hand; the second **C**; the third **G**; &c.

We now, for the order of the flats, commence with the fourth finger of the left-hand (B.)

Thus when only one note is made flat, it must be **B**; two flats, **B♭**, and **E♭**; three flats, **B♭**, **E♭**, and **A♭**; &c., &c., thus proceeding the reverse way round the circle. Exercise thus:

What number of flats are required in the key of D♭?

Hold up the Fourth   Finger   of the Right-Hand with
     the Fourth   „
     the Third   „
     the Second   „   } of the Left-Hand.
And the First   „ (D)

These *five* fingers point out that the key of D♭ requires *five* flats.

What notes are made flat? (Begin with the fourth finger of the left-hand, going the same way round the circle, and answer) B♭, E♭, A♭, D♭, and G♭.

Double flats are found in the same manner as the double sharps.

The key of F requires one flat.

The key of F♭ will require seven more, *i. e.*, eight flats.

The key of E♭ requires three flats.

The key of E♭♭ ten flats.

The first note made flat, is also the first to be made double flat, and so on in the same routine again round the circle.

Enharmonic Changes.

It will have been already perceived in analyzing the Diatonic Scale ascending (page 2), and descending (page 6), that each sound on the piano-forte may have two different names, for instance, the black key between G and A may be called G♯, because it is half a tone *above* G, or A♭ because it is a half tone *below* A.

This is called an Enharmonic Change, thus F♯ changed enharmonically becomes G♭. The Enharmonic Change of A♯ is B♭; D♭ becomes C♯; and A♭ becomes G♯: In like manner also B♯ enharmonically changed becomes C, and by the same rule F♭ must be the same sound as E.

For exercise, whole scales may be changed Enharmonically; thus the scale of D♯ changed Enharmonically becomes the scale of E♭.

Whilst upon this subject, we may take the opportunity of shewing how the Enharmonic Changes, being placed in order with the Chromatic Scale, form another, called the Enharmonic, Scale, which, though at present of no practical utility, may in future be referred to.

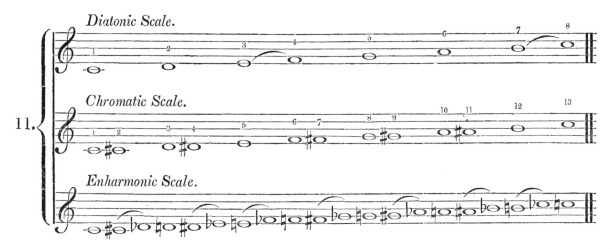

It will assist the memory, and serve as an amusing exercise, if we here observe that any key with a certain number of sharps when changed Enharmonically, will require as many flats as will make that number 12, and *vice versâ*—thus:

The key of C♯ has seven sharps, therefore its Enharmonic Change D♭ must have *five* flats.

The key of A♭ has four flats, and its Enharmonic Change G♯ must have eight sharps, &c., &c.

To shew much of the preceding matter in another point of view, let us divide a circle into 12 equal parts, representing the 12 keys, as in the following Ex. 12.

The numbers from 1 to 6 to the *right-hand* point out the keys with *sharps*, and those to the *left* shew the keys which require *flats*, commencing in both cases with the key of C, represented by a cipher as having no sharps nor flats.

By taking our course thus, from C, to the right, we perceive that the key of G has one sharp, D has two sharps, A three sharps, &c., &c.

Proceeding to the left, we find the key of F has one flat; B♭ has two flats; E♭ has three flats, &c., &c.

In this circle of keys it will be perceived that the numbers proceeding by different routes meet at 6, where an Enharmonic Change naturally takes place, for the key which has 6 sharps, and the one which has 6 flats are the same key on the piano-forte.

12.

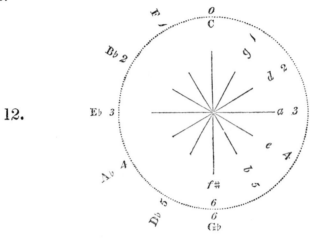

However, instead of thus making an Enharmonic Change at 6, were we to continue the figures completely round the circle to 13, we should pass through all the keys with double sharps and double flats, thus:

13.

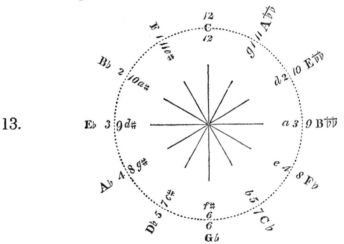

The above arrangement shews also the Enharmonic Change of each key; for instance:

The key of A♯ has 10 sharps; the Enharmonic Change of A♯ is B♭, which has 2 flats, &c., &c.

Having already compared the musical *scale* to an *alphabet*, we may now consider a *chord* as a *word* in the language of music.

A combination of letters selected from the alphabet forms a word.

A combination of notes selected from the scale forms a chord.

Let us write any Diatonic Scale, and select the 1st, 3d, and 5th notes, placing them one over the other, which is the method of writing when several sounds are intended to be heard at the same time.

The Common Chord extracted from the Scale.

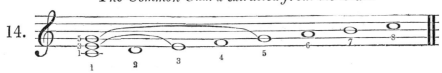

Whatever common chord we propose to write, (that it may be clearly understood) let us first write the scale of the key note of that chord, with the necessary sharps and flats, and then selecting the 1st, 3d, and 5th sounds, place them each over the other, as above.

The Common Chord of A extracted from its Scale.

To this combination may at any time be added the 8th, (or octave), it being merely a repetition of the 1st, thus:

Common Chord of E♭.

After sufficient exercise in thus extracting the common chord from different scales, the writing of the scale may be discontinued, and the chord may be written from reflection only; thus for instance, if the chord of E is required, write at once over each other the 1st, 3d, and 5th, as they arise, E, G, and B.

The key of E having four sharps, (F♯, C♯, G♯, and D♯), the G in the chord being one of these, must, of course, be made sharp, and thus the chord of E will be correct, E, G♯, AND B*.

---

* It is particularly recommended, for many useful purposes hereafter shewn, that in naming the notes of the common chord a strong emphasis should always be laid on this word " *And.* "

C 2

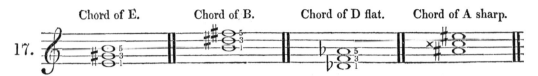

Bass of the Common Chord.

Every chord is supposed to have a Bass, on which it is founded*.

This Bass note, which is also called the fundamental Bass, is always the same as the first note of the scale from which the chord is taken; thus, the Bass to the chord of C, is C. The Bass to the chord of D, is D, &c., &c. Hereafter we shall write the Bass notes of the chords on a separate staff beneath, thus:

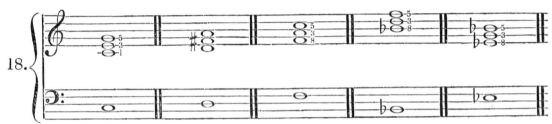

We always consider the Bass note as the first, from which all the others arise; therefore, the lowest note of the chord, before marked with the figure 1, now becoming the 8th to the Bass note, we shall hereafter continue to figure it with an 8, as in the latter chords of the above example.

It is recommended, as an exercise, first to write on the Bass staff a number of notes, and afterwards add (in the upper or Treble staff,) the proper chords, in a manner similar to the above, always preserving the order $\frac{5}{3}$.

The three Positions of the Common Chord.

As the Common Chord has been hitherto written, the 5th has always appeared the highest note, but the three sounds of this chord may interchange places; that is, the 3d, 5th, and 8th, may alternately appear in the upper, lower, or middle part of the chord.

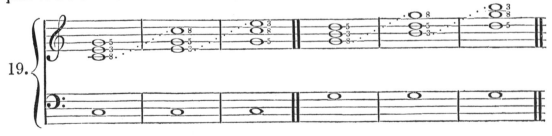

---

* This will be more particularly explained hereafter.

Let it be understood that when the 3rd is at the top of the chord, it is called the *first* position; when the 5th is there, it is called the *second* position; and when the 8th is there, it is called the *third* position*.

Melody and Harmony.

Melody is a succession of single sounds.

Harmony is a succession of *combined* sounds, or chords.

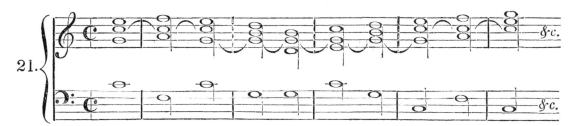

Such a succession of *chords* is similar to a sentence, which is a succession of *words ;* and, as between the words of a sentence there mus tbe some connexion to produce sense, so also it is necessary that a succession of chords should be similarly linked together.

The connexion required in this case is, that some one note at least of every chord shall be found in the chord which precedes it, and also in the chord which immediately succeeds it, as is pointed out by the curved lines in the above example.

A melody is said to be harmonized when properly accompanied by chords ; but before we can know the proper chords, it is necessary first

To find the Fundamental Basses to the Scale.

Let us take the scale as a melody to be harmonized, and, in order to find the Fundamental Basses, let us write over the notes the figures 8, 5, 3, repeated, as in the following example†.

---

* A reason for this arrangement may be seen in the introduction to Modulation.
See ~~remarks on Ex. 69.~~
note †, page 49

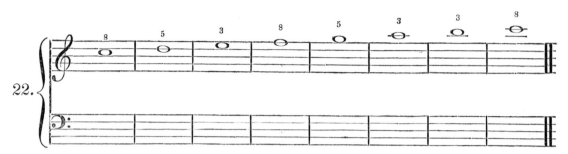

The figure 8 being placed over the first note, the 8th, or octave, must be written under it as the Bass.

The 5 over D directs the fifth note below it to be written in the Bass. To make sure of being correct, in the beginning commence by the note itself, D, calling that 1, and then count down 2, 3, 4, 5, pausing on the 5th below D, (which is G), write down G in the Bass staff underneath the D; and so with the rest, which when complete will appear thus.

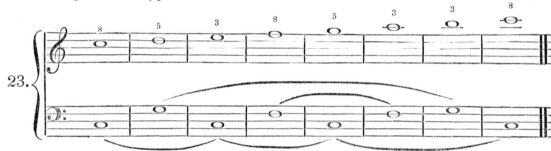

These then are the Fundamental Basses of the scale.

It will be perceived that there are only three different Bass notes. C is employed four times, G twice, and F twice.

Each of these three Fundamental Basses has its peculiar name.

The first is called the *Tonic*, which is always the same as the *Tone* which gives name to the scale; thus, the above example is the scale of C, consequently the Tonic in this scale must be C.

The second Fundamental Bass is called the *Dominant*, which *governs* all proceedings in modulation; it is the same as the fifth sound in the ascending scale, and may be also recollected by its being the last note spoken in pronouncing the common chord—always immediately following the emphatical word, " and."

Thus, to find the Dominant in the key of C, say the chord of C is C, E, AND G; therefore G is the Dominant.

The third Fundamental Bass is called the *Sub-dominant*, as it is the note in the scale immediately *under* the *Dominant :* or, perhaps it may easily be recollected as being a *whole tone* under the Dominant.

In the key of C, as in the preceding example, the Sub-dominant is F, because F is a *whole tone* under the Dominant G.

The Basses to other scales should, as an exercise, be now found by the same method as in Ex. 23.

Having first found the Basses as above directed, let us now figure the intervals of the scale in their proper progression, 1—2—3—4—5—6—7—8, in order to see which notes are accompanied by the Tonic, Dominant, or Sub-dominant.

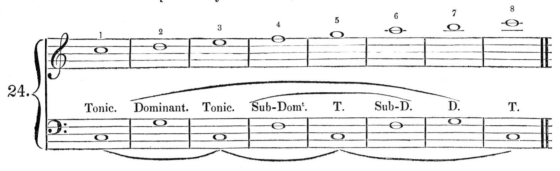

Here the Basses are placed as discovered in Ex. 23, and on examination we find that

    The 1st, 3rd, 5th, and 8th of the Scale are accompanied by the *Tonic*.

    The 2nd and 7th   .   .   .   .   . by the *Dominant*.

    The 4th and 6th   .   .   .   . by the *Sub-dominant*.

The Fundamental Basses to other scales ought now to be found by this method only, discontinuing the use of the figures 8—5—3 as at first employed.

Let us take, for instance, the scale of A.

First let us inquire, what are the three Bass notes belonging to this key.

    The key being A;   .   .   . the *Tonic* must be the same, *A*.

    The chord of A is A, C♯ *and* E; the *Dominant* therefore is . *E*.

    A whole tone below E is D; . the *Sub-dominant* therefore is *D*.

Having written the Scale of A in the Treble Staff, we proceed to write the Basses, as in Ex. 25, reasoning thus :—

    A the 1st of the Scale is accompanied by the Tonic   .   . A.

    B the 2nd   .   .   . by the Dominant . E.

    C♯ the 3rd   .   .   . by the Tonic   . . A.

    D the 4th .   .   . . by the Sub-dominant D.

    E the 5th   .   .   . by the Tonic   . . A.

    F♯ the 6th   .   .   . . by the Sub-dominant D.

    G♯ the 7th   .   .   . by the Dominant . E.

    A the 8th   .   .   . . by the Tonic   . . A.

Thus will have been found the proper Basses to the scale of A.

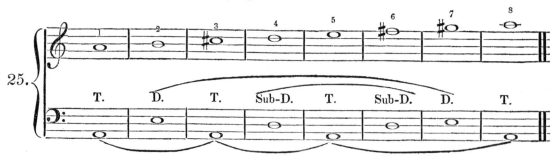

In the same manner, proceed to write the Basses to other scales.

Before proceeding to find the basses to other melodies, we shall spare ourselves some trouble by explaining here what is called

The Signature.

This is the *Sign* by which the key is known; that is, the number of sharps or flats belonging to the key, placed at the beginning of every staff, instead of being written before each note, which would occasion much inconvenience both to the composer and performer.

Thus in future, when we write a melody in the key of G, (which requires every F to be made sharp) instead of placing a sharp before every F as often as that note may occur in the course of the melody—we shall only place the sharp at the beginning of each staff, and this serves to make sharp every F which may be found on that staff.

If the melody is in the key of B♭, we shall place two flats at the beginning of the staff, *i. e.* one upon the third line, where B is written, and the other above the fourth line, where E is written. Proceed in the same manner with every other key; taking care to write the sharps or flats in the order in which they arise on the fingers, thus:

To find the fundamental Basses to other Melodies.

We have hitherto taken only the ascending scale as a theme, to which we found the Basses—but any other progression of notes must be treated in exactly *the same manner.*

If no other notes are used than those which belong to any given scale or key, the melody is said to be written in that key—for instance—in the following example no notes are used but such as belong to the scale of C, consequently we say this melody is in the key of C.

We may know this also from there being neither sharps nor flats placed at the beginning of the staff, which is the natural signature of the key of C*.

The key being ascertained, we must call to mind the three fundamental basses belonging to that key—thus,

In the key of C,

The Tonic is C, which is used to accompany the 1st, 3rd, 5th, and 8th, of the scale.

The Dominant is G . . . 2nd, and 7th.

The Sub-dominant is F . . . 4th, and 6th.

When a melody is given to be harmonized, examine each note, and remark what interval of the scale it is, and when that is known, the bass belonging to it is also known, by the rule at Example 2 .

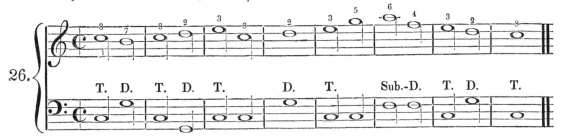

The first note C is the *first or eighth* of the scale, and requires the Tonic.

The following note is B, which is the *seventh* of the scale, and requires the Dominant, and so on†.

After having acquired, by sufficient practice, a readiness in distinguishing what part of the scale any note is, we may dispense with figuring the melody, and put at once the bass to each note as we proceed with the examination, thus—

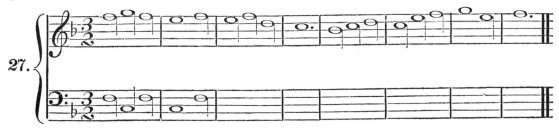

* An observation which might occur here, will be found in a more appropriate place.

† A variety of melodies proper for exercise at this and different subsequent stages will be separately published for the use of private students, and to spare preceptors the loss of time in writing themes for every pupil on every occasion.

D

We perceive this melody is in the key of **F**, from the signature, one flat.   The first note F is the 8th of the scale, and requires the Tonic F.

The second note G, is the 2nd of the scale, and requires the Dominant.

The third note F is the 8th, and requires the Tonic.

E is the 7th, and requires the Dominant, *&c., &c., &c.*

Writing the Common Chords to the Fundamental Basses.

When we have discovered the Fundamental Basses to a melody, they point out to us the chord which must accompany every note.

The Common Chord of each *Bass note* must be written under the note of the melody; which will itself be one of the intervals of the chord.

By way of exercise, let us write again the Scale of C; then write the Bass notes as before; after which add the chords; thus—

28.

The first Bass is C, consequently the chord must be C, E, and G:—C, the 8th, being already written in the melody, we add the 3rd E, and the 5th G; and thus the chord is complete, always letting the melody be the highest note, and writing the others, as near to it as possible, underneath.

It is also advisable to write down the notes of the chord, in the order we have been accustomed to pronounce them.   Thus, with the second Bass G, the chord must be G, B, and D.   Write first the G; then the B; and the D is already in the melody.

In this manner, exercise on different ascending Scales and Melodies written for this purpose*.   It is also recommended frequently to refresh the memory as to the three different positions of the Common Chord (explained at page 12), and in the course of these exercises to mark by a figure in which position each chord is written.

Consecutive 5ths and 8ths.

Let us now particularly examine the chain of connexion between the chords in the above Example (28), as marked by the curved lines.

It will be perceived that the G in the first chord, forms a part of the second,

---

* See Exercises, Class 1.

and the same note is continued in the third chord.—The C in the third chord is the connecting link with the fourth, &c., &c.

But no connexion is found between the 6th and 7th; here, according to our rule, the sense of the sentence is interrupted, and on being played it will produce a corresponding effect upon the ear. The fault lies in what is called consecutive fifths and octaves. They may be allowed to remain in the exercises on the scales up to this point, marking however the place where they occur by a ×.

But we will now explain this fault and the method of avoiding it.

Return to the last Example (28), and suppose four persons to *sing* this progression of harmony.

The *first* person would sing all the *highest* notes of the chords which, in this example, form the Scale of C. This we shall call the first part.

The *second* voice would take the range of notes next underneath.

The *third* part consists of that row of notes which is next above the Bass—and

The *fourth* part is the Bass or lowest row, written, in this example, in the separate Bass staff*.

Indeed each of these parts may be written thus, upon a separate staff, still placing over each other those notes which are to be sung at the same time; that is, the common chord of each Bass note must continue to be written exactly over it. Example 28 would appear thus:

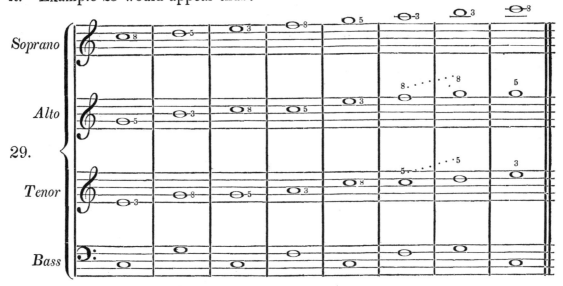

* The first or upper part is sometimes called the Treble and sometimes the Soprano, also the Descant.
The Second . . . is called the Alto or Counter-Tenor.
The Third . . . . is called the Tenor.
The Fourth or lowest part . the Bass.

This is merely spreading out the same Example upon a larger Scale.

To assist the eye in observing the chord written over each Bass note, we have *scored* bars across all the staves, and when the parts are thus separated from each other, Music is said to be written *in Score*.

Which way soever it may be written in future examples, let us still bear in mind that *each particular range of notes is a distinct part, and has its own individual progression.* It may be here observed also, that each particular part, being a progression of single sounds, may be called a Melody.

Referring now to the above Example (29) at the sixth note of the Scale, in the Alto (or second part) we find an F which is marked with an 8, as being the octave to the Bass note; and *in the same part*, the note *immediately following* is also an octave to the Bass note. These are *Consecutive Octaves*.

In the Tenor (or third part) we find a C, which is a 5th to the Bass note; and in the same *Part*, the note *immediately following* is also a 5th to the Bass note. These are *Consecutive Fifths*.

Observe that although an Eighth and a Fifth may, of course, be used in every chord, the *same interval* must not appear in the *same part* twice in immediate succession.

In the above Example (29), we discover the fault of Consecutive Octaves, in the second part; and the fault of Consecutive Fifths, in the third part.

It may be remarked, that these faults will always arise whenever the Bass and principal melody ascend together one degree.

As it must now be clear what the fault is, let us next consider how it is to be avoided.

To prevent Consecutive Octaves.

Let the note which is an 8th in the first chord, be continued in the second chord, in which it will become a 7th.

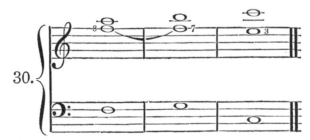

Here the consecutive 8ths are avoided, as the F is not allowed to proceed to the G as before. That this may be more distinctly observed, the Tenor part has been omitted in this Example. *Why* the 7th may be allowed to be heard in the second chord as it now appears, shall be explained when we have first shown how

To prevent Consecutive Fifths.

Take this as a rule,—" Whenever the Bass *ascends* one degree, the Fifth must *descend* one degree."

In Example 29, between the fifth and sixth notes of the Scale, the Bass ascends one degree, but in the Tenor we see the 5th (C) has *ascended* to D, instead of which, let it *descend* one degree, to B, and the fault will be corrected as in the following Example, in which, for the reason above stated, we shall omit the notes of the Alto.

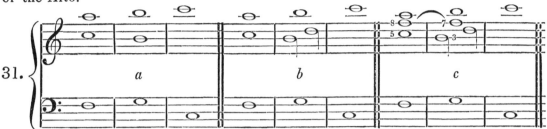

31.

a   *b*   *c*

But, having thus descended to the 3d, we are not obliged to remain there the full length of time which that chord of G may be sounded: we have already a B in the principal melody, and in this case we should ascend again to the nearest note of the chord (the 5th, as at *b* *.)

Thus the Consecutive 5ths are avoided—and the Consecutive 5ths and 8ths are *both* avoided in one Example at *c* †.

It will be perceived, that in the above three instances, we have not completed the last chord—the reason will be discovered in treating of

The Fundamental 7th.

Our Harmonies have hitherto consisted entirely of Common Chords, (that is, Chords composed only of the intervals of the 3rd, 5th, and 8th,) until, in avoiding Consecutive 5ths and 8ths, we have been introduced to a new interval, *viz.:* the 7th, which (as its name implies) is the 7th note above the Bass. Be careful to observe that this Fundamental 7th is not the 7th of the Scale, but must always be a *whole* tone below the 8th of its Bass ‡.

This interval is also called the *Dominant* 7th, as, whenever it is introduced into a chord, that chord immediately becomes a *Dominant chord*, and *must proceed to its Tonic*.

It is likewise sometimes called the *added* 7th, because it may be *added* to any perfect Common Chord such as we have hitherto constructed.

For instance; in Examples 30, and 31 *c*, to the chord of G we have added the Fundamental 7th, F, which is a whole tone below the 8*th*.

---

* See further on this subject Example **327**   † See Manual.

‡ See Philosophical Explanation in the Introduction to Modulation.

This chord of G, by the addition of this Dominant 7th, becomes a Dominant chord, and proceeds to its Tonic C, the next chord.

It is in this progression to its Tonic, that each interval of the chord of the Dominant 7th has its particular course appointed; which is called *its resolution.*

A satisfactory reason for this will be afforded in its proper place, but it will be sufficient for our present purpose, to give this simple rule for the

Resolution of the Chord of the Fundamental 7th.

The 7th of the chord must *descend* one degree.

The 5th   ,,   also must *descend* one degree.

The 3rd   ,,   ,,   must *ascend* one degree.

After what has now been said respecting the 7th, we can understand why, in Example 30, it was made to descend one degree, to E, in the succeeding chord.

Let us refer also to Example 31 *c.*

The chord of G has become a Dominant chord by the introduction of the 7th, and must therefore proceed to the chord of its Tonic C.

The 3rd must *ascend* one degree.   The B at the top is the 3rd, and it does ascend one degree to C.

The 7th must *descend* one degree.   F is the 7th, therefore it should descend one degree to E, in the following chord; but as this chord is not completed in Example 31, we shall here finish the resolution.

Thus, all is correct—B, the 3rd, ascends to C.

F, the 7th, descends to E.

and D, the 5th, descends to C *.

This part of the subject will be shortly resumed, but the student is recommended here to impress upon his memory what has been already said, by a variety of exercises, wherein Consecutive 5ths and 8ths are necessarily involved; as, for instance, where the Bass ascends one degree. The three last notes of different scales, will answer this purpose.

These faults must hereafter be carefully corrected wherever they arise in the course of harmonizing a Melody, as in Example 35 at *a.*

---

* It will be remarked that the 7th and 5th descending into the concluding chord leave that chord unavoidably without a 5th.

Diversification of the Common Chord.

It will afford some amusement in the course of these exercises, if we here point out the diversified effects to be produced by different methods of *playing* the same chord.

In a word of three syllables, each syllable is separately pronounced—yet it is still only one word.

In the same manner each of the three notes of the Common chord may be separately sounded, without in the least altering the nature of the chord *—thus :

A chord consisting of three different notes may be varied in six different groups, by employing the figures which represent the notes, in this order 8 5 3 8 5. To form the first group of three notes, write first the 8th of the chord, then the 5th, and then the 3rd. Tie these together, and then proceed to form another group of three, commencing at the 5, thus :

The first group will be . 8, 5, 3.

The second . . . . 5, 3, 8.

The third . . . . 3, 8, 5.

For the next three groups, reverse the above order; begin at the last figure 5, proceeding from right to left; then at the 8; and last at the 3. In this manner we will proceed to diversify the chord of C, writing at the bottom the fundamental bass, over it the chord which arises from it, and on the upper staff the six diversifications; and further, as the same process serves for each of the three positions, we will give the whole.

* This illustration is, of course, not intended to be carried further, as the syllables of a word will not bear inversion like the notes of a chord.

In this manner when a scale, or other melody has been harmonized, the chords may be placed with the notes thus separated, taking some one variation as a model, and proceeding with it through the exercise, repeating each group so as to fill up the time.   Let us diversify a melody, taking for example the bottom, the middle, and the top note of each chord.

We shall now take the scale of C, and write several variations.

---

* This is a mark of abbreviation, denoting that the preceding group of notes must be repeated.

Let other scales and melodies be taken as exercises for diversification, which will shortly be of great use, thus early giving some idea of writing variations.

These diversifications have been introduced in this place chiefly for amusement, and to afford a little variety in the exercises; but we must not allow them to interrupt the course of our proceeding.

Let us return, therefore, to what has been said respecting the chord of the Fundamental 7th, pages 21 and 22; having again carefully perused which, we may thus proceed.

The Fundamental 7th resumed.—Figuring the Bass.

It has been already said that this 7th is a whole tone below the 8th, and *may* be added to *any* perfect common chord. It should now be observed, that whenever we make this addition, we must mark the bass note with the figure 7 *.

A bass note without figures indicates that its common chord of 8, 5, and 3, only, is to be written above it; the 7 informs us that the 7th is also to be added.

This figure must represent the note in all respects; if the note requires a flat, the figure must also have a flat placed before it, &c. &c., as will be seen in the following examples.

It is scarcely necessary to observe that the 7th may be added to a chord in whatsoever position it is written, as in the following instance :—

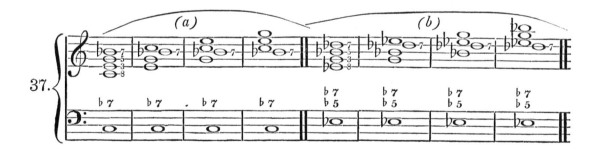

At (*a*) it will be perceived that the figure 7 has a flat placed before it, because the B, which is the dominant seventh in that chord, requires a flat, to make it a whole tone below the 8th. All the other intervals of the first chord are figured, but not

---

* It is immaterial whether this figure be written above or below the Bass note.

E

noticed over the bass, none of them requiring sharps or flats; and because it is always understood that its 3rd, 5th, and 8th, must be played with every bass note.

At (*b*), observe that we are obliged to mark the bass with a flat also before the 5th, as the 5th in the chord requires a flat. This information must, therefore, be attached to the bass note, which is thus made so complete, that if the chord were taken away, we should be enabled to write it again correctly from the figuring of the bass.

Thus when the 5th of the chord requires a flat, we place over the bass a figure of 5, with a flat before it; but had the 3rd required a flat, a flat alone would be sufficient, it being understood amongst musicians that an Accidental * placed alone over a bass note, shall always be considered as applying to the 3rd of the chord.

When we have occasion to make use of figures with *sharps*, instead of writing a sharp before the figure, we merely make a dash through it;—which rule will be understood by the following application:—

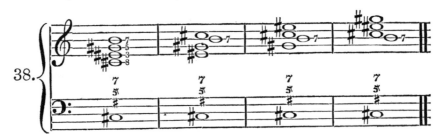

Resolution of the Chord of the 7th.

It has already been said, that by the addition of this 7th, a chord becomes a *Dominant*, and when we hear it, we feel an irresistible inclination to proceed to the harmony of *its Tonic*.

We shall not in this place enter into a philosophical inquiry how this desire arises; but it is the fact—and in order to prevent this expectation being disappointed, it must be considered as a law in the progression of Harmony, that the chord of the Dominant 7th shall be thus resolved:

The 3*rd* of the chord has an evident tendency to *ascend a half tone*. (Ex. 39, *a*.)
The 7*th* of the chord has the same tendency to *descend a half tone*. (Ex. 39, *b*.)
The 8*th* shews no disposition to move, and may *remain in its place*. (Ex. 39, *c*.)

---

* An Accidental is a Flat or Sharp occurring, which does not belong to the key.

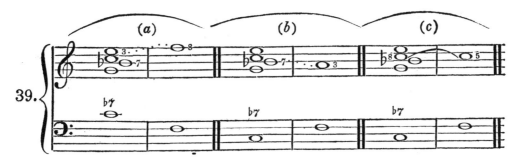

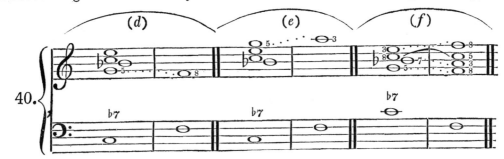

The *5th* is equally undecided, and may either descend (Ex. 40, *d*), or ascend (*e*); but it will generally be found best to allow it to *descend*.

Allowing this chord, therefore, to proceed as it appears itself to dictate, we find the succeeding chord will always be its Tonic, as in the following Ex. at (*f*).

C is the Dominant to F, the succeeding chord, and into which it resolves.

Example of the resolution of the chord of the Dominant 7th in its various positions:

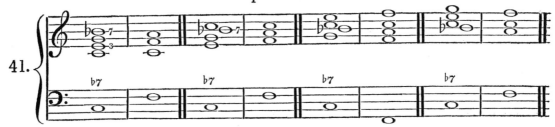

In resolving the Dominant Chord, first dispose of its 3rd, and the note to which it proceeds will always be the octave of the Tonic, the chord of which must succeed.

The Tonic may also be known by reflecting, that its key requires one sharp less, or one flat more than that of its Dominant.

It is of essential importance that we should be very well exercised in the use of this Fundamental 7th, and its resolution. Let us commence a course of exercises at C; add the 7th; and proceed (as we should) to F. The addition of a 7th to that chord will lead us to B♭; thus proceeding through all the keys.

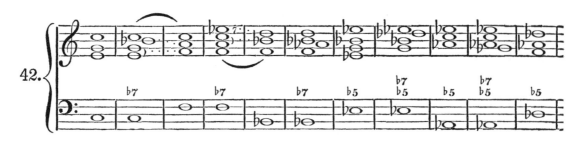

Be careful to figure the Basses correctly : there being no signature, every accidental sharp or flat required must be properly marked before the note, and also before the figure which represents that note.

As an exercise in figuring the sharps, let us pursue the same course as in the preceding example, commencing with B♯.

By the introduction of the Fundamental 7th, the progression of harmony acquires a more decided character, and produces in effect a certain degree of light

and shade, of which a progression of mere Common Chords is incapable : thus
the advantage of perfectly understanding it cannot be too strongly enforced. It
is unnecessary to multiply examples here; but it is strongly recommended frequently to play the chords, with, and without the 7th, by which means the
ear will be early accustomed to compare and acknowledge the difference of
effect.

Harmony in Four Parts.

An instance of this has already appeared in Example 29, which we have called
writing in Score.

By being thus *drawn out on separate staves,* the progression of each of the four
parts is more clearly distinguishable, than when the Harmonies are *compressed* into
two staves, as we have hitherto usually written them, and as they are always
written for the Piano-forte.

Although we have, in our remarks on the above-mentioned example, entered a
little upon the subject of writing in four parts, nevertheless, that it may be perfectly understood, we will here place it in another point of view.

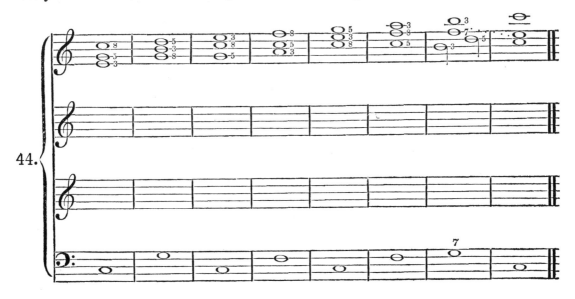

Here the *Harmonies* are compressed upon the upper staff. Let us now leave the
Melody only there, and place the other parts each on a separate staff in its proper
relative situation, i. e. the note next under the melody must still retain that
place.

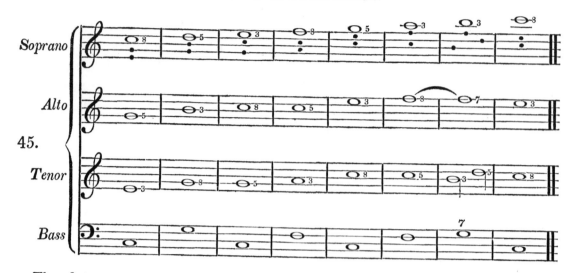

The dots now appearing on the upper staff mark the places from which the notes composing the other parts have been taken.

The proper name by which each of these parts is to be known is marked in the margin.

Many other Scales, and also some of the melodies already employed*, should now be taken as exercises, and harmonized thus in score.

The improper progression of consecutive 5ths and 8ths must, of course, be always avoided. The same interval (as has already been explained) must never appear twice in immediate succession in the same part: thus the intervals will be found continually changing places amongst themselves, rendering each part a distinct melody with ever-varying effect. It is by the union of these several melodies that perfect harmony is produced.

The following is a Melody, harmonized in four parts:—

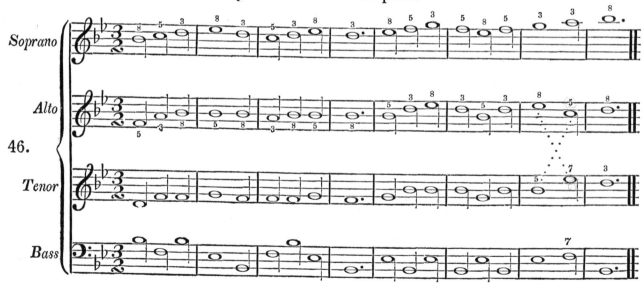

* Belonging to Class 1 of the Exercises in Harmonization.

In this Exercise (bar 7,) we have introduced another method of preventing consecutive 5ths, by allowing the Alto and Tenor to change places.—Had the B in the Tenor proceeded to the c, two 5ths would have appeared in immediate succession in the same part, which are by this means avoided.

This method may be employed, where convenient, in our future exercises, without entering into any further discussion here*.

To what Chords this 7th may be added in a Progression of Harmony.

We can introduce the 7th in *any* chord, *provided* we can make the following chord the chord of its Tonic, for the proper resolution of the 7th †; and it must be clearly understood, that we *cannot* introduce the 7th into any chord which *is not* the dominant to the one which immediately follows it. Thus,

> " When the Bass proceeds from Dominant to Tonic, we may introduce the 7th in the Dominant Chord."

This rule will always be a correct guide, where a progression of Basses is fixed, and cannot be altered.

Wherever we wish to introduce a 7th, we have only to examine if that Bass note is the Dominant to the one which immediately follows; if it is, we may introduce a 7th in the chord. As, for instance, in Example 44, bar 7, we can have a 7th in the chord, because the Bass note G is the Dominant to C, which follows.

Thus, then, we know in which of the chords we are at liberty to introduce the 7th. Let us now inquire,

In which part (in Harmony of Four Parts) the 7th must be written.

" The 7th must be placed in that part where its resolution is found."

As the 7th always descends into the 3d of the following chord, we have only to look forward to the next chord, and wherever *its 3rd* is written, in the *same part* write the 7th.

Thus in the following Harmonization of the Scale of A♭ (bar 3), the 7th is written in the Tenor part, because the 3rd of the following chord is there.

In the last bar but one, the 7th has been introduced in avoiding the Consecutive

---

* This subject is fully treated in a separate article.　　† More will be found on this subject hereafter.

5ths and 8ths by the second method, yet still it is found in the same part as the 3rd of the following chord.

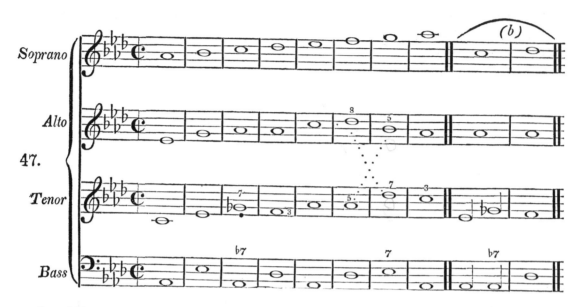

In adding this 7th to any chord, we cannot fail to remark, that as the Harmony must at present consist throughout of only four parts, if we admit the 7th, some one of the former notes must be expunged. Thus, in the above Example, (47, bar 3,) in the Tenor, the 5th has been expunged, and its place is marked by a dot.

In the same manner, whatever interval happens to be placed immediately before the 3rd of the Tonic chord must be displaced to make room for the 7th.

Referring again to the 3rd bar,—if we may be permitted to have two notes in one part, we may employ both, and divide the time of the bar between them, as at (b); still, however, it will be observed that there is really no 5th, when the 7th is sounding.

Now let us examine the Bases of the above Example, (47.)

Upon the first Bass, A♭, can we have a 7th? No. Because that A♭ is not the Dominant to the next note.

Upon the next Bass, E♭, can we have a 7th? Yes. Because it is the Dominant to the note A♭, which follows it.

In which part should it then be introduced? In the Soprano—because the 3rd of the following chord is there.

This is true—but if we should introduce the 7th there, and consequently take away the note which is already in that part, we should alter the melody or theme given to us as an Exercise, and this we are not (for the present) permitted to do;

we are therefore compelled in such case to omit the 7th altogether, although from the progression of the bass it might be admitted.

In bar 5, a similar circumstance occurs; the 3rd of the following chord being in the principal melody, we cannot introduce the 7th, although the progression of the bass would allow it.

Here exercise upon Scales in other Keys, avoiding the consecutive 5ths and 8ths by the two different methods, and also introducing the 7th occasionally, as at Example 47, *b*.

A few Melodies should also be taken for a similar exercise; proceeding always according to the routine already indicated: thus,—

First, write the Basses;—then the common chords;—avoid consecutive 5ths and 8ths:—and lastly introduce the 7ths; carefully examining where the progression of the bass will admit of them: properly figuring the bass, and observing that the several intervals of the dominant chord proceed to their respective destinations.

Example of a Melody Harmonized in Four Parts, with the Fundamental 7th added.

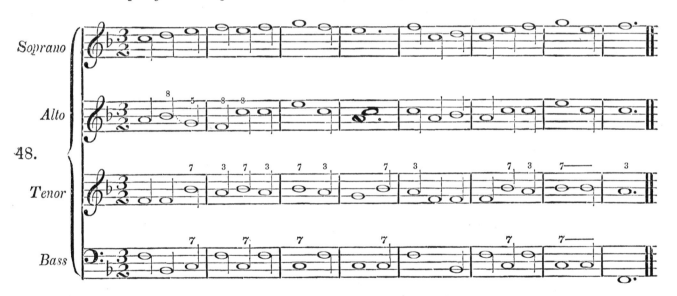

The pupil is recommended carefully to examine the above example; first to make his own remarks strictly on what has taken place at every bar; and afterwards to compare them with the following observations.

In the first bar, though the first bass note is the dominant to the second, still the 7th is not introduced, because the 3rd of the following chord is in the Soprano.

F

Moreover it is not usual to commence with the chord of the 7th, though there is no absolute law against it *.

In this bar, also, where the bass ascends one degree, the consecutive 5ths and 8ths are prevented by the second method, *i. e.*, by the crossing of the parts.

In the second bar, in the Alto, appear two 8ths in immediate succession. How can this be allowed? Because that part and the bass proceed by contrary motion—*in which case alone* they may be admitted †.

In the fifth bar there appear to be two chords over one bass note, but these are merely the same chord in two positions.

In the seventh bar the figure 7 is placed over the first note only of the bass. It must be understood that a line drawn from any figure, and extended over other bass notes, signifies, that the interval which that figure represents, shall be continued in all the chords over which the line is extended.

In the third bar a 7th is introduced in the chord of C, and yet the 3rd of that chord does *not* ascend : this appears to be an infraction of the rule laid down, that, " When the 7th is introduced, the 3rd *must* ascend one degree," but, in the present instance, if E (the 3rd) is made to ascend to F, it will, in proceeding to the following chord, occasion consecutive octaves with the bass.

This however might be prevented, by letting the bass ascend from the F to the C, producing *contrary motion ;* or, by allowing E, the 3rd of the chord, first to ascend to F, and immediately to descend again in the same chord to C ‡.

In the above examination of Example 48, having mentioned contrary motion, we may here explain that—contrary motion between any two parts, is, when one of them ascends, and the other descends; and it should be clearly understood that no improper consecutive progression can possibly arise by contrary motion.

Now let the pupil pause, and reflect on the progress which he has hitherto made, and on the effect he is enabled to produce by the application of the materials with which he has been already supplied. This is a practice productive of the best effects, and cannot be too early or too frequently introduced.

Up to this period we have been enabled to harmonize melodies by the simple application of only *three* fundamental basses. It will be profitable, and also amusing, to trace back the means by which we have arrived at this point.

---

* Should we wish to introduce a 7th on the first chord of any Theme, it will be better to let the chord be first heard as a simple common chord, and introduce the 7th only on the latter part of it, as in the first bar of Examples 52 & 54.

† Further observations on this will be found hereafter.

‡ See Ex. 52, Bars 2 & 3.

Melody and Harmony having been described, (page 13.) we proceeded to the discovery of the Fundamental Basses, by writing the figures 8—5—3 over the scale, by which we found that

The 3rd, 5th, and 8th of the scale were accompanied by the Tonic.

The 2nd and 7th . . . . by the Dominant.

The 4th and 6th . . . . by the Sub-dominant, which may be called *the first rule of accompanying the scale.*

By this rule we were enabled to write the Fundamental Basses to a given Melody. (Ex. 26, 27.) The chords were added, (Ex. 28,) producing a Harmony of Four Parts, (Ex. 29.)

In preventing consecutive 8ᵛᵉˢ we were introduced to a new interval, the fundamental 7th, (Ex. 30,) which has been variously employed, in producing new effects, and avoiding the monotony arising from a too frequent succession of common chords.

Having now availed ourselves of all the effects arising from the application of the three Fundamental Basses, let us see whether we cannot, by some change in their application, produce a still further variety in their effect.

An opportunity presents itself, arising from the introduction of the Fundamental 7th, with which the pupil is already acquainted.

We find on examination, that in every key the 4th of the scale is, in reality, the fundamental 7th of the dominant; consequently we *may* accompany the 4th of the scale by the dominant as its bass, deviating in this one note only from the first rule; and this we call

The second Rule of Accompanying the Scale.

" When the 4th of the scale *descends one degree,* it *may* be accompanied by the Dominant."

Thus the 4th of the scale *in descending* may hereafter be accompanied by two fundamental basses, producing the variety desired.

This rule is illustrated in the following Example :—

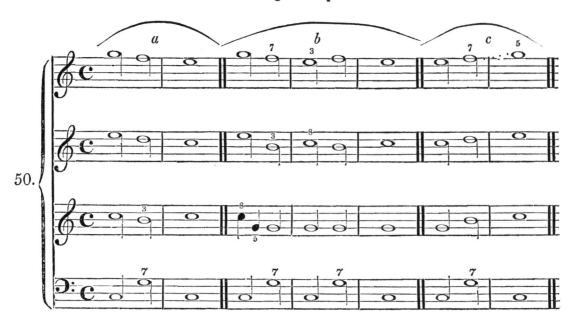

If we write the harmonies as at (*a*), we are forced to leave the concluding chord incomplete, because the 3rd of the dominant chord must ascend. Therefore it is better to omit the 5th in the dominant chord, (as at *b* *.)

In the first bar of this Example (*b*), in the tenor, the octave falls to the 5th on the same bass: this is merely an instance of one part taking two notes of the harmony: as a matter of taste it may be observed, that the effect is thus somewhat improved, by not permitting the bass and tenor to proceed at once from C to G, even though the contrary motion avoids a direct offence against the rule concerning consecutive 8ths.

The Ex. (as at *c*), is inserted, to shew that the 4th of the scale, when it *ascends*, *cannot* be accompanied by the Dominant; for in such case, *the 7th would improperly resolve upwards.*

Recollect that this second rule is only introduced to produce variety, and *should not be too frequently applied.*

When the descending 4th occurs frequently in the course of a melody, it may be alternately accompanied by the Dominant, as in the following Example 51, at (*a*), and the Sub-dominant as at (*b*.)

---

* Another reason will be found in treating of the peculiar character of each of the 4 parts.

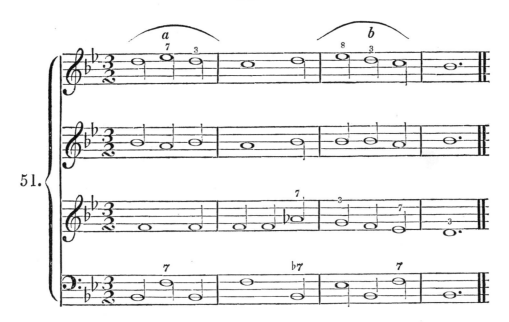

Should the 4th of the scale, after being several times repeated, at length descend, the last note may be accompanied by the Dominant, even though the preceding ones had the Sub-dominant : as at (*a*) in the following Example.

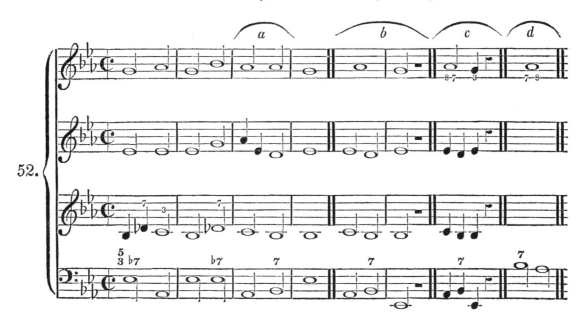

By the same mode of reasoning, had the melody at (*a*) been written as a semi-breve, in place of the two minims, still the *two* basses might have been given, dividing the time, (as at *b*.)

Another instance, where the time of a minim is divided into two crotchets, is found at (*c.*)

Were we, by mistake, to use the Dominant *first,* and the Sub-dominant after it, we should find the 7th would remain unresolved, (as at *d.*)

In order clearly to ascertain the variety which has been produced simply by the introduction of the second rule, the pupil should harmonize the 4th of the scale descending, by both rules alternately, noticing particularly the change which takes place in the inner parts.

Melodies, in which the 4th of the scale frequently descends∗, arranged for Exercises on this rule, should here be harmonized in sufficient variety, before proceeding farther.

The Third Rule of Accompanying the Scale.

" The 8th of the scale *may* be accompanied by the Sub-dominant."

This rule, as well as the last, affords us additional variety; but it is to be employed with discretion, and merely for diversity of effect.

Where the 8th of the scale is frequently repeated, a monotonous effect would be produced by a continued repetition of the same harmony; in such case, therefore, the occasional application of this rule will be found to produce an agreeable relief: as at (*a*), in the following Example:

Suppose the two first crotchets had been written as a minim, still two basses might be used, (as at *b*) which is a similar instance to (*c*) in the last Example, (52.)

Indeed this third rule may occasionally be employed even where the 8th is not repeated, as at (*c*); but it should be avoided where the melody forbids it; as in the two instances at (*d*), where direct consecutive 5ths would be produced.

And further, it should not be employed so as to conclude the harmonization of any melody with the Sub-dominant.

∗ Will be found in Class 2 of Exercises.

By this third rule, it will be observed that we are enabled more frequently to avail ourselves of the powerful influence of the fundamental 7th, and to render still more evident the pleasing variety which may be given to the harmony by the diversity of the application of only the three fundamental Basses.

As an instance, let the Melody of the following Example be harmonized by the first rule only, and afterwards contrasted with the same Melody treated as it here appears.

In bar 1, the 7th is introduced in the Alto, because its resolution is in that part ; and it is introduced only on the latter part of the chord, in order to commence with a Common Chord, as recommended in Note, p. 34*.

In bar 5, it is introduced in the Alto, at the commencement of the Chord.

In bar 3, the second rule of accompanying the Scale has been employed.

" Where one dominant Chord is immediately succeeded by another, the 3rd of the first dominant Chord needs not ascend, but may descend, and become the 7th of the following chord: as in bars 4 and 5."

Let the pupil now exercise on melodies adapted to the application of these rules†.

---

* The Bass note is here figured, first with $\frac{5}{3}$, and then with a 7 ; this is to show that two different chords are employed to that Bass, the first of which is the Common Chord of the 3rd and 5th, the 8th being always understood. Similar instances occur in bars 3 and 4.

† Class 3.

The fourth Rule of Accompanying the Scale.

" The fifth of the scale *may* be accompanied by the Dominant."

We have hitherto accompanied the fifth of the scale by the Tonic, and this last rule is, like the others, only to be used for the sake of variety in the harmony; chiefly where the fifth of the scale is frequently repeated in a melody, or heard in notes of long duration: as in the following Example.

Exercise first on airs fitted for the application of this rule in particular*, and afterwards use, *with discretion*, all the four rules combined: thus,—

(*a*) The fourth rule, (*b*) the second rule, (*c*) the third rule, and (*d*) the first.   At *x* and *y* compare the same progression of intervals in the Melody, differently accompanied.

The four rules above given for the accompaniment of the scale, may be safely left as here stated, with the few observations attached to each.   Sufficient has

---

* Class 4.

been said to direct the choice on all future occasions. In harmonizing a Melody, each interval should be examined to discover whether it admits of two Basses, and if so, which of them will be most effective. The following is a short Example, as a further guide in this particular.

57.

The second note of the Melody is D♭, which is the fourth of the scale, and may be accompanied either by the Sub-dominant, or (as it descends) by the Dominant. In this instance we prefer the latter, because D♭ occurs again in the second bar and ascends; consequently *there* we have no choice; it *must* in that case be accompanied by the Sub-dominant. Thus by looking forward a few notes, we have produced an agreeable variety.

Whilst only one rule for accompanying the scale was known, little study was necessary, but now we are led to reflect on the consequences of every step we take; the Melody must be carefully examined; prudence and circumspection must be employed in forming a plan for the succession of the several Basses, and the judgment called upon for the selection of those which are calculated to produce the best effect.

One reflection is here very consolatory; that though we may err in a mere matter of taste, we are sure of being generally correct; and that moderate care in the application of the rules already given, will produce results which could be little anticipated by those who have already studied harmony by any other process.

Definition of the peculiar Character of each of the four parts of Harmony.

The Soprano, Alto, Tenor and Bass, produce each a melody peculiar in its effect, chiefly arising from the chord of the Fundamental 7th.

G

The different intervals of this chord, in their progression, have each a marked peculiarity ; and, as each interval is generally found attached to one particular part, it gives to that part its own decided character; by which we are enabled clearly to distinguish and describe it.

The Soprano progression is *that which passes direct to the Octave of the succeeding Tonic,* whether ascending from the 3rd, or descending from the 5th.

The Alto, or Counter-tenor, *that which remains in its place and becomes a 5th.*

The Tenor, *that which proceeds direct to the 3rd,* whether descending from the 7th, or ascending from the 5th.

The Bass progression is *that which ascends a 4th, or descends a 5th,*—or, in other words, *that which proceeds directly from Dominant to Tonic.*

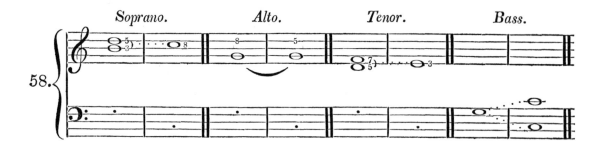

In harmonizing a melody by the first rule, all these progressions are in their proper places ; each of the four parts retains its peculiar character throughout.

In the application of the other rules, a variety of effect is produced by an interchange of character amongst the different parts ; as will appear on an investigation of Ex. 50. *b,* bars 1 and 2.

This interchange of character may perhaps be more clearly distinguishable by directing the attention particularly to that part wherein the 7th is found.

In the above-mentioned Example it will appear that the Tenor character (*the progression into the 3rd of the Tonic*) is in the Soprano part.

The Soprano character (*the progression into the Octave*) is in the Alto part.

The Alto character (*remaining in its place*) is in the Tenor part.

The Bass part retains its own character.

We may hereafter have occasion to observe more at large on this characteristic distinction of the four parts ; as it will frequently serve to throw a light on our subject : for the present, we shall only make one more remark, on the same Example 50 (at *a*), the impropriety of which arrangement of the parts will appear from the following analysis as to the interchange of character.

The Part of The Soprano has the character of the Tenor.

The Alto   . . . . .   that of the Soprano.

and The Tenor   . . . also that of the Soprano.

The Alto character being entirely omitted.

But in the arrangement of the parts as at (*b*), in the same Example (50), the whole of the four characters are preserved; from whence will be perceived the propriety of the recommendation there given, to leave out the 5th, when the 4th of the scale descending is accompanied by the Dominant.

Major and Minor Chord.

This term relates to the 3rd of the chord only, which is MAJOR or *Minor* as it may contain a GREATER or *less* number of Semitones.

All the chords hitherto written have been MAJOR, containing FIVE Semitones in the 3rd; commencing with the key-note, and calling that one (Ex. 59, *a.*)

The *Minor* chord contains in its 3rd only *four* Semitones (*b*), which is one Semitone *less* than the major, and hence its name.

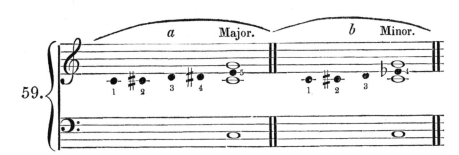

All chords are understood to be MAJOR if not otherwise marked, or expressed. Thus if the chord of C is required; C, E, and G, is the answer. The *Minor* chord of C, is C, E♭, and G. In pronouncing the common chord hitherto, it has always been given major; for the minor we need only to lower the 3rd a half tone, by putting a flat before it, or taking away the sharp (if there be one.)

The chord of G   is G B and D.
The chord of G minor is G B♭ and D.

The chord of D   is D F♯ and A.
The chord of D minor is D F and A.

The chord of E♭   is E♭ G and B♭.
The chord of E♭ minor is E♭ G♭ and B♭.

Whenever a minor chord is to be written, care must be taken to mark the Bass note with any accidental required.

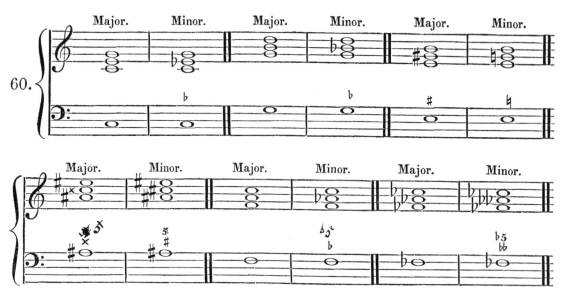

To accustom the ear to distinguish the difference of effect, the same chord should be frequently struck, alternately major and minor. Also as a farther exercise, a continuous progression of alternate major and minor chords should be written and played, commencing at C, as a major chord: descending first a *Minor* 3rd, to a *Minor* chord (A minor); then a MAJOR 3rd, to a MAJOR chord (F) and so on alternately.

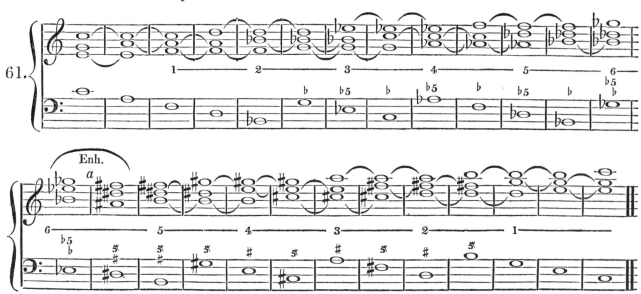

It will be observed that the foregoing example proceeds by flats round the circle of keys, interposing on each occasion a minor chord, which is called the *relative minor* to the major which precedes it, and which will be further explained hereafter.

By the Enharmonic change at (*a*), the progression is conducted back again to the key of C, from which we set out.

Although we shall afterwards resume the subject, it may be well in this place to state, that every *Minor Key* has always the same number of *sharps or flats* as its *relative major*.

In order to find the number of sharps or flats belonging to any *Minor Key*, we must examine the *3rd* of that *minor* chord, and whatever number is necessary in the key of that *3rd*, (as already learned by the fingers,) is the number required; for instance:

The chord of C minor is C E♭ and G.

The *third* of this chord is E♭.

The key of E♭ requires three flats; therefore,

The key of *C minor* requires *three flats*.

This is one of the stages noticed in the Introduction, where the subject may be allowed to pause for a while; and in order that the student may render his further progress easy, advantage should be taken of this opportunity fully to assure himself that he has well understood all that has preceded; for henceforward we shall make free use of it, applying our observations chiefly to the new matter as it occurs.

Having by this recapitulation secured firm possession of the fund of materials already supplied, we shall proceed to apply them on a more extended scale, and open a wider range into the agreeable regions of Harmony. First, however, we shall endeavour to shew, by some introductory remarks, that in adopting this system, we have done nothing more than follow the simple dictates of nature.

We would willingly have deferred any philosophical discussion until the pupil had been practically acquainted with more of the subject; but as the following observations form the most proper introduction to modulation, and at the same time comprise a developement of the principles on which we proceed, a more suitable situation could not elsewhere have been found. These observations being, however, directed to the philosophical inquirer and the matured mind, the young pupil is recommended to pass on, for the present, to the definition of Modulation and Progression which precedes Example 69, and after having advanced some little way beyond that, to return to this part, which he will then be better able to understand.

For the sake of brevity, the exercises throughout this work will generally be written as concisely as possible, but the pupil is recommended frequently to vary his style of performing them.

The following specimens will be sufficient to shew the very extensive variety of effect which may be given in the performance of any exercise written in simple chords, as in Example 61.

No particular rule is necessary in this case, it being entirely a matter of taste; but probably it would be found less to distract the attention from the progression of the harmonies, were the performer to select some particular diversification, and continue the same throughout the exercise.

A few Specimens of Diversification, which may be employed in performing Example 61 and other Progressions of Harmony.

Origin of Melody and Harmony, Explanation of the Diatonic Scale, and Discovery of the Fundamental Basses.

WHEN a musical string is put into vibration, we may imagine we hear but one single sound; but on listening attentively we shall discover, particularly if it be one of the deep tones of the piano-forte, that the principal sound is accompanied, though faintly, by other sounds, called its "Harmonics."

In sonorous bodies, as a bell for instance, the principal sound and its harmonics appear to be produced at the same time, and all to be heard at once; but in wind instruments, as the French Horn, Trumpet, &c., they may be produced separately, so as to be distinctly analyzed, and these prove to be exactly the same in order and proportion as those produced from the vibration of a string.

Thus a Tube, or String whose lowest sound is C, will produce the following

Harmonics.

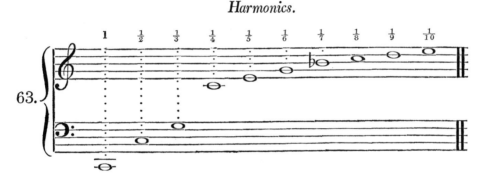

These, as they are written, are the sounds, and in the order in which they are actually produced from the French Horn, &c.

The lowest sound we shall call the foundation and *generator* of all the rest, which are called its Harmonics, and which, it will be perceived, are regular portions or fractional parts of the Generator.

The first note above the Generator, being the *octave C*, may be considered as one half of the whole Tube: in fact *one half* of this Tube would really produce, as its lowest note, this very octave C.

By the same rule, G would be produced by a tube which should be only *one third* the size of the above; and so on with the rest, as marked in the preceding Example.

To illustrate this still further, let us extend a musical *String* over two bridges, until its grave sound be the same C as that produced by the above *Tube.*

If we then place another bridge exactly in the middle, *each half* will produce the *Octave* of the whole.

If we divide the *same string* into *three* equal portions, *each portion* will produce a G; and so with all the other proportions.

It will be remarked, on referring to the Scale of the Harmonics, that the sounds are produced in a succession of gradually diminished distance from each other, until they end in a progression of whole tones; a real diatonic progression,

Thus: The note first appearing above its Generator is the 8th.

The next is a 5th above that.

The distance to the next is a 4th.

And the next a major 3rd, &c., &c.

As far as E, the last in the Example, all the sounds are perfect, but the one immediately following that is involved in obscurity; we are left in uncertainty whether F, or F♯ should follow*; however, our attention must be directed to another circumstance which offers itself as our guide.

Let us take the three last sounds produced, as a scale or melody to be harmonized;—How are we to proceed?—We must discover the Fundamental Basses; but by what means?—Let us take as basses the three *first* sounds produced by the same Tube, and our object is effected.

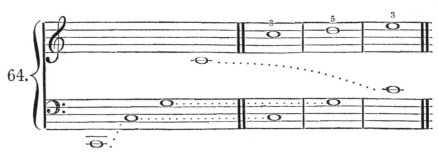

The Fundamental Bass being discovered, we may now add the Chords.

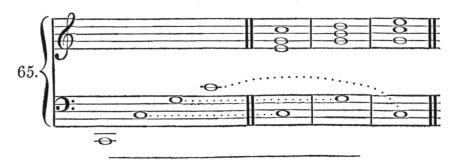

---

* As is well known to all performers on wind instruments.

Let us now turn to Example 63, and let it be observed, that amongst the harmonics of C, the 7th sound is a B♭.

This, in fact, is not the 7th note in the scale of C; but the *Fundamental 7th*, being a whole tone below the 8th.

When the chord of C is heard with this 7th added, it at once assumes all the character of the chord of the Dominant 7th, and produces an irresistible inclination to proceed to its Tonic *. The ear acknowledges in the 7th a decided tendency to descend, and in the 3rd, an equal tendency to ascend into the nearest sound in the following chord.

Having harmonized (as in the last Example) the scale produced by the harmonics of C, let us bear in mind that the Dominant 7th is actually produced amongst the harmonics of the last bass note C. Should we bring this 7th prominently forward, and write it in the harmony, we must be irresistibly forced to proceed next to the chord of F †. Now, therefore, if we are disposed to extend the scale further than these three sounds which Nature has given, the next sound here pointed out to us is *F natural*.

Having thus ascertained that our next bass note *must* be F, let us take that sound as a new generator, and treat it exactly as we did the preceding one, C.

We have only to consider this new generator as a Tube of smaller dimensions, and it will give us, amongst its harmonies, the Melody F, G, A; to which let us write the Basses, as on the former occasion, and thus we shall have formed a scale of six notes, properly harmonized ‡.

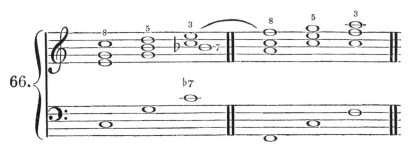

Here then we have united two scales of three sounds each, the first scale having been produced from the Tube C, and the second from the Tube F.

---

* See pages 21, 22, and 26.

† Example 40, *f*.

‡ It will be perceived that the Bass to the first note of the scale is found an 8th below; the Bass to the second note is a 5th below, &c. &c., explaining why we used these figures in first discovering the Fundamental Basses, page 14.

H

These two scales are united by an interval of a half tone, as marked by the curved line in the last Example ; as also in Examples 3, 11, &c*.

We have now six notes, and if we desire to extend the scale still further, to what note must we next proceed ?   To B♭.   Why ?

To answer this, let us apply the same reasoning which guided us in discovering the second generator F.

The generator of the last scale of three notes being F, let us add the 7th to the last chord, and the F, thus becoming a dominant, will lead us to B♭, and we gain a third scale of three notes, B♭, C, and D, as in the following Example 67, fig. 3.

Another 7th may be added on the B♭, which will lead us to the scale of E♭, and thus we might continue to proceed—adding scales of three notes *ad infinitum*†.

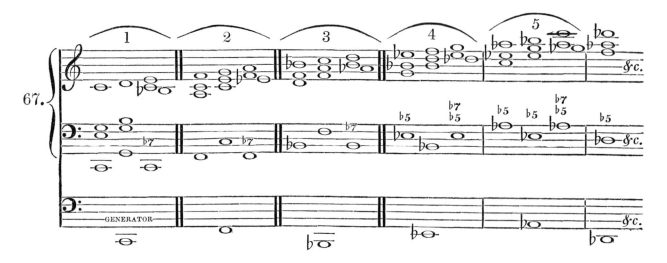

It will appear clear from this examination, that no scale can naturally consist of more than three sounds, for which there are only two Fundamental Basses required, *viz.*, the Tonic and Dominant. The Sub-dominant which we have hitherto employed, appears now to be really the generator, or Tonic, of another scale.

The pupil will now clearly comprehend the nature and origin of *Modulation*. which may be shortly summed up in the following rule.

---

* Here will be perceived the reason why between the 3rd and 4th of the scale is only *a half tone* ; the 3rd of the Dominant chord ascending *a half tone* into the 8th of the succeeding **Tonic.**

† Such a progression, however, has a fatiguing effect upon the ear, like a never-ending series of digressions, and should always be confined within proper limits.

" Whenever *we use a 7th*, and thus proceed to a new key, we *modulate* into that key."

In the above Example, for instance, a modulation takes place in proceeding from the scale of C to that of F ; another, by the same rule, in proceeding from the key of F to that of B♭, *&c. &c.*

Let us now apply these observations in an

Examination of (what is called) *the Diatonic Scale.*

The first three sounds (as in Ex. 68 below), are in the key of C. A modulation then takes place into the key of F, in which key are the three sounds immediately succeeding.

Were we after this to proceed as in Example 67, we should diverge still further from the point at which we set out, and the ear would be offended by a continuance of such a progression, for we already feel an inclination to return to the original key : but having modulated from that key into another, we can only return again by the same means, *i. e.* by a modulation, which forces us to introduce the chord of G, the Dominant to C, in order that we may conclude upon the latter chord.

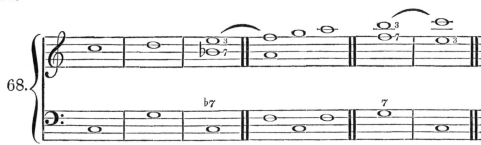

Thus we complete a scale of eight sounds, and it will be perceived that the 7th note in this scale *cannot* be B♭, as it is found in Example 67.

It must here be B♮; the dominant chord of G, thus forcibly introduced, being G, B, and D. This B♮ also, being the 3rd of the Dominant chord, must ascend a half tone to the C, which makes the half tone occur between the 7th and 8th of this scale, though, as in Example 67, it would naturally occur between the 6th and 7th. It is this forced deviation from the order which nature seems to point out, that involves us in so many difficulties with respect to consecutive 5ths and 8ths between the 6th and 7th of the scale ; for, had we followed the progression which nature points out to us, these difficulties would never have occurred.

H 2

In order still better to define what Modulation is, and to place it in a still clearer point of view, we may contrast it with what we shall call

Progression.

By which is meant a succession of chords in which the Fundamental 7th is not employed, and in which, consequently, no modulation takes place.

The following instances will illustrate this.

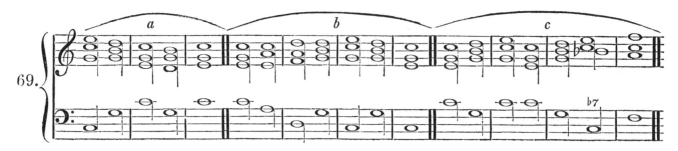

At (*a*) we use only the chords properly belonging to the key of C.—This is Progression.

At (*b*) some chords are introduced which do not belong to the original key— yet still it is only Progression, no Modulation having yet taken place by the employment of the Dominant 7th.

At (*c*) the harmony remains in the original key until the 3rd bar, in which a Dominant 7th is introduced, and a Modulation takes place to F *.

Harmony thus appears to divide itself into two distinct branches, Progression and Modulation; the peculiar characteristics of which will be sufficiently distinguished as we proceed. It has been shown at Example 67, that nature points out to us the means by which we must proceed from one key to another, and thus gives us

The Rule of Modulation.

" In proceeding from one key to another, the Dominant of the key to which we are *going*, must be introduced immediately *before* it."

We shall find that in the *Intervals* of the *Common Chord*, nature supplies us with Dominants to lead us to those keys which produce the most pleasing effect.

---

* Indeed we might have given as an instance the first four sounds of the scale, as nature gives them to us, in which the three first chords move by progression, and a modulation takes place between the 3rd and 4th.

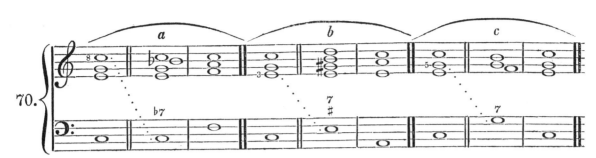

As at *a*: If we take the 8th of the chord of the Tonic, and employ it as a Dominant, it leads us to the first Modulation pointed out by nature (as shown in Example 67) on modulation; as it is an extended exercise which will be found below in Example 71.

As at *b*: If we take the 3rd as a Dominant, it modulates to the relative minor. See Example 72.

As at *c*: The 5th of the Tonic, being the same as the Dominant, does not modulate out of the key, but serves, after any modulation, to bring us back to it.

By continuing to employ, as a Dominant, the octave of the key *at which we have arrived,* we modulate to every key round the circle by flats; and, making an Enharmonic Change at G♭, we return back to C by sharps.

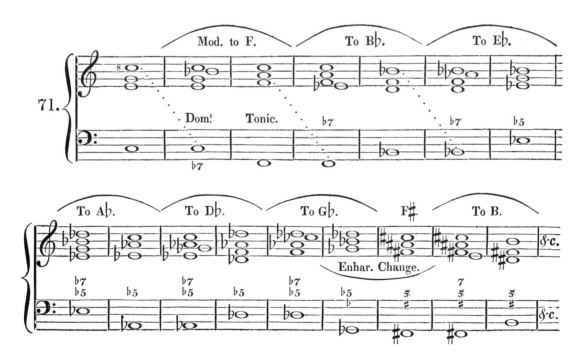

By continuing to employ the 3rd of the key *at which we have arrived*, as a Dominant, it leads us through the same circle of keys—interposing, on each occasion, a Modulation to the relative Minor.

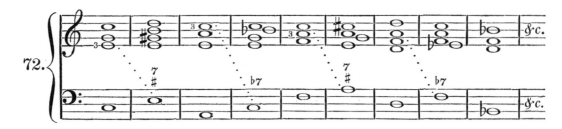

Supposing we are in the key of C, let us now take the sounds of the chord of the Dominant (G), and see what modulations they will afford.

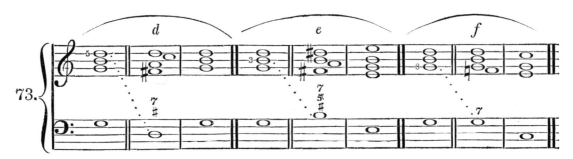

As at *d* :   D (the 5th) affords us a Modulation to G.

As at *e* :   B (the 3rd) leads us to E, which is the relative minor to G.

As at *f* :   G (the 8th) brings us back to our key of C.

By thus employing the Intervals of the chords of the Tonic and Dominant, we find we can modulate to four new keys; and if we take, in the same manner, the Intervals of the chord of the Sub-dominant, we shall obtain two more.

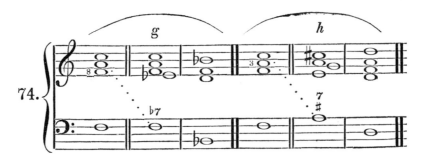

As at *g* :   F (the 8th) leads us to the key of B♭.

As at *h* :   A (the 3rd) leads us to the key of D Minor.

From the above examples, it is clear that the keys most nearly related to any given key are

> Its relative Minor.
> The Dominant and its relative Minor.
> The Sub-dominant and its relative Minor *.

But it is by no means necessary that, in our modulations, we should confine ourselves to those keys which may be considered as nearly related to the original key from which we set out: we may modulate occasionally with great effect to keys further remote, which are called *extraneous keys;* in doing which, however, we must carefully observe that there is a proper connexion between all the chords †.

In the preceding exercises we have modulated by means of a Dominant supplied to us: let us now *first* determine the key to which we choose to modulate, and then interpose the proper Dominant.

On a Bass staff, (having a blank treble above it,) let us write a Bass note, for instance C, from which we will set out.

Having determined to modulate to the key of D, write a D; leaving a space for the insertion of its Dominant.

A (being the Dominant of D) will accordingly be inserted in that space.

Choosing to modulate still further to E, write the bass note E; leaving, as before, a space for its Dominant B, which must be there inserted:—and thus proceed further at pleasure.

The proper dominants will thus be placed before their tonics, and should be figured with a 7. The chords may afterwards be written on the treble staff‡, adding the 7ths where the bass is figured, and thus completing the exercise as follows.

---

* The Fundamental 7th, and its relative Minor are rather too far removed to be noticed at present.

† See page 18.

‡ The upper notes of the successive chords should be kept as near each other as possible, and the intervals of the dominant chords must be properly resolved.

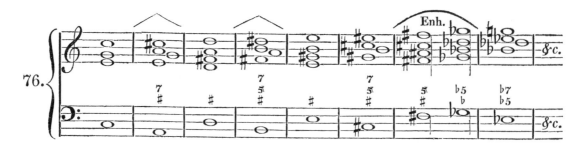

The above is a continued modulation by whole tones ascending.

At F♯ an enharmonic change takes place, and instead of proceeding to G♯, &c., we should thus return back to C by keys requiring flats.

We may in the same manner modulate by whole tones descending; thus,

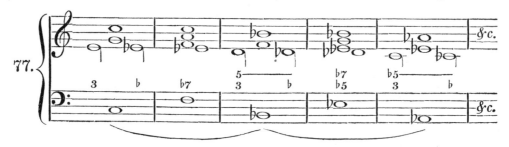

We may at any time, as in the above Example, change a major chord into minor, and *vice versâ;* which will often afford us an additional connexion with the succeeding dominant, and soften the harshness of effect which might otherwise be produced in modulating to *extraneous keys:* as in the following Example.

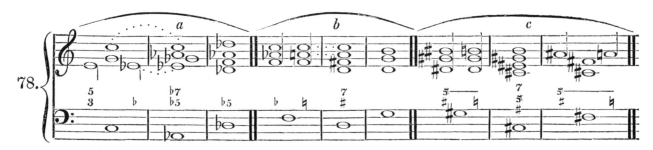

At *a*: The major 3rd is changed to minor, because we are modulating to keys with flats; and the chord, when so changed, has a double connexion with the next.

At *b*: The minor 3rd is changed to major, because we are proceeding from a key with flats to one with sharps.

At *c*: There would be no connexion with the succeeding chord, were we not to make this change.

The following Example will show how useful *Enharmonic changes* are in modulating.

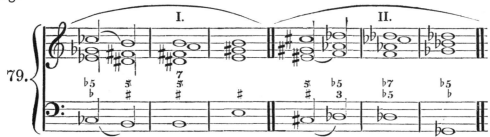

I. Here we commenced in the key of C♭, which chord we have been forced to change Enharmonically, before we could modulate directly to E.

II. Here we are in C♯, which being Enharmonically changed to D♭, enables us to modulate at once to G♭.

In Example 72 we selected the 3rd of the Tonic chord to form a new dominant, but that was a *major 3rd*. As we are at liberty to make the Tonic chord minor, let us take that *minor 3rd* as a new dominant.

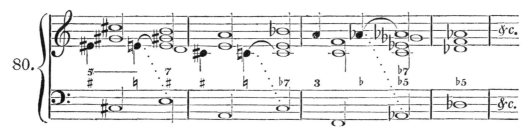

Let us now try the effect of modulating at each step, to a *major half tone* * above.

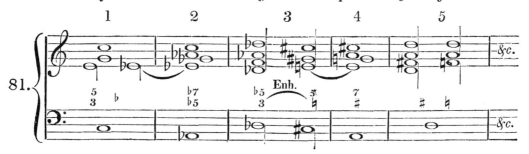

At bar 1: The chord is changed to minor because we are going to keys with flats.

At bar 3: The chord of D♭ is made minor and changed enharmonically, which avoids the necessity of going to E♭♭.

And thus we may proceed, ascending a major half tone, until we arrive again at C.

* See Explanation of major and minor half tones.

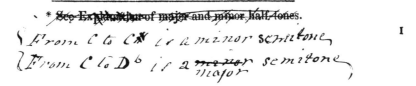

I

We will now select the *5th of the Dominant* of every key to which we proceed, and modulate to the key of the 5th above, or (which is the same thing) the 4th below.

In the above Example, as the bass ascends one degree, the Pupil must not forget the rule for preventing consecutive 5ths and 8ths, by making the 5th fall one degree.

We will now modulate to the *major 3rd above ;* in doing which, it will be found that there is no connexion between the interposed Dominant and the preceding chord.

In this case, we must find some chord to place where the chain of harmony is interrupted, thus introducing a *progression* into the course of modulation.

N.B. We shall generally find that the chord of the minor 3rd below, or of the major 3rd above, will answer this purpose ; we will try them both here, in modulating from C to E.

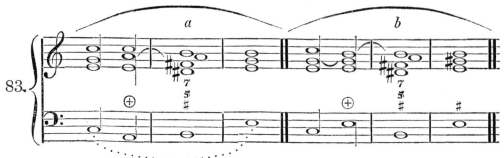

The chords marked thus ⊕, are interposed.

The circumstances are the same in modulating to *the minor 3rd above.*

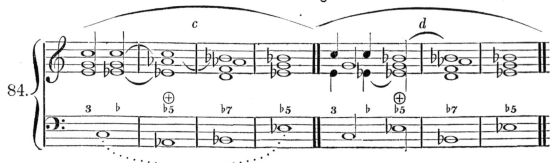

In modulating to the *half tone below*, although the 3rd of the Tonic seems to mark a connexion with the 7th of the Dominant, yet the relationship between these two keys is so very far removed, as scarcely to be admitted ; and the effect of such a succession is extremely harsh and disagreeable, as in the following Example at (*a.*)

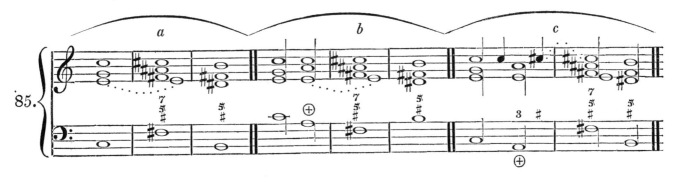

A much better effect is produced by the intervention of a chord, as at (*b*); or still better as at (*c.*)

Now let us go to the key farthest removed, *i. e.*, a sharp 4th, (or, which is the same thing, a flat 5th) above.

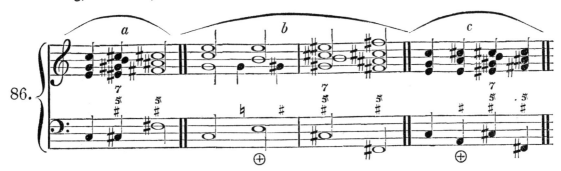

At (*a.*) There is no connexion between the two first chords.
At (*b.*) The chord of the major 3rd above is interposed ; and
At (*c.*) That of the minor 3rd below.

By the preceding rules for selecting Dominants, it appears that we can modulate from any given key to six others.

We must now particularly remark, that, when we have thus modulated to any new key, we may consider ourselves placed in the same situation as if we were commencing at that key; and we may, in the same manner, employ any of the intervals of the Tonic, Dominant, or Sub-dominant of that key, for the purpose of further modulation.

An Exercise on all the preceding Rules.

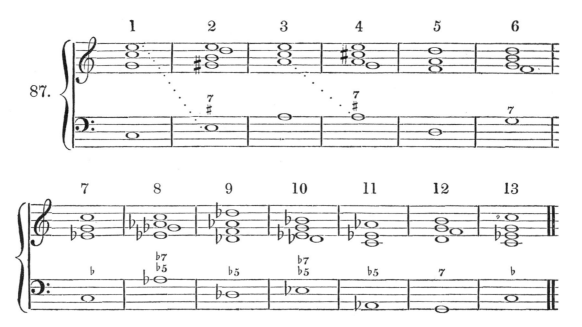

At bar 1: We have taken the 3rd of the *Tonic,* and modulated to the relative minor.

At bar 3: We have chosen the 8ve, and modulated to D minor, the *Sub-dominant* of which key we have taken (in bar 6,) and thus modulate (in bar 7) to C minor.

At bar 8: Being in C minor, we take the 3rd of the *Sub-dominant,* which modulates to D♭.

At bar 10: We are in the key of D♭, and, taking the 5th of its *Dominant,* modulate to A♭.

At bar 12: Being now in A♭, we take the 3rd of its *Dominant,* and modulate to C minor.

The foregoing Examples will sufficiently show the inexhaustible variety of modulations to be produced, by the application of the preceding simple rules; which, let it not be forgotten, have all arisen out of the original three fundamental basses.

The Pupil will not fail to avail himself of the extensive power of modulation now placed at his command, varying his selections from the different intervals on each occasion, by which he must inevitably produce ever new, and only the best, effects; all harsh and extraneous modulations being totally excluded by the nature of the rules themselves.

He is strongly recommended on all occasions to play the modulations he may write; and in order to produce a diversity of effect, he may arrange them in various ways, of which a few specimens are given in the following Example.

This, in fact, will constitute an elementary introduction to extempory playing, and afford hints for different styles of accompaniment.

EXAMPLE 88.

Harmony is divided into Concord and Discord.

The common chord is a Concord, and the sounds comprising it (*i. e.*, the 3rd, 5th, and 8th) are called *Consonances*.

When a Concord is heard, the effect upon the ear is agreeable and perfect in itself: the sounds of which it consists may be allowed gradually to subside, for they excite no expectation of any others to succeed them.

But when any one of the sounds composing the concord is removed, and some other sound substituted in its place, the very opposite effect of a Concord is produced.

The sound which occasions this difference of effect, is called a *Dissonance;* and The chord in which this Dissonance is heard, is called a *Discord.*

A constant succession of Consonances would cloy the ear.

A judicious intermixture of Dissonances creates more interest, adds greatly to the variety, and may indeed be said to give light and shade to harmony.

If the following descending melody be played, accompanied by its fundamental bass (as at *a*), the ear will be perfectly satisfied.

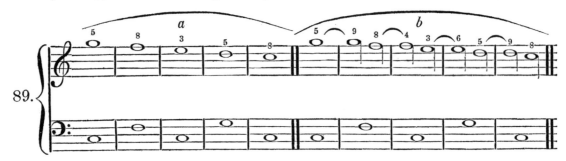

But let the sound G in the melody be continued in the succeeding bar without altering the bass (as in the above Example at *b*), and the ear will be immediately in a state of anxiety to hear the sound F.

When an interval of a melody is thus kept back in *descending*, we shall call it *suspension;* for instance.

G suspends F.

F . . . . E.

E . . . . D ; or, in other words,

The 9th suspends the 8th.

The 4th . . . . the 3rd.

The 5th . . . . the 6th.

These comprise all the *Dissonances by suspension.*

The chord of the Dissonance of the 4th produced by suspending the 3rd.

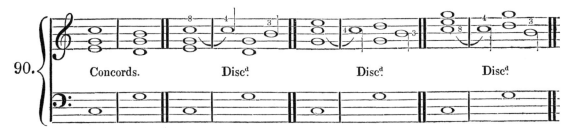

The chord of the Dissonance of the 9th produced by suspending the 8th.

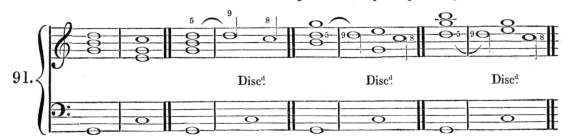

Chord of the Dissonance of the 6th produced by suspending the 5th.

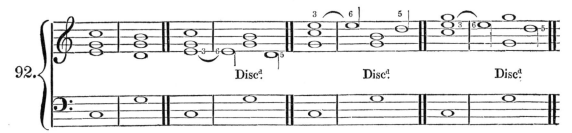

From the preceding Examples, it is evident that those sounds which produce discord naturally present themselves, in their descending progression, first as *Consonances,* and then as *Dissonances :* from this circumstance arises a very natural and a very important rule, *viz.,* that

> " All *Dissonances must be introduced by Consonances,"* or (in other words), " *the sound which becomes the Dissonance, must first be heard in the preceding chord as a consonance.*"

This is technically called *preparing the Dissonance,* or simply *preparation ;* and

> " *In whatever part the Dissonance appears,* (whether soprano, alto, &c., &c.,) *in that part must it likewise be prepared.*"

This rule for the preparation of Dissonances would be quite superfluous, were we to introduce the *suspensions* only when the melody *descends;* but as this is not the case, the preparation must be strictly attended to.

N. B. On referring to Example 89, (*b*) it will be observed that the Dissonance always descends one degree upon the following Consonance.

In order to give a proper notion of *preparing* Dissonances by suspension, instead of taking the *descending scale*, we will make use of the *ascending*, in which no Dissonance will be found naturally prepared.

At (*a*) in the following Example, the three chords are all Concords.

At (*b*) the Dissonance of the 4th is introduced in the alto, because its resolution (the 3rd) is in that part. But, as it here appears, it is *not prepared!*

At (*c*) it *is* prepared, and in the same part, by dividing the 5th (G) of the preceding chord into two minims, and allowing the latter to ascend to C, (the 8th of the same chord) which is the proper preparation for the following 4th.

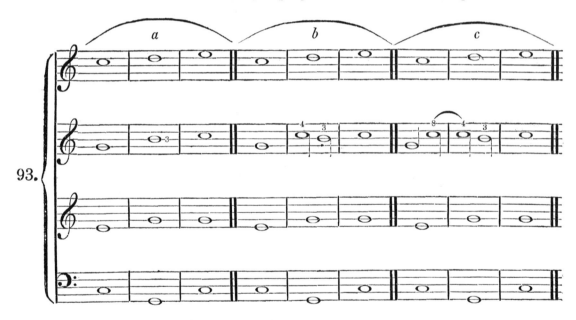

All the above observations, as to preparation, &c., apply equally to the other Dissonances of the 9th resolved into the 8th, and the 6th into the 5th.

After having harmonized a melody, or having otherwise obtained any progression of harmony, in order to know in what chords we can introduce dissonances, we must examine the progression of the Fundamental Bass, and observe the following rule.

" When the Fundamental Bass *ascends a fifth**, we can introduce the dissonance *of the 4th resolved into the 3rd.*"

As shown in the following Example.

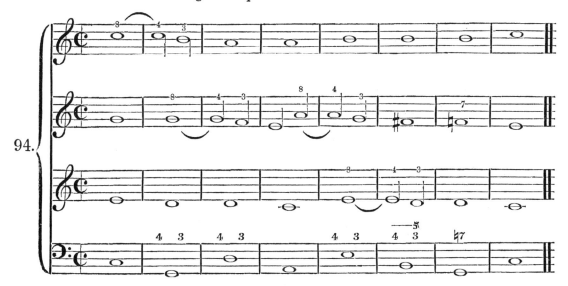

Observe that in bars 2, 3, and 6, the dissonances are already prepared in the same part where their resolution appears, because the melody *descends ;* but in bar 5 the case is otherwise, the melody *ascends,* and we are obliged to ascend to obtain a preparation for the dissonance.

N.B. The pupil may take the basses of some of the melodies which he has formerly harmonized, and employ them as exercises on the above or the following rules.

" When the Fundamental Bass *ascends a 4th†,* we can introduce the Dissonance of the *9th resolved into the 8th.*"

On referring to Example 91, we observe that the bass *ascends a fourth,* and, in the chord to which it has ascended, the 9th is introduced, prepared by the preceding 5th, which is the ground of this rule, and of which the following is an Exercise in score.

At *a :* The 9th is introduced in the alto, because the 8th is there ; but it will be observed that it is not yet prepared in that part.

At *b :* The 9th is prepared, by the 3rd of the preceding chord having ascended to the 5th.

---

* Which is, of course, the same as *descending* a 4th.   † Which is the same as *descending* a 5th.

K

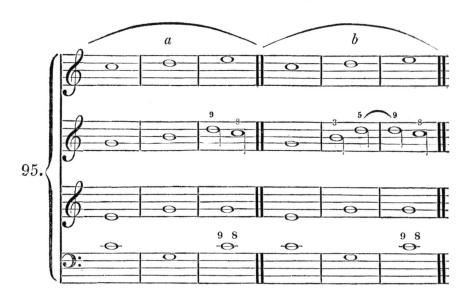

We will now harmonize the ascending scale, introducing both the 4th into the 3rd, and the 9th into the 8th *.

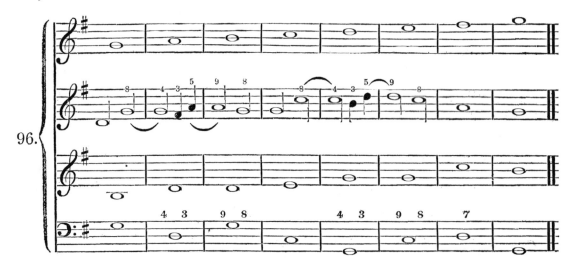

At bar 2: The bass has descended a 4th, (the same as ascending a 5th,) consequently we can have a 4th resolved into the 3rd. The 3rd being in the alto, the 4th is put there also. As the 4th was not already prepared in that part, the alto ascends to G, the 8th in the first bar, for that purpose.

At bar 3: The 9th requires the alto to ascend again in bar 2, for its preparation.

At bar 4: The alto ascends to C, in order to prepare the 4th in the following bar.

---

* Some future remarks on the strict and free styles will refer back to this Example.

It will be observed, that in this bar 4, the bass has descended a 5th; therefore, by the above rule, we could have the 9th into the 8th. Why is it not introduced? Because the 8th is in the soprano; and, as the 9th must be placed there also, we cannot, in this instance, admit the dissonance without materially altering the melody.

At bar 7: The consecutive 5ths and 8ths are avoided by the second method.

In this manner should the pupil exercise on scales in different keys, introducing these two dissonances*, performing them thus harmonized, and comparing the difference of effect with Examples 45 and 47.

The Harmonization of the Descending Diatonic Scale.

The Diatonic Scale considered as a Melody, is the same ascending and descending; but there are many reasons why it should be differently harmonized.

In the introduction to modulation we explained in what manner the forced construction of the scale, between the 6th and 7th intervals, produced consecutive 5ths and 8ths, and we have already shown two methods of avoiding these in the ascending scale, but the same methods cannot be employed in descending. Instead, therefore, of allowing the Bass to fall from the Dominant to the Subdominant, (as at *a* in the following Example,) it is made to ascend one degree, (as at *b*,) and thus by proceeding in contrary motion to the rest of the parts, consecutive 5ths and 8ths are prevented †.

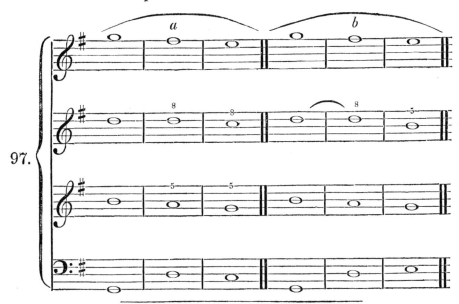

* The 6th into the 5th will be found noticed in Example 101.

† This introduces into the scale a minor chord, which had not been explained when we treated of the ascending scales. This will account for our thus long delaying Exercises in the descending scales.

K 2

The following is an Example of the Diatonic scale descending, in four parts, in which is introduced the dissonance of the 4th resolved into the 3rd, and the 9th resolved into the 8th [*].

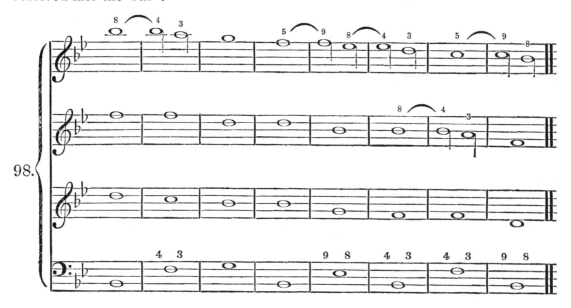

In bar 2: Why does the 4th appear in the soprano, and in bar 7 in the alto? Because its resolution is there.

Why can we introduce the 4th in that chord? Because the Bass has ascended a 5th.

In bar 3: Why has the bass ascended one degree? To prevent consecutive 5ths and 8ths.

" No interval can be suspended, and also *be heard at the same time.*"

Let us therefore be careful when we introduce the 9th, (for instance,) in one part, that the 8th shall not appear in another. This remark applies, of course, to the other dissonances.

As we are now about to employ the Fundamental 7th in conjunction with the Dissonances above explained, we will take this opportunity to point out some peculiarities worthy of attention.

1st. The dissonances by *suspension* are always *prepared.*

The 7th is introduced *without* preparation.

---

[*] The dissonances thus appearing in the soprano, are not to be considered as any material alteration of the melody, which is merely suspended in its progress.

2nd. The dissonances by suspension are resolved upon the *same* bass.
The 7th is resolved upon the *succeeding* bass.

Thus the fundamental 7th appears to partake of the nature of a consonance—as requiring no preparation ; and of a dissonance—as requiring to be resolved.
Another distinction in the effect is also to be observed.
A dissonance by suspension has a tendency to come to a state of rest upon the same bass ; but the 7th urges us forward to another chord.

The Diatonic Scale Descending

With the 4th into the 3rd, the 9th into the 8th, and the fundamental 7th.

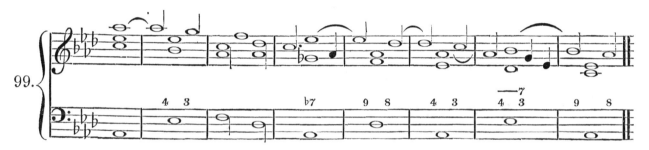

From the progression of the bass it appears that, in the above Example, we can introduce the fundamental 7th on only two chords.
In bar 3 : After the consecutives have been prevented, the bass descends to the sub-dominant, the original bass of the scale ; by which we produce still greater variety.
In bar 4 : The 3rd of the dominant chord descends to the 8th on the same bass, in order to admit the 9th in the following chord, for had the 3rd continued until the end of the bar, it must have ascended to the 8th of the following chord, and thus the *8th and 9th would have been heard together.*
N.B. This method must be adopted whenever the bass proceeds from dominant to tonic, and the 9th is introduced on the latter chord.
The following is a melody harmonized in score, introducing *occasionally* the dissonances already explained : to introduce them on *all* occasions allowed by the progression of the bass would crowd the exercise, and frequently injure the effect of the melody *.

---

* It may be remarked also, *en passant,* that no attention is here paid to disputed points, they will be noticed hereafter. Our object is simply to exercise the pupil on what has been *already* said.

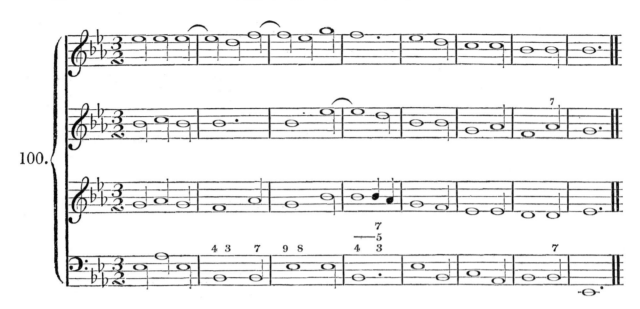

100.

In bar 6: Two fundamental basses are employed to the 6th of the scale, as in Example 99, bar 3.

At the conclusion of this Example, the alto progression appears in the soprano, and of course there is an interchange of character in the other parts. It is not usual to close thus, but for variety of effect it may be permitted.

Compound Dissonances.—Two Dissonances introduced at once upon the same Bass.

We have seen that when the bass ascends a 5th, we can have the dissonance of the 4th into the 3rd, and

When the bass *thus proceeds*, we can *also* have the 6th into the 5th, and

These two may be used either separately, or together, as in the following Example (at *a*.)

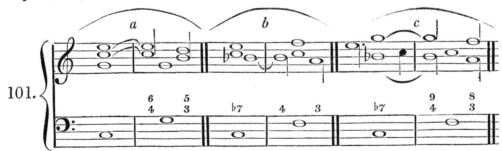

101.

When the bass ascends a 4th, we already know that we can have the 9th into the 8th, and

We can *also* have the 4th into the 3rd prepared by the 7th; provided the harmony admits of a 7th being used in the foregoing chord, (as in the above Example at *b*:) and

The 4th into the 3rd may be compounded with the 9th into the 8th, (as at *c*.)

The following Exercise is the same melody as Example 100, arranged for the piano-forte; by which the pupil will begin to perceive the variety of effect which may thus be produced. The harmony is still strictly in four parts, and the same as in Example 100, with the addition only of the compound dissonances explained in Example 101.

In bars 2 and 4: The compound dissonance of the 4th and 6th is used.

In bars 3 and 8: The 4th is combined with the 9th.

In bars 6 and 7: The 9th is prepared by the 3rd, (as will be explained in the next Example, 103.)

The melody in this above Exercise has been made to close with a *tenor progression*, which has a peculiar softness of expression; this should be compared with the same melody at Example 100, which will also render the effects of the dissonances, here added, more particularly observable.

N.B. Descending scales may be here employed as Exercises.

The Introduction of the Dissonances is regulated by the Progression of the Bass.

The two chief progressions of the bass are already shown, and we shall only briefly display the rest, as every thing respecting preparation, &c., is now understood.

When the bass ascends a 2nd, } the 9th prepared by the 3rd, } as in Ex. 103.
we may introduce . . . . . . } & the 4th . . . . 5th. }   (a)
When the bass ascends a 3rd,   the 6th . . . . 8th.   (b)
When the bass ascends a 6th,   we can have no dissonance.

When the bass ascends a 7th, {
we can have the 4th prepared by the 3rd. (c)
. . . . 9th . . . . 8th. (d)
. . . . 6th . . . . 5th. *(e)

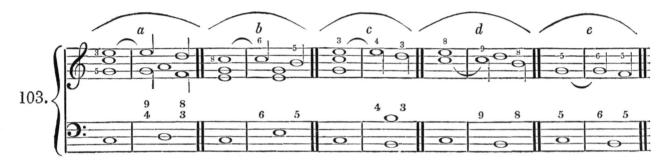

In order to acquire a facility in introducing dissonances, proceed thus,
Take any succession of fundamental basses, such for instance as the following,

Write the chords on a treble staff left blank for the purpose above this bass, always avoiding unnecessary skips in the melody.

Figure each bass note with all the dissonances which its particular progression admits of.

Introduce into the harmonies such of these dissonances as your own taste may suggest, or as may be dictated by circumstances; for (as has been already observed) the whole ought not to be introduced on every occasion.   And lastly,

Take care that those which are employed are properly prepared and resolved.

The pupil may easily supply himself with exercises of this description, to any extent, by taking the basses of any course of modulation, which he has already written, or which he may write for himself by following the instructions at Example 87.

* It will be better to postpone the employment of these two latter dissonances on this progression of the bass, until the introduction of the subject of inversion.

We shall conclude this part of the subject, by an exercise, of which the former part is complete, the full chords having been first written over the basses, and the dissonances afterwards introduced. The latter part of the example is yet incomplete; the chords not having been first written as in the former part, the dissonances only are introduced with their preparations and resolutions, leaving the remaining notes of the harmony to be afterwards added.

This latter plan will be found advantageous if frequently employed, as it more distinctly displays the dissonances, and will ensure a more perfect acquaintance with the subject.

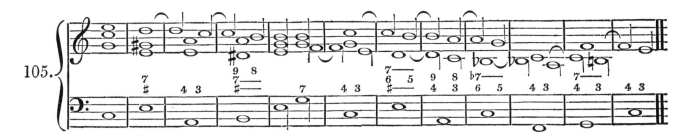

Inverted Basses.

It must have been observed that Fundamental Basses move generally by great intervals, (5ths, 4ths, &c., &c.) which is the peculiar characteristic of a Bass melody, and gives an unconnected effect to that part when compared with the melody of the others.

There appears something too decided and too peremptory in this progression of the Bass, which does not sufficiently amalgamate with the smooth and equal progression of the other parts. It has the effect of a bluntness of expression, which we wish exchanged for a softer and more pleasing phraseology.

The mode of accomplishing this is, to adopt occasionally other intervals of the harmony in place of some of the Fundamental Basses, thereby producing a melody in the Bass, which still preserves in a great measure its natural character, whilst at the same time it participates also in that of the other parts, thus promoting an intimate union of the whole, and producing a graceful and flowing harmony.

Any of the intervals may be taken out of a chord and written as a Bass, which is then called an *Inverted Bass,* and under which must be supposed to stand the Fundamental Bass, to sustain and direct the whole superstructure.

L

The Fundamental Bass *may,* indeed, be written underneath on a separate staff, but must not be considered as a fifth part, for it may be entirely expunged after the inversions have been completed.

What is meant by Inversion will be understood, when described as a chord wherein the note written in the bass is not the real fundamental bass, but some other note of the harmony. Thus, when we take for the bass the *first* note of the chord above the fundamental bass, it is called the *first inversion;* when we take the *second* note above the fundamental bass, it is the *second inversion;* and so on.

In selecting intervals of a chord for inverted basses, we will, for the present, attend to the chord of the dominant 7th only. This chord has (besides its fundamental bass) *three intervals,* therefore we can have *three inversions.*

When we thus adopt for the bass a note belonging to any other part, we must take out from the harmony that note, and also the note to which it proceeds: to shew this, in the following example the part which has been selected for a bass is marked by black notes.

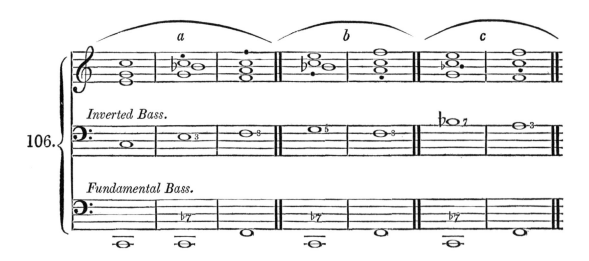

Whenever any of these intervals are written in the Bass, they must proceed exactly the same as if in their own places, and we shall thus transfer to the Bass the peculiar character of the part from which they have been selected.

But, supposing that the *chords* are *not* written above, how are we to know which is a Fundamental, and which an Inverted Bass?

The *fundamental bass* of the chord of the dominant 7th we have always figured with a 7, and we will continue to do so: when we use an Inversion, we will count upwards from the *borrowed Bass note* to the other intervals of the chord, and write the figures corresponding with each over the Bass note; which is, in fact, describing the notes by figures instead of writing them on a staff*; and an Inversion is thus distinguished by its figuring.

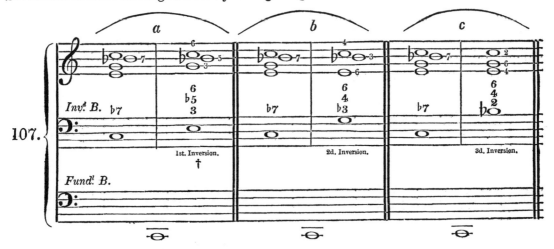

The pupil must, however, at all times look for the true explanation of the chord to the *Fundamental Bass* only, and consider the *Inverted Bass* merely as the lowest of four melodies; for we shall continue to name all the intervals of the chord, as hitherto, counting from the fundamental bass. Thus in the above example:

At (a): Is the first inversion of the Fundamental 7th, where the real 7th of the chord is figured by a 5; but we shall still continue to call it the 7th.

In the same inversion also, by the same rule, we say the 3rd is in the bass; the 5th in the Tenor; the 7th in the Alto; and the 8th in the Soprano; and the same observations will apply to all other inversions.

By this means the subject is much simplified, as our attention is directed only to the intervals of one chord, of the Fundamental 7th.

At (b): Is the second inversion of the same chord, (the 5th being in the bass) which is called the chord of the *third, fourth, and sixth; or fourth and sixth.*

At (c): Is the third inversion, (the Fundamental 7th being in the bass) which is called the chord of the *second, fourth, and sixth.*

---

* This may be called a musical stenography. It is, indeed, of very little real utility; but as there is much valuable music still extant, wherein the harmonies are only to be found by a knowledge of these figured basses, and as that knowledge is very easily acquired, we have thought it right not to omit this part of the subject.

† The 3 is usually omitted in figuring this inversion.

L 2

Modulation by the first Inversion of the Dominant 7th, or chord of the Fifth and Sixth ($^6_5$).

As an exercise on what has just been said, let us take a course of modulation, for instance the one ascending a whole tone, as in Example 76; between the fundamental bass and the chords, we will leave a blank staff, on which may be afterwards written the inverted bass.

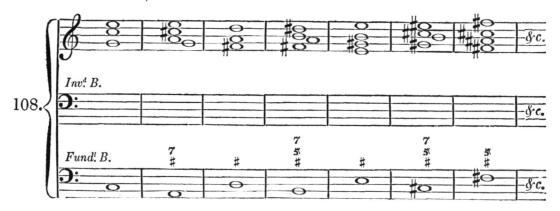

Having prepared the exercise as above, let us commence by writing upon the blank Bass staff, the fundamental bass to the first chord; from the second chord, which is a Dominant, take away the 3rd, and place it on the bass staff, continuing to select the 3rd out of each *Dominant* chord throughout the exercise; thus,

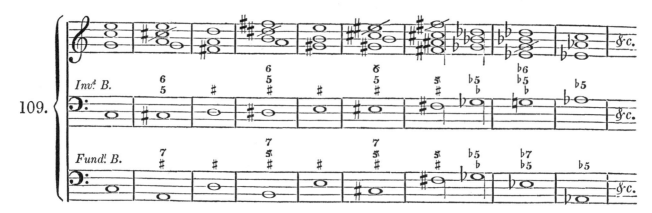

In filling up the inverted bass staff of the above exercise, the Pupil should proceed thus:

Bar 1: Commence with C: the Fundamental Bass, as is usual at the commencement of any composition.

Bar 2: C♯ is the 3rd of the dominant chord, and must ascend. Write this C♯ as the bass, and take away the note from the chord (as marked by a dash). Then figure that bass note with a 5th and 6th (it being the first inversion of the fundamental 7th).

Bar 3: The last note C♯, of course, here ascends to D. In this case the D in the *melody* is allowed to remain, because E (the 5th) in *that part* has descended to it; and the same occurs at bars 5 and 9.

Bar 4: D♯ is here chosen, being the 3rd of the dominant chord, and proceeds exactly the same as in the former instance (in bar 2).

Here, in the figuring, a sharp is marked without a figure, as applying to the 3rd, because the 3rd (F♯) requires this accidental, which must never be omitted.

Bar 5: E is the fundamental bass, and must be figured as the fundamental bass, which bears a ♯, on account of the 3rd being sharp.

Bar 6: In this first inversion of the dominant 7th, the 6th also requires to be made ♯, and has consequently a dash through the head of it.

The rest is similar to the preceding, and sufficiently explains itself.

The above example we have modulated by the *First Inversion only.*

In the same manner let us now modulate through all the Major and Minor Keys, as in Example 72.

The pupil should proceed as before, writing the exercise upon three staves; but to avoid occupying more space than necessary in this work, we will, as often as practicable, merely mark the *fundamental bass* with a *point*, allowing the inverted bass to stand conspicuous. The pupil, however, should continue to write the fundamental basses on a separate staff, and also carefully figure them.

In this example it may be perceived that we have, as in the former instance, selected only the *first inversion* of the dominant chord on all occasions, without regard to the formation of a good melody; this has been done, in order to make the pupil perfectly acquainted with the *first inversion.* We shall now proceed to employ the others in a similar manner.

Modulation by the Second Inversion of the Chord of the Dominant 7th, or Chord of the Third, Fourth, and Sixth $\left(\frac{6}{4}\atop 3\right)$

Through all the Major and Minor keys, as in the last Example.

In Bar 2.   The B, taken as a bass note, is the 5th of the true fundamental Bass, and, consequently, the second inversion. This, as well as the first inversion, gives a soprano progression to the bass. The B is taken away from the chord in the staff above, but the note to which it proceeds is allowed to remain, because the 3rd must ascend to it; and the same occurs at bars 4 and 5.

In Bars 6 and 7. The note itself and the one to which it should proceed are both removed; otherwise consecutive octaves with the bass would be the consequence.

Modulation by the Third Inversion, or Chord of the $\frac{6}{4}\atop 2$ *through the Major and Minor Keys.*

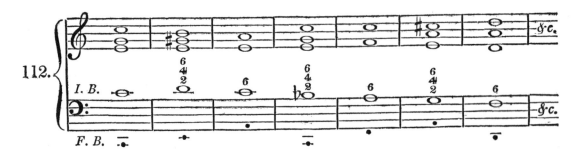

In Bar 2.   D, in the Bass, is the 7th of the chord of E, which is the third inversion, and gives the Tenor progression. The note itself, and also its resolution, are taken away from the chord above, to prevent consecutive octaves.

In Bar 3. D, the 7th, properly resolves upon C, the 3rd of its Tonic chord. This not being a fundamental bass, but the first inversion, must be figured with a 6*.

Having employed the three inversions separately, now let us take the same modulation through the Major and Minor keys, employing all the inversions in the same Exercise. No rule for this need be given, for, by observing what has been already said, it is not possible to err.

As in other cases variety of effect has been our chief object, so let it be here; and in writing the chords, let care be taken to avoid skips, as before recommended.

A few chords of the commencement may serve as a specimen.

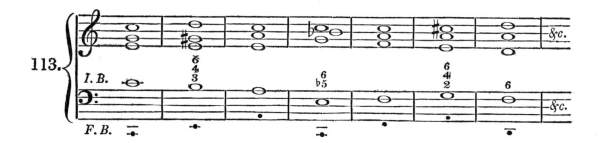

N.B. When we write *diversifications* for exercise, in order to preserve the uniformity of the variation with which we set out, we may be allowed to relax a little the rule laid down respecting the progression of the 5th and the 8th† in the resolution of the Dominant chord; this, however, will only be necessary when employing the 3rd inversion of that chord. Instances of this relaxation of the rule will be found in the following Example, where

In Bar 6.　　　　The 5th ascends to the 5th in Bar 7.
In Bar 12 and 13.　The 5th ascends to the 5th, and the 8th to the 8th.
In Bar 14.　　　The 5th ascends and doubles the 3rd of the following chord, which should be sparingly used.

---

*This first inversion of the common chord is sufficiently represented by the 6 above the Bass note; the note corresponding with this figure is in reality the real octave of the Fundamental Bass.

† See pages 22 and 26.

Specimen of Diversification in the Performance of an Exercise.

The preceding is the *same* modulation as Example 87, which, it will be recollected, was discovered, merely *by selecting a Dominant* from the intervals of the chords.

In the present example, it will be perceived that the inverted basses have been also selected, by a similar easy process, from the intervals of the chords; from these it will be very evident that the pupil must, of necessity, produce excellent effects in modulation, even without further instruction, merely by putting in practice the simple rules hitherto given.

Let us suppose a pupil, thus far advanced, desirous of writing for himself an exercise in modulation:—

He must first determine the key from which he will set out. This being fixed, the question he will propose to himself will be—

How shall I first modulate?

I will take the 3rd of the above first-determined chord, employ it as a Dominant, and I find it leads me to ———.

To where shall I next modulate?

I will now take the 8th of my present chord as a Dominant, which brings me to ———, which, for variety, shall be a minor chord*.

I will now take an interval from the chord of the Sub-dominant of this last key, suppose the 8th, which leads me to ———.

Here I will take the 5th of the Dominant of this last key, which brings me to ———.

Now let us have the 3rd of the Sub-dominant of this key which modulates to ———.

And this shall be a minor chord

Here I wish to close the exercise, and will, therefore, take

The present dominant which shall be minor, and

The 3rd* of ~~this last chord~~, which presents the Dominant I require; and thus I shall conclude in the key with which I commenced.

In whatever key the pupil commences his exercise, should he choose to follow this process exactly, he will return again to the same key, which will be a proof of the exercise being correct. It may, however, be further extended, or brought to a conclusion at any time, or in any key, by employing the Dominant of that key. Should no connexion be found between the Dominant thus employed and the preceding chord, he will interpose another chord, as directed in Example 83.

It is unnecessary to point out how infinitely such an exercise may be extended. From the immense variety producible, new effects will continually occur, and no two examples can ever be alike.

N. B. The pupil should frequently write variations upon his exercises, for which purpose the above Example 114 will serve as a specimen.

---

* It may be mentioned as a useful hint, that a Major 3rd taken as a Dominant, will lead to a key with three sharps more, and a Minor 3rd to a key with four flats more.

M

Cadences in Modulation.

When the chord of the Fundamental 7th, or Dominant harmony proceeds *direct* to the Tonic, it is called " a perfect Cadence," as at *a* in the following example.

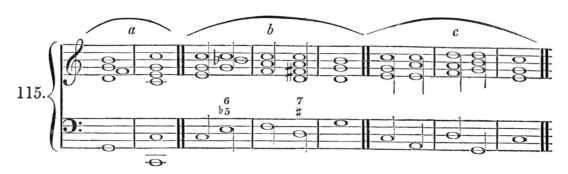

It must have been observed, that by a continued Modulation from key to key, we are kept in a state of constant excitement, approaching even to a painful sensation, so that the ear becomes desirous of rest. Therefore, when we have modulated for some time, it becomes necessary either to return to the key from which we set out, and there conclude, or, if we wish to proceed still further, first to make a close in the key at which we have arrived, and, afterwards modulating for some time longer, to come at last to a final close.

We must not, however, suddenly stop upon any Tonic at which we may have arrived (as at *b*, in the above example); for, as the great object of a Cadence is to lead the ear to a quiet state, an abrupt termination must destroy the effect intended. It might be supposed that the perfect Cadence described above would be sufficient for this purpose, yet we find that this is really not the case. It is true, that proceeding direct by the chord of the Fundamental 7th to its Tonic forms a perfect Cadence, with which the ear would be sufficiently satisfied, where modulations have not recently occurred (as at *e* in the above example); yet the frequency of its occurrence in a course of modulation, although it may not destroy, materially weakens the decisive and concluding effect it would naturally produce under other circumstances. Therefore, when we arrive at the Tonic of any key to which we have modulated, and desire to come to a decided and satisfactory close, the ear must be gradually soothed into a quiescent state by the introduction of a few chords, so constructed, that they shall not only have a tendency to conduct the ear to a state of rest, but shall also be calculated to produce a strong impression of the key in which it is intended the close shall take place.

The chords best calculated for this purpose are those of the Sub-dominant and Dominant; for, the intervals of these chords (including also those of the Tonic) embrace the whole of the Diatonic Scale: so that, in fact, by hearing these three chords at the close of a modulation, we receive an impression of every interval of the key in which we thus conclude.   See *d* in the following example.

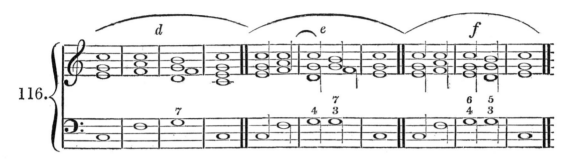

However, a frequent recurrence of the simple chords of which this Cadence is constructed would produce a heavy and rather monotonous effect, which is much relieved by the introduction of the Dissonance of the 4th upon the Dominant, as at *e*.

On account of the frequent occurrence of the Final Cadence, composers have been induced to seek for every possible variety, and great liberties have been taken for this purpose.   The 4th, as it appears in the last example (at *e*), was properly prepared; but a sixth is also sometimes introduced, which, it will be perceived, cannot be prepared, and must be considered as a licence, as at *f*.

Another liberty was afterwards taken with the chord of the Sub-dominant in this Cadence, by *adding* to it a 6th, calling it then " *The Chord of the added Sixth*," (as at *g* in the following example.)

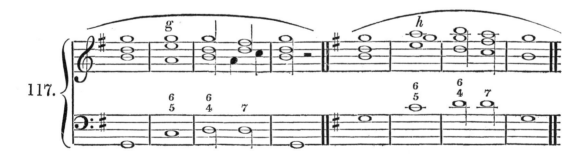

N.B. The 5th in this chord is prepared as if it were a dissonance; and, in four parts, the octave should be omitted, as it appears above, at *g*.

This chord sometimes of the added sixth is also written as at *h*.

M 2

Sometimes the 5th of the Sub-dominant Chord is entirely omitted, and the added 6th doubled, as at *i* in the following example; and sometimes the 8th is used in place of the 5th, as at *k, l, m**.

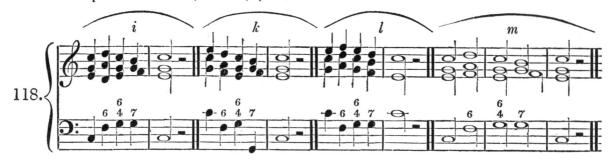

N. B. This part of the subject will be resumed hereafter.

Let the pupil now write an exercise on what he has acquired up to this point. Let him proceed step by step, exactly as hereafter directed, and *afterwards* compare what he has done with the exercise completed as in Example 119.

Brace together three staves; the top for the chords, the middle one for the Inverted Bass, and the bottom for the Fundamental Bass.

Draw bars across these, and number each bar:

In the first bar, "write the chord of C in the third position, *four crotchets* in the bar," which may be continued in each bar, throughout the whole exercise.

Let the first Bass note be C.

"Make a Cadence with the $\frac{6}{4}$ upon the dominant." The chord of the Sub-dominant occupies the second bar; the Dominant the 3rd bar, with the $\frac{6}{4}$ on the first half, and the 7th on the other, resolving on C in Bar 4.

"Modulate to the relative Minor by the second inversion." *This occupies two bars.*

"Modulate to the key of F by the second inversion."

"Modulate to the relative Minor of F by the second inversion." Make a Cadence in that key, which brings us to the 12th bar.

"Modulate to B♭ by the third inversion," and make a Cadence in that key.

"Make another Cadence in B♭ with the added 6th."

"Modulate by the 2nd inversion to the relative Minor of the last key."

"Modulate to E♭ by the 2nd inversion, and make a Cadence in that key with the $\frac{6}{4}$ on the Dominant."

"Modulate to C by the 2nd inversion, and thus proceed further at discretion."

---

* We must not suppose that when the chord of the Sub-dominant appears as in the above example, it is the first inversion of the chord of D Minor, though it has that appearance. If we take the trouble to trace the final Cadence throughout its different stages, it will be evident that the 6th on the Sub-dominant is derived from the chord of the added 6th.

The following example will be found to correspond with the preceding directions. It is of no consequence, if the pupil should find that he has given the time of a full bar to some chords which may here only occupy half a bar; the principle is the same, and as to effect, he should early begin to exercise his own taste.

In order to give some appearance of periods, and regularity of effect, let a Cadence be introduced after any *even* number of bars (as 8, 10, 12, &c.)

To repeat the same modulation with a different inversion has sometimes a good effect.

A modulation may sometimes, for variety, be made to take place at the half bars (as at bars 18 and 19 of the above example), and may gradually lead to distinguishing periods, &c.

A variety of effect may be also produced by changing the time of an exercise.

Suppose, for instance, the last example of four crotchets in a bar is to be changed to ³⁄₄ time of three crotchets in a bar: there can be no difficulty in doing this, if there be only one chord in each bar; and should there be two different chords in the same bar (as in bars 18, 19, and 20), let the first half bar be written the value of two crotchets, and the latter half only one, as at *a* in the following Example 120.

The same example may be changed to ⁶⁄₈ time, by writing the second and fourth crotchets as quavers, as at *b*.

Nine-eight being an unequal division of the time, must again have (as at *a*) the larger portion to the first chord: thus two dotted crotchets would belong to the first chord, and only one to the latter, as at *c*.

The following example will serve many useful purposes.

It will elucidate what has just been said as to varying the time of any progression of harmonies.

It will gradually give some ideas of rhythm, and the construction of periods, and open the mind to the different styles of diversifying chords, by way of accompaniment.

It consists of specimens of various styles of performance of *the same* progression of harmonies not intended to be played altogether, as they here appear scored, but in many different ways, as may be thus explained.

First, let it be understood by any one performing this exercise, that whatever style of accompaniment may be first selected, the whole should be played *through* in that same style. Suppose the pupil commences as written in the first four bars, at *a* and *b*, playing steadily four crotchets in each bar, he must continue the same to the end of the exercise and not change the style on arriving at II.

He may commence with the variation in triplets as at II., and proceed through the whole of the exercise in the same character; or he may commence and proceed through with *any* of the variations or different specimens of accompaniment as introduced on the two lowest staves, and marked from I. to XII.

Any one of these accompaniments may be performed whilst another person plays one of the melodies at *c, d,* or *e,* or any other similar one which the pupil may hereafter write upon the same succession of harmonies. Care must be taken, however, to regulate the time of the accompaniment, as directed above, to correspond with the melody chosen.

EXAMPLE 121.

cres - - cendo

Continue the Accompaniment according to the preceding specimen.

VII.

Introduction of the Dissonances in Modulation.

In this there is nothing new: we have only to consult the progression of the Fundamental Basses, and observe the rules preceding Examples 103, 4, 5.

The following Example (122, at *a*) is a course of Modulations with Inverted Basses. Let the pupil take this, and having at every step introduced whatever Dissonances the progression of the fundamental bass will admit, let him compare what he has done with the Exercise completed below at *b*.

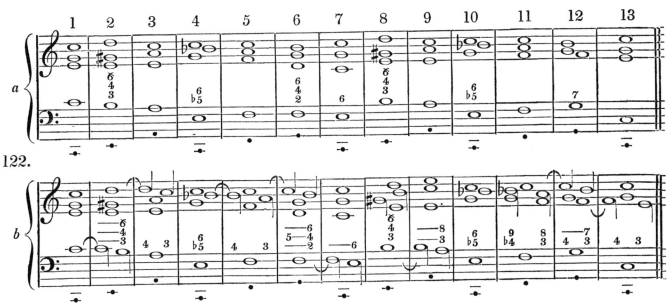

Examination of the above Exercise.

Bar 2. How has the Fundamental Bass here proceeded?

It has ascended a third.

What Dissonances can we introduce?

The 6th into the 5th prepared by the 3rd.

In what part ought we to introduce the 6th?

In the Inverted Bass, because the 5th (its resolution) is there. Therefore (B) the 5th in the Inverted Bass must be removed a little to the right, written as a Minim, and have (C) the 6th placed before it.

N.B. At present take no notice of the figuring.

Bar 3. The Fundamental Bass has here ascended a fourth:—what Dissonances may we introduce?

The 4th prepared by the 7th.

In what part must this 4th be written?

In the soprano, where the 3rd (its resolution) is.

Bar 4.   No Dissonance by suspension is used.

Bar 5.   As the Dominant 7th was employed in the preceding chord, that 7th will prepare a 4th in this bar; and this 4th is introduced in the alto where the 3rd is.

Bar 6.   The Fundamental Bass has ascended one degree, and the 4th is introduced, resolved into the 3rd in the soprano.

Bar 7.   The 4th into the 3rd is introduced in the Inverted Bass, prepared by the preceding Dominant 7th in that part.

Bar 8.   No Dissonance is employed.

Bar 9.   The Fundamental Bass ascends a fourth, and the 9th is introduced in the Inverted Bass, because the 8th is there.

Bar 10. The 7th only is introduced, which prepares the 4th in

Bar 11. Where also the 9th into the 8th is used at the same time, as the Fundamental Bass ascends a fourth.

Bar 12. The Fundamental Bass ascends one degree, and the 4th into the 3rd is in the soprano; the 7th also is here introduced, which prepares the 4th in the following bar.

Thus the Exercise is completed, and the whole process explained.

We will now say something more respecting the

Figuring of Inverted Basses when Dissonances are employed.

It must always be recollected that the Inverted Bass is merely a melody selected from the harmonies of the Fundamental Bass, and in the course of this melody the Fundamental Basses themselves are frequently used, as in the above example, Bars 1, 3, 5, 11, 12, 13.

What has been already observed respecting the figuring of Fundamental Basses is sufficient, and may be referred to at Examples 37, 60, 89, and following.

By the practice we have had up to this period, we may be supposed to be well acquainted with the figuring of the inversions of the common chord, and the chord of the fundamental 7th. (Example 107, &c.)

If this be the case, we have little more to learn. The introduction of a Dissonance, for instance the 4th into the 3rd, is merely placing the 4th before the 3rd; therefore in the figuring of any Inverted Bass, if the Dissonance of the 4th is to be introduced into the chord, let a figure, which will represent that 4th, be placed before the figure which represents the 3rd: this is the whole business.

To illustrate this, let us turn to the last Example. In bar 6 of the upper part (*a*) the bass note is figured $\frac{6}{4}$, being the third inversion of the chord of the dominant 7th. Here there is no suspension. The bass note itself is the real 7th.

Which of the figures represents the 8th?

The 2 represents the real 8th, and therefore a 3 would represent the 9th; consequently if we would have the dissonance of the 9th introduced into this chord, we must write the figure 3 before the figure 2; thus $_3\frac{6}{4}$, and in order to shew that the 4 and 6 are to be played when the 3 is struck, a line may be drawn back from them as far as the 3; thus $\overline{_3\frac{6}{4}}$.

Let us look again at the same bar 6:—As the figure 2 represents the real 8th, so the figure 4 represents the real third of the chord; and, of course, a 5 would represent the real fourth. Therefore if we would introduce into this chord the dissonance of the 4th into the 3rd, we must place a figure of 5 before the 4, thus $_5\frac{6}{4}$; and, for the reason above stated, we must draw the lines back from the other figures, thus $\overline{_5\frac{6}{4}}$; as is found in the same bar completed in the lower part of the Example at (*b*).

At the first glance upon this figuring, we perceive the nature of the chord. The $\frac{6}{4}$ inform us that it is the 3rd inversion of the fundamental 7th; and the 5 placed before the 4 tells us there is a suspension employed. By a very little practice, we know at once what dissonance it is.

This reasoning may be applied to all other cases. Suppose, for instance, we meet with this figuring $\overline{_7 \flat\frac{6}{5}}$; the $\flat\frac{6}{5}$ inform us that it is the first inversion of the dominant 7th, and that there is a suspension.

What interval does the 6 represent? The original 8th; therefore the dissonance is the 9th into the 8th : and the line drawn from the 5 tells us that the Fundamental 7th must be struck at the commencement of the chord. Had it been intended that the Fundamental 7th should not be heard until the dissonance was resolved, then the line from the 5th would have been omitted; thus $_7\flat\frac{6}{5}$.

It is unnecessary to multiply examples, for the same reasoning will apply to all cases. Let us turn, for instance, to bar 2 (*b*) of the last Example. The $\frac{6}{3}$ over the B, tell us it is the second Inversion of the chord of E with the Fundamental 7th; and the lines drawn back from all the figures over the preceding note C inform us that the same chord exactly must be played with that note C. On examination we shall find that this is merely the dissonance of the 6th into the 5th introduced in the inverted bass.

At bar 7, the figure 6 placed over the E denotes the first inversion of C, and the line drawn back over the F, points out that E is the real note of

o

the chord, and that the F is merely a suspension: in reality it is the 4th into the 3rd.

At Bar 9, $\frac{8}{3}$ are written over the A to denote the common chord, and the lines point out that the common chord of A is to be played also to the B, which shews it to be merely the 9th into the 8th written in the Inverted Bass.

This principle of figuring will, with very little practice, be found so exceedingly simple, that it is a waste of time to say more on the subject. Should any thing occur deserving remark, it will be hereafter noticed in its place; but we must never forget that thus figuring the bass is merely writing the harmonies by a sort of short hand, using figures instead of notes, and which is now in a great measure useless. As it is seen that the figures are intended merely to represent the notes required to be played, the hints already given cannot fail to enable the pupil to describe what he intends, so as to be clearly understood.

We will now return to the subject of the

Introduction of Dissonances.

Recurring to Example 122, bar 9, (*b*) we find the 9th is introduced in the bass, because the 8th was in that part. Now had the bass been allowed to remain as in bars 8 and 9 (at *a*), and had the 9th been introduced in the alto, consecutive octaves would have been produced, as in the following Example at *a*.

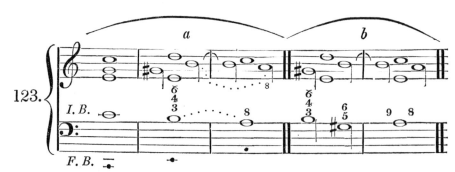

The Dissonance however might be thus introduced in the alto if desired, provided the bass were allowed to quit the 5th, and take the 3rd, as at (*b*), where all is correct.

It is advisable that the pupil should write some of the preceding exercises on modulation in four parts, adding the dissonances; of which it must be unnecessary to give any further specimen.

On employing Inverted Basses to harmonized Melodies.

The pupil is already acquainted with nearly all the essential matter here required, but we shall now arrange it in such a form as imperceptibly to lead to its more extended and more elevated application.

At Example 58, we explained the peculiar character of each of the four parts of the harmony which became interchanged amongst themselves, with an agreeable diversity of effect, from the application of the four rules of accompanying the scale.

The bass, which had then only the restricted movement of the Fundamental progression, may now, by the introduction of inversion, partake of this variety, and be allowed its share in the interchange of character; producing thus a graceful flow of melody and harmony.

In the following examples of harmonized melodies, the soprano, being the theme given for exercise, will not be allowed to be altered; therefore the bass will be found to borrow largely from the alto and tenor; generally, however, preserving its own peculiar characteristic at the final close. Let it be again enforced, that the pupil should hear every exercise performed, to be enabled to judge of the difference of effect, which it is not in the power of words to describe.

We will now take a melody, and harmonize it with fundamental basses only, writing the chords on the upper staff, and leaving a staff vacant for the inverted bass. We will add the 7ths upon the dominant chords, and take care that they are properly resolved: thus

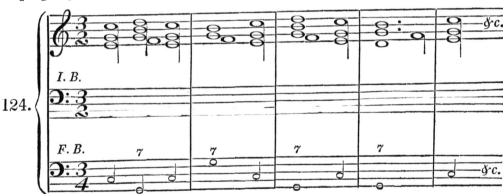

Having thus prepared the melody, our object is now to choose from the harmony some of the intervals with which to form an effective melody in the inverted bass: we will endeavour to give a few hints as rules to direct the choice, and, in doing this, we shall direct the attention only to the *Dominant Chords,* as the rest will be found to regulate themselves accordingly.

For the choice of Inverted Basses.

First Rule.

" When the 5th of the Dominant chord is in the melody, it is recommended to take the 3rd for the Inverted Bass."

This will be the first inversion $\frac{6}{5}$, and gives to the bass the soprano progression.

With this rule let us proceed to the selection of a bass melody for the vacant staff in the last Example (124), making use, for the present, of the Fundamental Bass, wherever this first rule will not apply.

Bar 1, *First Note.* Not a Dominant chord.   Use the Fundamental Bass.

   Second Note. What interval is in the melody ?   The 5th ; therefore the third is to be taken for the bass.   Take out B the 3rd from the chord, and write it in the vacant Bass staff ; after which, being the third of the Dominant, it must, of course, ascend to C in the following chord.

Proceed thus with the rest, and when completed, the Example will appear as follows : the notes selected for the Inverted Bass, and which are therefore to be removed from the chord, are marked with a dash through them.

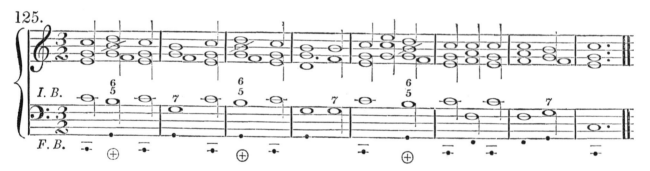

The Bass has now got rid of its monotonous effect, by taking the soprano progression where marked thus ⊕ ; in every other respect it is exactly as it was before.

Let the pupil well observe the gradual interweaving of the parts now commencing, which will at last bring the bass to a full participation in all the various movements.

Second Rule.

" When the 3rd of the Dominant chord is in the melody, take the 7th for the Inverted Bass."

The 7th being taken as a bass must, of course, descend; and thus gives the tenor progression. It is the 3rd inversion of the chord, and is figured $\frac{6}{4}$.

The soprano and bass being the extreme parts of the harmony are the most conspicuous, and to them are generally given those intervals which are considered to produce the best effect, viz. the 3rd and 7th; on which this rule is grounded.

We will now take another melody with which the pupil is recommended to proceed exactly as before, introducing the first rule in all cases where it applies, and afterwards the second; trying the effect on each occasion.

At (m) The 3rd is in the melody, and the 7th is taken for the bass.

(n) The 5th is in the melody, and the 3rd in the bass.

(p) The first inversion of the common chord is in the bass (figured with a 6) on account of the resolution of the preceding 7th.

Bar 4. The 7th is not introduced until the latter half of the bar, the ear requiring a certain degree of rest at the fourth bar, which will be further explained in treating of periods. The introduction of a 7th always inspires a desire to proceed, and would, consequently, be improper at the commencement of this bar; but, for the same reason, when the movement commences again, the 7th has a good effect.

Bar 5. The introduction of a 7th upon a Dominant so near the final close, weakens the full effect which that close should produce; this, however, is merely a matter of taste, and we admit it here for practice.

Bar 7, at (y). The 3rd is in the melody, but the 7th could not with propriety be used in the bass, as it would destroy the decisive effect of the final close; consequently the fundamental bass is employed; and on this is founded the next rule.

THIRD RULE.

" When the 3rd is in the melody, and the 7th cannot be taken as the Inverted Bass, take the Fundamental Bass."

N.B. This rule applies to all common chords also, though they may not be dominants.

The foregoing three rules may be *reversed ;* that is, the intervals of the bass and melody may change places: for instance, in the first example, where the 5th is in the melody, the 3rd may be taken as a bass; therefore, when the 3rd is in the *melody,* the 5th may be taken as a bass, &c., &c.

FOURTH RULE.

The following rule is set apart, as not being quite so good as the former, but it is sometimes used to produce variety.

" When the 7th is in the melody, take the 5th for the Inverted Bass," and its reverse, " When the 5th is in the melody, the 7th may be taken for the Inverted bass."

The following example shows the whole at one view.

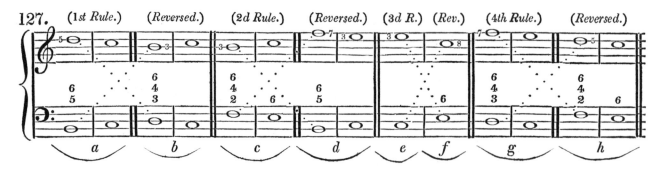

And the whole may be still more condensed thus:—

Intervals in the Melody: 3rd — 5th — 7th — 8th.

May have as Inverted Basses: 7 8 5—3 7—3 8 5—3

Arranged in this order, we are to understand that when the 3rd is in the melody, we should choose, for the Inverted Bass, the 7th; next in preference is the 8th; and the last the 5th, &c.

In the following example will be found two distinct bass parts to the same melody, in which all the foregoing modes of selecting Inverted Basses are put in practice. A comparison of the different effects which they produce will tend to improve the taste. Of course it is unnecessary to observe that these two Inverted Basses are two distinct exercises, and cannot both be used at the same time: each of them should be taken as a separate exercise, employing the same melody, and adding the two other parts of the harmony.

The letters refer to Example 127, pointing out which rule has been followed.

On looking over the second bass part, it will be perceived that had the G♯, in the latter part of bar 2, continued to the end of the bar, it must have ascended to A; instead of which, it first ascends to the 5th of its own chord, and then *descends* to A: meanwhile the 5th in the melody* also divides itself into two notes, and, instead of *descending* to A in the next chord, it first takes up the 3rd, which the bass has quitted, and afterwards ascends one degree (as that interval should) to A.

The occasional use of this interchange of intervals has the effect of rendering each part still more melodious†, as will be perceived from the following Examples.

---

* Let it be remembered that these intervals are always calculated from the Fundamental Bass.

† It will be perceived that this interchange takes place during the continuance of one chord; and the different intervals, wherever they may be found when the harmony advances, proceed in their own proper progression.

129.

Melodies which have already been harmonized with Fundamental Basses only, should now be taken as exercises on the above rules, and by a comparison of the different effects, the subsequent improvement will be shewn.

Licensed Introduction of the 7th where the 5th ascends.

If we take as a melody the four first notes of the scale; we find, at the second note, the chord of the Dominant, where the 5th is in the melody, and ascends to the 3rd of the following tonic. Now as the 7th ought to be introduced where this 3rd is, and as we cannot alter the melody, it would appear from our former rules that in such a case as this we must be deprived entirely of the 7th, unless we can find some other place to introduce it. The effect produced by this Fundamental 7th is however of too much consequence to be easily relinquished; therefore, by what we must call a license, we may introduce the 7th at once in the tenor; as in the following Example 130, bar 2.

On resolving this 7th, the 3rd of the following tonic is necessarily doubled, but the tenor may immediately ascend to the 5th on the same bass after the 7th has been resolved; as at bar 3.

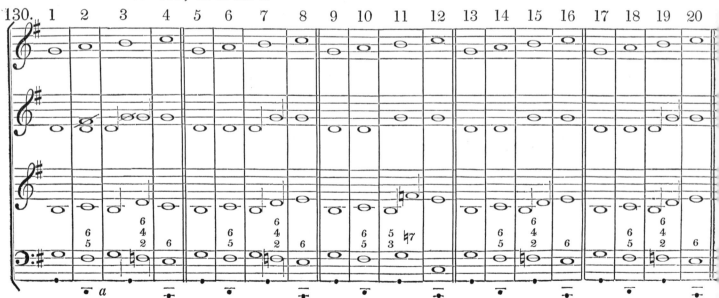

130.

In Bar 2. There is a 7th by license which descends at bar 3, whereby the 3rd of the tonic chord is doubled; but immediately after the resolution of the 7th, the tenor ascends to the 5th in the same bar, and thus prevents the octaves which would otherwise have occurred between the tenor and soprano. Any ambiguity, however, on this subject is avoided at bar 7, by the 5th again ascending to E, instead of descending, as in the former instance, on the same note to which the 3rd must proceed. In consequence of this, in bar 8, the 3rd is necessarily doubled, it being already in the bass; still it is generally safer to allow the 5th thus to proceed in an ascending melody.

Bars 4 and 8. Compare the two methods of proceeding in the tenor.

Bar 10. The 7th by license resolves in bar 11 upon the 3rd, as before, and immediately ascends to the Fundamental 7th.

Bar 14. The 3rd is chosen for the Inverted Bass, but instead of ascending, it descends into the Fundamental 7th in the following chord; which may always take place when one Dominant Chord is succeeded by another.

Ascending Scale harmonized by Inversion.

Write the scale with the fundamental basses on a fifth staff below. Write the harmonies on the alto and tenor staves as before, without correcting the consecutive 5ths and 8ths.

Introduce the 7ths and also those allowed by license; then proceed to select the Inverted Basses as recommended, and write them in the blank staff left for the purpose, expunging the note borrowed by the bass from the part where it was found, and supplying its place by some other note of the harmony.

The following is an example of a scale thus harmonized (but not written in score), and the notes borrowed for the Inverted Basses are marked out by a dash.

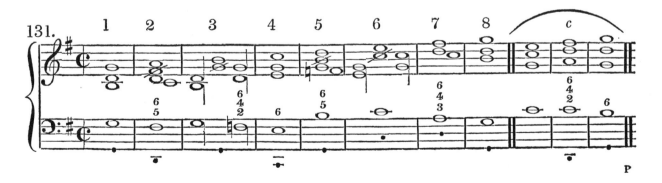

P

The three last notes are again given (at *c*) to show, that were we to take the 7th as the Inverted Bass when the 3rd is in the melody, we should conclude with an inversion, which ought not to be allowed: it is better to consider it as a general rule, that every composition should commence and conclude with a common chord and the fundamental bass.

On Doubling any Interval of a Chord.

As there are frequently only three notes in the harmony, one of them must necessarily be doubled when we write in four parts; or, in other words, the same interval must appear in two parts at the same time.

At 1. The 3rd is doubled, which may be permitted as one of them afterwards descends.   But it is recommended not to double the 3rd, where it can with propriety be avoided.

The effect, however, of doubling the 3rd is not so objectionable in the minor as in the major.

At 2. The 5th is doubled to produce a melodious progression, and contrary motion.

At 3. The 8th is doubled.

Descending Scale with Inverted Basses.

Proceed in the same manner as directed for the ascending scale, with this difference, that the consecutive 5ths and 8ths should be first corrected.

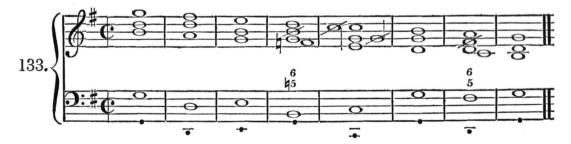

After this, the ascending and descending scales may be harmonized by inversion with the dissonances introduced, proceeding thus:

First harmonize the scale without dissonances, and select Inverted Basses.

The Fundamental Basses being written on a separate staff, place over them the figures denoting the dissonances which can be introduced, as pointed out by their progression; and introduce them according to the rules given: as in the following examples, which, for the sake of brevity, are compressed into two staves, and the fundamental figuring omitted.

The Ascending Scale with Dissonances.

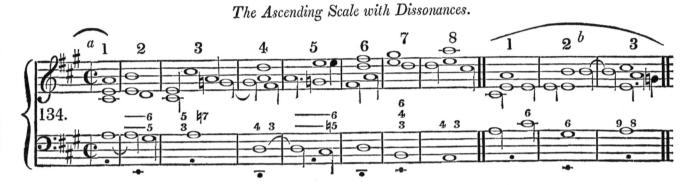

Bar 2. The dissonance of the 4th appears in the bass part, as its resolution was found there.

Bar 4. The same dissonance is in the tenor, for the same reason: and so with the rest.

Bar 3. The 7th is introduced in the tenor, in order to prepare the 4th in the following bar. The dissonances thus appearing alternately in the different parts produce a variety of effect.

Had the 7th been taken in the bass in this bar, dissonances would have appeared twice in succession in that part.

A still greater variety might be produced by the introduction of the 9th into the 8th in the alto at bar 3 (*b*).

The Descending Scale with Dissonances.

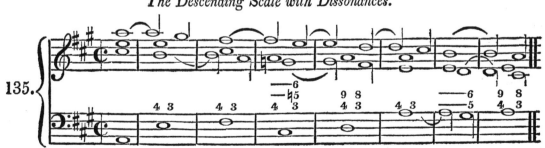

It will be perceived that no dissonance could be introduced in the alto, except in bar 7, where the dissonance of the 4th might have been introduced in that part instead of in the bass.

> " The dissonance and the note which it suspends must never be heard at the same time."

Although this rule has been fully enforced and continually in practice, yet an error in this particular is so easily committed in employing inversions, that it is considered necessary again to repeat it as a caution; especially where the licensed 7th is introduced, as at (*a*) in the following Example; or where the 7th is used in the Inverted Bass, and the octave doubled, as at (*b*); in both which instances the error is shewn.

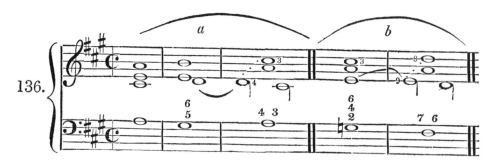

In the following example (at bar 1) the 5th of the Dominant chord in the melody *descending*, is accompanied by the 5th in the Inverted Bass *ascending*, producing contrary motion and a more melodious effect.

In bars 3 and 6. The fifth in the melody ascends, and the 5th in the bass descends, with the licensed 7th added.

And in bar 5. The same with the 7th omitted.

We may here with propriety offer a few observations regarding the 2nd and 4th Rules for employing Fundamental Basses.

We are aware that when the 4th of the scale descends one degree, and is accompanied by the dominant, the chord of the Fundamental 7th is produced.

We may now add that the 4th of the scale, though it may not descend one degree as hitherto, may still be accompanied by the dominant, provided it proceeds to any of the other intervals of the chord before it is resolved; as in the following example:—

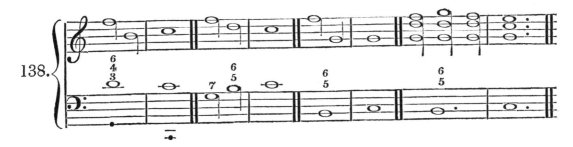

Should the 5th of the scale be accompanied by the dominant, when it proceeds immediately to the 3rd of the following tonic; as at (*a*) in the following example; and should we wish to employ the 7th on that dominant, we must introduce it in the soprano (as at *b*); for were we to place it in any other part, it would produce hidden octaves (as at *d*), between the soprano and tenor, or unisons (as at *c*), between the soprano and alto.

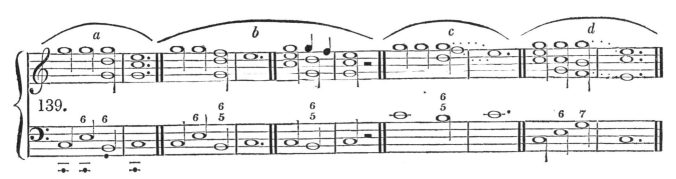

Let us now recapitulate what we have obtained up to this point, and put into practice the knowledge we have gained. Henceforward much must be left to the ripening judgment and discretion of the student. The recommendations already given for the choice of Inverted Basses will be found quite sufficient. It will not be expected that definite and absolute rules should be laid down for every possible case which may occur; the attempt, if practicable, could only tend to fetter the imagination, and degrade the art itself.

Recapitulation.

Let us take now some melody, and see what can be effected by the mere application of the simple rules hitherto laid down.

Suppose an air were given us to be harmonized.

We know that this can be done in various ways.

1st. By employing the four rules of Fundamental Basses. These rules, if used with the least degree of judgment, or even common attention, will of themselves produce extraordinary variety.

Each part, except the soprano, will, through their different application, produce each time a different effect; and even the soprano is not left entirely uninfluenced by this change; for though that part is not *altered*, yet, as the different rules are introduced, the same interval which at one time is heard as the 8th, will at another be heard as the 7th or 5th, and *thus*, with relation to the other parts, produce a different effect.

2ndly. By employing Inverted Basses.

Here again the different parts interchange characters, because by introducing an Inverted Bass a change will necessarily be produced in the Bass Melody, and thus a corresponding change will likewise take place in that part or melody, out of which the Inverted Bass has been chosen.

3rdly. By employing Dissonances.

By means of which a wide field is opened for the production of a great variety of light and shade. In one place we introduce a Dissonance of the 4th prepared by the 7th, 8th, or 5th. In another a 9th prepared by the 3rd, 8th, or 5th. In another a 7th or a 6th: again, we employ them in conjunction with others, or produce imitations amongst the different parts.

In one word, it is amazing what variety can be produced by means which present themselves to us every moment in a form so simple and comprehensible, that it requires no more than ordinary reflection and industry to produce effects the most agreeable and unexpected.

With respect to Inversions, the great object to be attained is the production of a *graceful* and *flowing* melody in the bass, in order that it may be more intimately blended with the other parts, and thus produce a beautiful *whole*.

It should not be forgotten that this is not the progression which nature has pointed out (see Introduction to Modulation, page 49). Each of the four parts is naturally distinguished by its own characteristic (see page 42), which must always be kept carefully in view, when we are about to introduce Inversion in harmonizing a melody.

Let us, however, ere we proceed to harmonize a given melody, once more explain the routine to be observed.

1st. Write Fundamental Basses according to the four rules, upon a fifth staff below*.

2ndly. Write the common chords in score.

3rdly. Add the 7ths and resolve them.

N.B. Consecutive 5ths and 8ths need not be prevented; the second or third inversion will always accomplish that.

4thly. Select Inverted Basses.

5thly. Introduce Dissonances.

Suppose, then, the following melody to have been given, and to have been thus treated, it will produce the following finished exercise; in which the Dissonances only have been omitted.

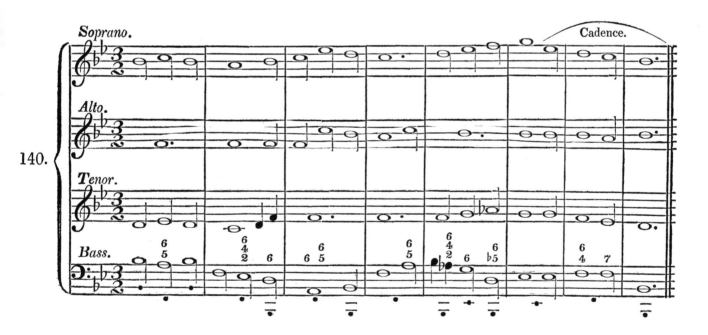

We shall now take the same air, with the same Fundamental and Inverted Basses, and add the Dissonances.

---

* They are written here in our examples only as points, as much as possible to avoid extending the work.

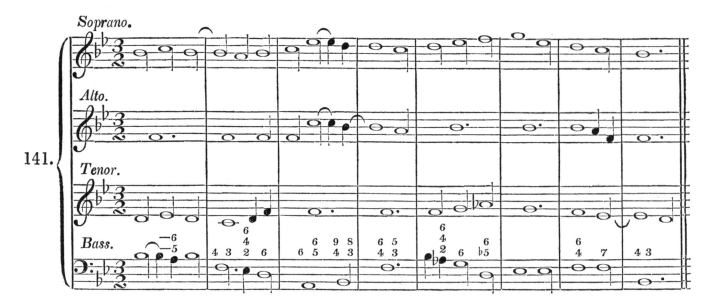

N. B. When the Dissonance of the 4th is introduced as in the last bar, the 5th of the chord must never be omitted.

Here follows the same air with the same Fundamental basses, but with different Inverted basses and some selected Dissonances.

If we compare the Inverted Basses and inner parts of the two preceding examples, we shall find a continual interchange of character; for instance, the soprano progression, which, in Example 141, bar 1, was in the bass; is, in Example 142, in the alto.

The inverted bass in the same bar, Example 142, has the progression of the tenor, and the tenor that of the alto.

Thus should the whole be analyzed, and the various effects compared.

The melody in the preceding examples has been harmonized by the *same Fundamental Basses*, and the variety of effect has been produced only by Inverted Basses and Dissonances.

In the following examples, a variety of effect in the harmonization of the same melody is produced, not only by the employment of different inverted basses, but the *fundamental basses* also are occasionally *changed*, by the application of the four rules.

Each melody is written with two distinct inverted basses, and should be harmonizedwith each of them separately. Dissonances may be added at pleasure; after which the pupil should endeavour to produce a still greater variety by the choice of other Fundamental and Inverted Basses, according to the rules laid down.

The same melody also, by way of exercise, may be transposed into various other keys, &c.

N. B. The Fundamental Basses have been chosen in the three following examples.

At (*b*). By the Second Rule.
(*c*). By the Third Rule.
(*d*). By the Fourth Rule.

The 1st Rule is not noticed, as being generally employed where no remark is made.

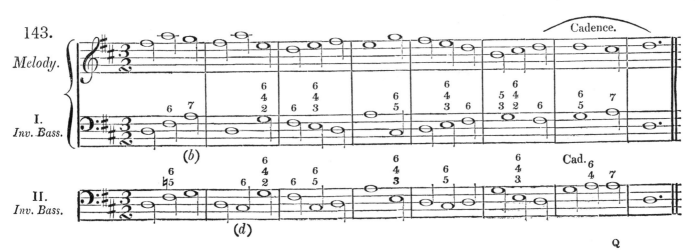

Q

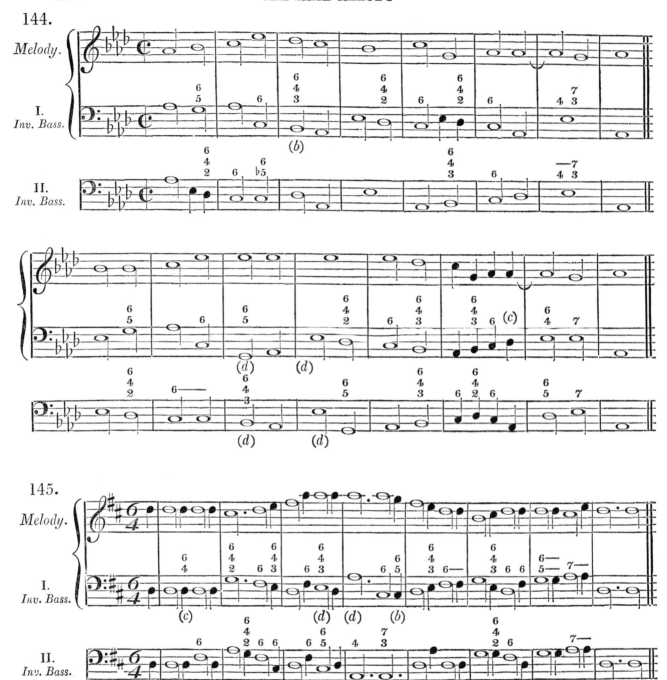

At Example 145, bar 1, of the first bass, we have taken the 5th of the chord as the inverted bass, producing the chord of the $\frac{6}{4}$, the second inversion of the common chord.

The monotony between this and the soprano will be thus sufficiently relieved, by the richness of the inner parts.

To shew the endless variety which may be produced by the employment of the preceding simple rules alone, we will here take the two first bars of the last example, which may be considered as a subject in itself the least interesting possible, containing only two sounds.

The third and fourth bars of the same air may also be harmonized thus:

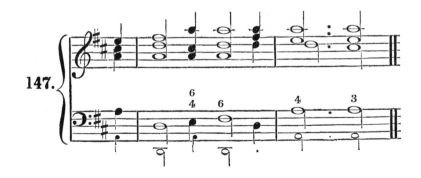

The same air harmonized, with Dissonances occasionally introduced.

N. B. The corresponding letters of reference, in this example, are intended merely to point out how the same subjects are occasionally transferred into different parts.

We will not pursue this subject further at present: it is presumed that sufficient has already been said to shew to what an extent it may be carried.

The pupil, before he proceeds further, will, of course, so exercise himself as to be well assured that he fully comprehends the subject thus far. He is once more earnestly recommended to perform the exercises he has written, in order to hear and compare the effects at each change; by which practice his taste and judgment will become gradually matured, and his eye will imperceptibly acquire a facility in reading a score.

Extended or open Harmony.

Hitherto our harmony has been so written, that between the soprano, alto, and tenor parts, no space has been left for the introduction of any other.

A harmony constructed thus, and which arises from the manner in which the three original positions of the chord are written, we shall call *compressed harmony*.

It shall now be shown how a compressed harmony may become *extended*, by which a new and beautiful effect is produced.

If we examine the three positions of the common chord, we find that in the second position the 3rd of the chord *lies under the* 5th. In the third position, the 5th *under the octave*. In the first position, the *octave under the* 3rd (as at *a*), in the following example.

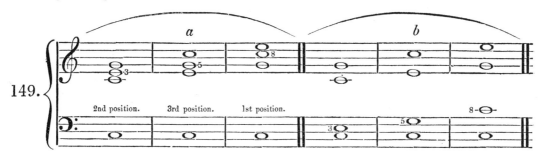

If we remove the 3rd from the chord in the second position, and place it an octave lower (as at *b*), we shall find that the alto has changed place with the tenor.

If we take the 5th from the chord in the third position, and write it an octave lower, a similar change takes place in the same parts. Lastly,

The octave when removed in like manner from the chord in the first position, produces the same change in the *same* parts.

The following Ex. (150, *a*) is written with compressed harmonies as usual. The alto is then (at *b*) written an octave lower, and transferred to the place of the tenor, and the tenor to the place of the alto.

The figures 2 and 3 denote the parts which have been interchanged, by which an extended harmony has been produced.

The effect of this extended harmony will be best perceived by playing the alto and tenor *alone*, first as at (*a*), and then as at (*b*): and pupils may be still more interested in this by playing the harmony thus written, as duets on the piano-forte; the parts being, on these occasions, sometimes too far extended for one performer.

As the alto, when thus interchanged with the tenor, will appear generally too low for the treble staff, it is advisable, in order to avoid ledger lines in that part, to write it for the present in the bass clef; subsequently, when we have been made acquainted with the alto and tenor clefs, this plan of resorting to the bass clef will be unnecessary.

The extraordinary diversity of the effect in these two methods of writing the same harmony, is produced not only by the parts moving at greater distances, but also by two of the parts having exchanged places; in consequence of which, those two parts which, in compressed harmony, produced between themselves 3rds, 4ths, and 5ths, &c., &c., will, when changed to extended harmonies, be heard as 6ths, 5ths, and 4ths, &c. For instance, by this change,

A unison becomes an 8th.

A 2nd . . . . a 7th.   *Note.* When two parts are

3rd . . . . a 6th.   thus interchanged, it

4th . . . . a 5th.   is called double coun-

5th . . . . a 4th.   terpoint in the oc-

6th . . . . a 3rd.   tave.

7th . .. . . a 2nd.

8th . . . . a unison.

From this it will be clear that

" No progression of *consecutive 4ths* can be permitted, in the compressed harmonies, between the two parts which are to be thus interchanged in extended harmonies."

For by changing places, they become *consecutive 5ths.*

Therefore, should consecutive 4ths appear in the compressed harmonies about to be changed, an alteration must be previously made in the arrangement of the parts.

The following rule must also be observed.

" *The Bass part must not approach the alto nearer than an octave.*"

Otherwise the alto, which, in the extended harmony, takes the place of the tenor, will be found lower than the *Inverted Bass.*

In the following Example at (*a*) the bass is nearer than an octave to the alto; in consequence of which, when the harmonies are extended, the tenor is found *below* the *Inverted Bass* (as at *b*).

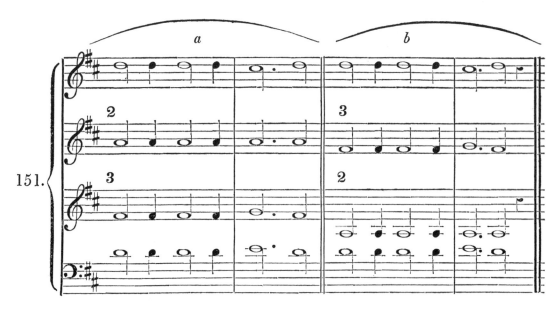

When the melody rises or falls by great intervals, a *partial* extension of the harmony becomes sometimes necessary, in order to preserve a smooth and graceful progression of the inner parts, which would otherwise be destroyed. An occasional extension of the harmony is also frequently necessary to prevent the bad effect produced by too many parts proceeding in *similar motion*.

At (*a*) in the following example, the soprano ascends a fifth, and as the alto and tenor, in compressed harmony, must ascend with it, the consequence is a progression of three parts in a similar motion.

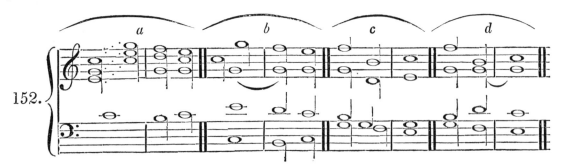

This is avoided by the partial extension of the harmony (as at *b*), where the alto, instead of ascending with the soprano, remains stationary, and the tenor falls by single degrees.

When the harmony is already in an extended position (as at *c*), and the soprano falls by a great interval, a partial compression of the harmony must take place (as at *d*).

When the harmony is compressed, and the soprano falls by a great interval, the alto may sometimes be permitted to appear over the soprano as in the following Example 153, at *a*, which otherwise would be written as at *b*.

On Major and Minor Keys.

To each major key is attached another, called its *Relative Minor*, which is found a *Minor 3rd below* *.

The 3rd of a chord determines whether it be major or minor.

No minor chord is produced by nature, for the chord which is formed by the harmonics of a musical string is major; the explanation of which appeared at page 47. The construction of a minor scale is therefore artificial.

In constructing the minor scale, let us draw our reasoning as much as possible from the formation of the major†.

If we examine the scale of three sounds, we find, that its third sound is the same as the third of the chord of its generator, as appears in the following Example, (at *a*).

---

* (See Example 61 and 62) which are exercises on major keys and their relative minors in regular succession.

† On which we have already treated in the introduction to modulation, page 48.

R

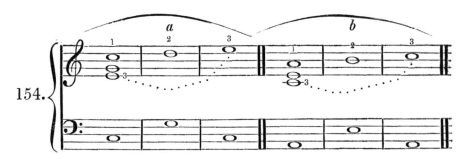

The Tonic chord has a *major 3rd*, and the distance from the 1st to the 3rd of the scale is therefore a *major 3rd*.

Should we give the Tonic chord a *minor 3rd*, the distance from the first to the 3rd of that scale must also be a *minor 3rd*, (as at *b*).

N. B. The first chord of a scale we shall call the key chord.

Let us now proceed to construct a minor scale, pursuing the same plan as before in forming the major scale; that is, first forming and uniting two scales of three sounds each.

In the following Example at I, is the major scale as we first discovered it*, in which all the chords are major; but at II they are all minor, which is an entire departure from nature, and the effect upon the ear is intolerable.

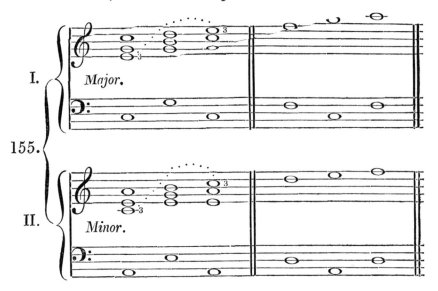

But we may unite nature and art, so as to retain the impression of a minor **key**, and still adhere in a great measure to the principles established, making the minor to resemble, as much as possible, the major scale.

---

* See page 48.

This is accomplished by changing *one* of the three minor chords, at II in the preceding example, into major; but, as the first and third chords must be **minor** for the reason stated in the last page, the second chord only can be made **major**; the Example will then be as follows, at (*a*).

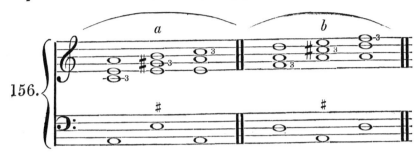

It must be remarked also that this second chord is the dominant of the **key and** *therefore* must be major.

Having arranged the harmonization of the first scale of three notes (as at *a*), let us proceed to arrange the second scale in exactly the same manner (as at *b*).

Having placed together these two scales of three notes each, the two remaining notes may be added to complete the *Minor Diatonic Scale of A*, as follows.

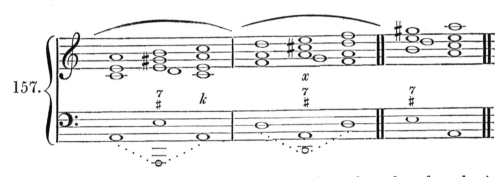

In the above Example no absolute modulation has taken place from the A minor to the D minor at the fourth chord, because the chord of the preceding dominant (at *k*) has no major 3rd, and, consequently, no fundamental 7th can exist; but a modulation takes place immediately afterwards (at *x*) because the chord, being major, admits of a Fundamental 7th; and, as a modulation to D has thus taken place, it is necessary to modulate back again to the original key, A minor; which obliges us to place a sharp before G, the 7th note of the scale, in order to make the chord major. This produces between the sixth and seventh of the scale a distance of three half tones, which constitutes a distinguishing characteristic of the minor scale.

R 2

On examining the preceding scale (Ex. 157) we perceive that the second, fifth, and seventh sounds are accompanied by major chords, all the others being minor.

With respect to the fifth of the scale being accompanied by a major chord, there are various exceptions which shall be explained in due time. The second and seventh, however, *must always* be accompanied by major chords, which may have the Fundamental 7th added.

Chord of the Minor 9th.

Let us now carefully examine the Dominant chords in the above Example 157. We find that the Fundamental 7th, which has hitherto always descended a semi-tone, now descends a whole tone. This arises from the succeeding chord having a minor 3rd. The equal progression of the two principal intervals of the Dominant 7th (where the 3rd ascends, and the 7th descends *a half tone*) is thus destroyed. The expectation which arises on the introduction of the 7th, is disappointed in the resolution, because the ear is prepared for the succession of a major, and not of a minor chord. Thus we are forced to resort to some other means of preparing the ear for the following minor.

Our object will be attained, if we remove from the Dominant chord the 8th, and insert in its place the sound which is a major half tone above it, or in other words, the minor 9th to the fundamental bass: at the same time allowing the 7th to remain.

This minor 9th will descend a *half tone* into the 5th of the succeeding tonic.

It may be introduced into the Dominant chord, like the 7th, without preparation; which circumstance will sufficiently distinguish it from the 9th by suspension, which must be always prepared.

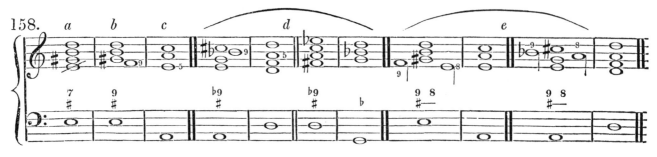

At (*a*) the 8th is marked to be expunged.

At (*b*) the minor 9th is inserted in its place.

At (*c*) the 9th is resolved, descending a half tone into the 5th.

At (*d*) the same in other keys and other positions of the chords.

At (*e*) the minor 9th is relinquished, and the 8th of the same chord taken in its place.

This may be permitted, because the 9th, having been once heard, has already prepared the ear for the succeeding minor chord.

It must be observed with respect to this useful and effective interval, that, when by its means we have once introduced a minor key, there is no necessity for our employing it upon every subsequent dominant; a little discretion should be used in this particular.

It may also be here remarked that when the 9th happens to be written in the chord above the 5th, (as in the following Example at *a*) consecutive 5ths will take place, if not avoided by allowing the 5th to ascend (as at *b*).

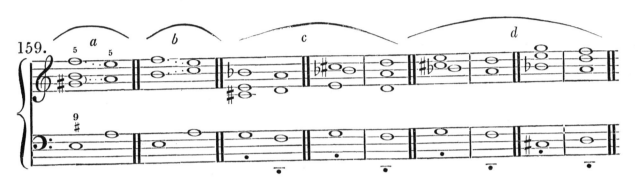

Many modern composers however do not observe this rule very strictly, for this progression, is often written as above (at *c*)*. However, when the 9th lies under the 5th, no improper progression can occur (see *d*).

From the introduction of the 9th, arises another preparation for the dissonance of the 6th. The rule is,

> " *When the Fundamental Bass ascends a fourth*, the Dissonance of the 6th, prepared by the 9th, *may* be introduced."

As in the following Example at (*a*).

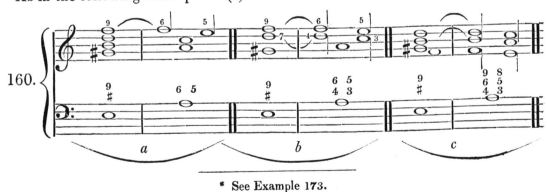

---

* See Example **173**.

As the same progression of the Fundamental Bass admits of a 4th prepared by the 7th, and a 9th prepared by the 5th, these Dissonances may be combined (as in the preceding Example at *b* and *c*).

We ought now, as an exercise, to modulate through all the major and minor keys with fundamental basses only; and, on modulating to the *minor*, introduce the *minor 9th*, with which the 7th also should always be employed; thus—

Inversions of the Chord of the Minor 9th.

In the chord of the fundamental 7th, we have but *three* inversions; but in the chord of the minor 9th we have *four* intervals besides the fundamental bass, and therefore we can have *four inversions*.

The chord of the fundamental 7th is changed into that of the minor 9th, by merely removing the octave and replacing it by the 9th, and when we write the inversions of the latter chord we have only to observe the *same* process as we have already done with the chord of the Fundamental 7th. If from *any* inversion of the fundamental 7th, we take away the original octave, and write in its place the interval which is a major half tone above, it will become an inversion of the chord of the minor 9th.

All the other intervals, remaining exactly the same as before, are treated in the same way as if the chord had never been changed; thus—

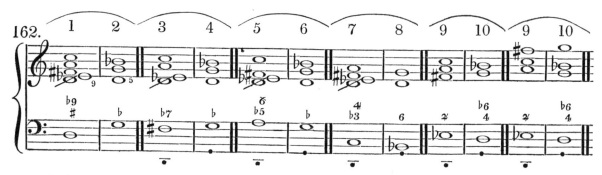

In bar 1, the chord is fundamental, with the octave marked to be expunged; and the 9th written in its place resolves by descending a half tone on the 5th of the succeeding chord in bar 2. All the other intervals proceed as they usually do in the chord of the fundamental 7th.

At bar 3, this chord of the minor 9th appears in the *first* inversion.

By expunging the 6th (which here represents the original 8ve of the Fundamental Bass) and substituting the half tone above, we find that note to be a 7th to the present bass note (F$\sharp$); but as this 7th is a half tone less than the fundamental 7th, it is called the *diminished* 7th. The first inversion, therefore, of the chord of the fundamental 9th, is called the chord of the diminished 7th.

Had the 9th not been introduced, it would have been the chord of the $\frac{6}{5}$.

As the most essential intervals of the chord of the fundamental 7th are the 3rd and 7th, so the intervals of most consequence in the chord of the 9th, are the 3rd and 9th.

In figuring any inversion of this chord, we shall in future place over the bass the figures only which correspond with these two intervals; for instance, in bar 3 of the last example, the real 3rd is already in the bass, therefore, it is merely necessary to write over that bass the figure 7, which will represent the real 9th. However, should any of the other intervals of the chord require an accidental $\sharp$, $\flat$, or $\natural$, it must of course be noticed.

At bar 5, is the *second inversion* of the chord, and the bass is figured thus $\flat\frac{6}{5}$, the 6 represents the original 3rd, and the 5th the original 9th.

Had the 9th not been introduced, it would have been the chord of the $\frac{6}{3}$.

At bar 7, is the *third inversion*, figured $\flat\frac{4}{3}$. The 4 represents the original 3rd, and the $\flat$3, the original 9th.

Had the 9th not been introduced, it would have been the chord of the $\frac{6}{2}$.

At bar 9, is the *fourth inversion* of the chord, the 9th being in the bass, we are required to notice, in the figuring, only the original 3rd which is now represented by a $\natural$.

Exercise on the *First* Inversion of the Minor 9th, or chord of *the Diminished* 7th.

163.

The following is an exercise on the *second* inversion of the minor 9th, in which the Inverted Bass always ascends, in order to prevent consecutive 5ths.

Exercise on the *Third* Inversion of the Minor 9th.

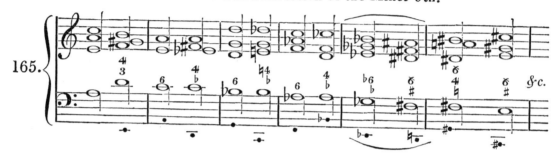

Exercise on the *Fourth* inversion of the Minor 9th; or, as it is sometimes called, the chord of the *sharp second*.

The 9th being the Inverted Bass in bar 1, resolves of course, upon the 5th of the following chord, which forms the second inversion of that chord, figured $\frac{6}{4}$. *

The pupil may perhaps observe some similarity of figuring in the inversions of the chord of the fundamental 7th, and those of the minor 9th.

The figures representing the *first* inversion of the *fundamental 7th* (are $\frac{6}{5}$) and the *second* inversion of the *minor 9th*, $\flat\frac{6}{5}$. The figures are the same, but those which denote the inversion of the minor 9th have this characteristic; they are

---

* A common chord having but *two* intervals beside the bass can have but *two* inversions, viz., the chord of the sixth (6), and that of the fourth and sixth ($\frac{6}{4}$).

marked by accidentals of *an opposite nature;* that is, the 6th has a sharp, and the 5th a flat placed before it.*

This combination of two opposite accidentals, which is the same in all inversions of the minor 9th, can *never* take place in an inversion of the fundamental 7th; and thus no difficulty will be experienced in distinguishing the two chords.

The Minor 9th resolving into the 8th on the same Bass in the different Inversions.

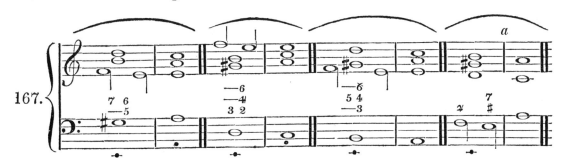

In Example 166, bar 2, the chord of the sharp second (✗) resolves into that of the $\frac{6}{4}$ in bar 3.

Now this resolution, of all others, produces the most *unsatisfactory* effect—the effect of a discord unresolved.

Several modes of avoiding this present themselves; first, by letting the 9th descend into the 8th, as at (*a*) in the last example; or, secondly, as at (*b*) and (*c*) in the following example, where the chord of the $\frac{6}{4}$, into which the 9th resolves, is not considered as an inversion, but is treated as a compound discord and resolved accordingly.

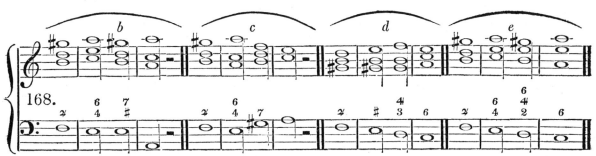

At (*d*) and (*e*) are shewn two other methods of treating the resolution of this chord.

---

* The figure before which a sharp is placed, represents the real 3rd of the fundamental chord, and that before which a flat is placed is the real 9th.

s

The following is an exercise on the four inversions of the chord of the minor 9th in four parts.

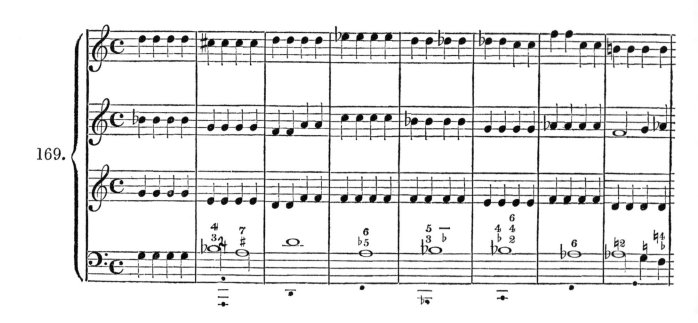

169.

At bars 8, 10, 12, 15, the 7th in the alto ascends, merely to change places with the 9th in the bass, producing a very pleasing effect.

Let us now modulate through all the major and minor keys by inversion, commencing, as in the following example, in extended harmonies.

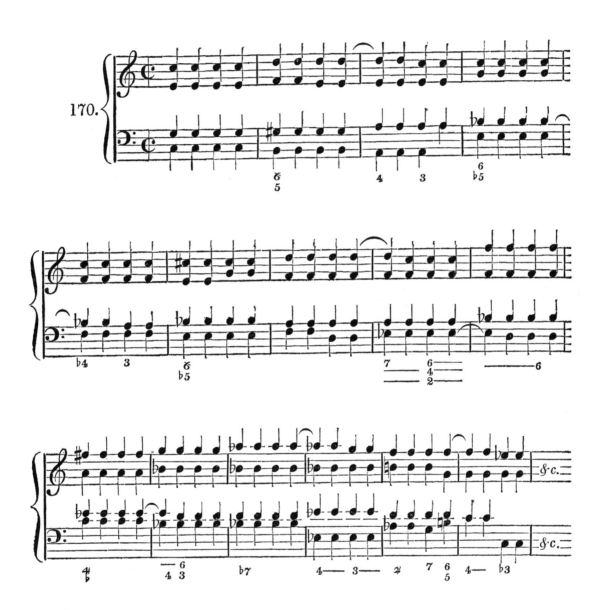

170.

The ingenuity of the pupil should be frequently brought into action by turning progressions of harmony, such as the above, into a variety of practical exercises for the piano-forte, thus:—

171.

The Variations in bars 1, 3, and 5, are diversifications of the chord, ascending and descending in different positions. This exercise may be continued regularly through all the major and minor keys, or by any other modulations which may be thought proper.

Before we proceed to harmonize minor scales and airs, it will be necessary to introduce

The fifth and last rule for employing Fundamental Basses.

" *When the* SIXTH *of the scale descends one degree, it may be accompanied by the* DOMINANT, *to which it will be a 9th.*"

N. B. It must be recollected that the second rule for employing fundamental basses is, " *When the* FOURTH *descends one degree it may be accompanied by the* DOMINANT."

From the above two rules arise some of the exceptions to the 5th of the scale being accompanied by a major chord, as remarked in page 124. For instance, should the sixth of a minor scale descend and be accompanied by the dominant according to the above rule, the fifth of the scale, whether preceding or succeeding, must have a minor chord, (as at *a, b,* in the following example.)

In like manner should the fourth of the scale descending be accompanied by the dominant; the fifth of the scale, which immediately precedes it, must also have a minor chord (as at *c.**)

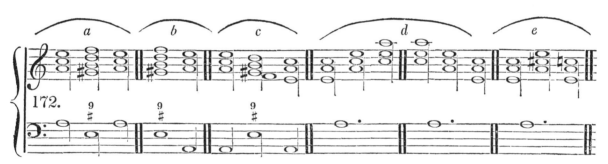

When several different intervals of the chord of the tonic immediately succeed each other in a melody (as above at *d*), they must all be accompanied by minor chords, and it would therefore be incorrect to accompany the fifth as at *e*.

Hence it follows that when the fifth of the scale in descending is accompanied by a *minor chord*, the sixth and fourth may be accompanied either by the dominant or sub-dominant; but when the fifth is major, the fourth and the sixth must be accompanied by *the sub-dominant only*.

---

* It is scarcely necessary to observe, that when the fifth of the scale commences or concludes a minor melody, it must have a minor chord.

In order to preserve the subject of the minor scales in a clear and connected form, the student is recomended to refer back to page 121, and peruse again what is there stated as far as page 124.

He may then proceed to harmonize the minor scale ascending and descending, with inverted basses, partly in compressed, and partly in extended harmonies, introducing the minor 9th, &c.

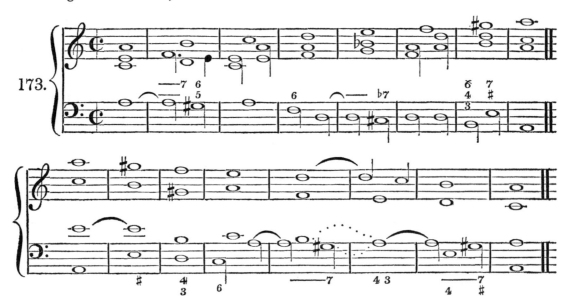

It will be found productive of great advantage, to submit every exercise, when completed, to a rigid examination, bearing upon every branch of the subject; as for instance,

Examination of the above Exercise.

Is this a major or a minor scale?

    A minor scale; because the first, or key chord, is minor.

From whence comes the G♯ at bar 2?

    It is the major 3rd to E; because the second of the scale must be accompanied by a major chord.

From whence comes the F in the alto?

    It is the minor 9th, which may be introduced because it is a dominant chord.

Is not A, at bar 3, the dominant to the succeeding Bass? and why have you not introduced the 7th and 9th there also?

    Because it is a minor chord, and we are therefore not permitted to use those intervals.

From whence comes the B♭ in the alto at bar 5?

It is the minor 9th; because the 5th of the scale has been accompanied by a major chord.

How has the sixth of the scale been accompanied at bar 11?

By the dominant.

Why is the fifth of the scale at 12 accompanied by a minor chord?

Because the sixth in descending has been accompanied by the dominant.

How has the fourth at bar 13 been accompanied?

By the dominant.

Could the sub-dominant have been employed? &c. &c.

Respecting the Consecutive 5ths at bars 13 and 14, see remark after Ex. 159.

Observe also that the descending scale is in *Extended Harmonies*.

It is evident that the minor scale is capable of producing much more variety than the major, from its harmonies consisting of a mixture of major and minor chords; and from the introduction of the minor 9th, which places at our disposal an additional interval, not incident to the major scale.

A curious coincidence will be observed in the harmonization of the minor scale; it is accompanied, in the tenor, by a perfect *major* scale, which is its *relative major*.

174.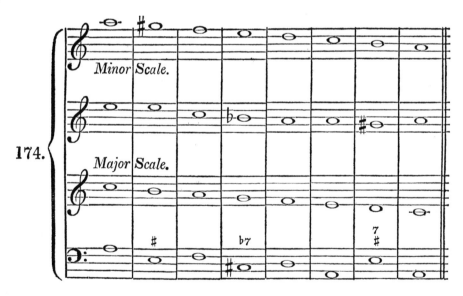

Let us now harmonize a few melodies in minor keys. The following Example (175) is in the key of A minor; the fundamental and inverted basses are the same as if it were in A major; in fact were we to place the signature (three sharps) at the beginning, the exercise might be played in A major.

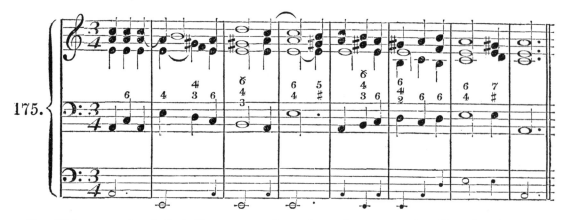

It will be perceived that dissonances have been here occasionally added.

In the following example, the first four bars of the melody are the same as in the preceding, but in the third bar different basses are employed; *viz.*, the 4th of the scale is accompanied first by the *sub-dominant*, and then by the dominant. In bar 6, the 6th of the scale also is first accompanied by the sub-dominant, and then by the dominant, which explains why the 5th preceding is accompanied by a major chord, and the succeeding one by a minor*.

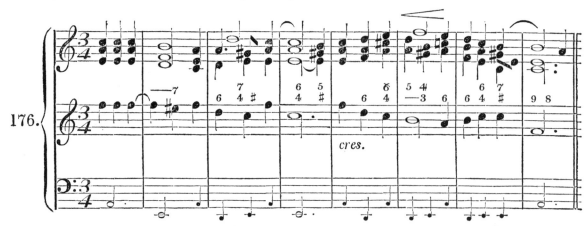

N.B. The subject of the Minor is resumed at Example 20⁗

Rules for the employment of the Intervals of a Melody, for the purposes of Modulation.

From what has been said respecting the vibration of a string, it appears that a scale consists in reality of only three sounds, accompanied by two fundamental basses, called the Tonic and Dominant; the intervals of which chords (including the 7th of the dominant) make in number *six*. (See the following Ex. 177, *a.*)

---

* See remarks at page 133.

Should no other than these six sounds be employed in writing a melody, and no other fundamental Basses be used than the before-mentioned Tonic and Dominant, the melody and harmony would remain in the key in which it commenced, and no departure from it could possibly take place. (See *b*.)

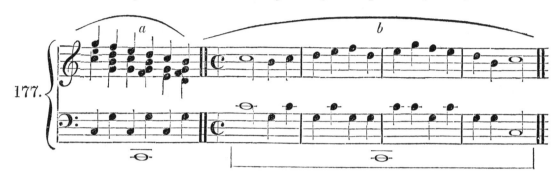

From the above example, it is evident that no sharp or flat could have been introduced, without disturbing the natural order of the original intervals of this scale. When, therefore, we perceive either an accidental sharp, flat, or natural, before any interval in a melody, a sound, foreign to the original key has been introduced, and it is an indication that a modulation out of it is taking place. Suppose we are required to harmonize an air in the key of C, and we meet with an F♯; it is evident that this F♯ is no part of the key of C, and therefore it cannot be accompanied by either of the Basses belonging to that key; but as this F♯ belongs to the key of G*, to the octave of which it ascends by a half tone, we conclude that the modulation is proceeding to that key. Therefore, whenever an accidental sharp † is found before any note which directly ascends a half tone, that note must be considered, for the present, as *the third* of the *Dominant* of the key to which we are proceeding.

When an interval of the melody is thus employed, we shall call it the *Note of Modulation*.

After a modulation has taken place, every succeeding note must be considered as being in the key to which we have modulated, and must be harmonized accordingly; until another modulation is indicated by a subsequent accidental, or otherwise, as hereafter explained.

N. B. In the following Examples, the notes placed below the fundamental

---

* F♯, being the first note made sharp, may be considered as leading to a key with only *one sharp*, viz., the key of G.

† A natural, in keys with flats, has of course the same effect.

T

Basses point out the generator of the key in which we are for the time being; and the Dominant, marked thus ⊙, must be considered as the door which leads us to the new key.

It is a general rule, that a composition shall be concluded in the key in which it is commenced. It is, therefore, necessary that, after having modulated, we should return to the original key. In the above Example, the modulation to **G** was performed by its Dominant (D): so the modulation back to **C** must be by its Dominant (*viz.* G), thus—

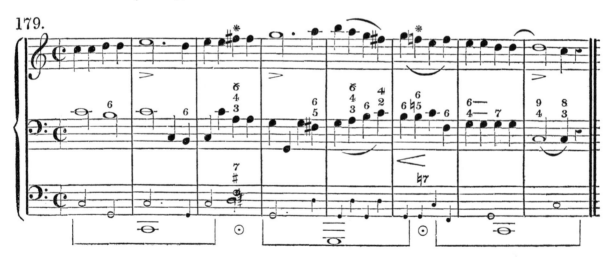

The above melody remains in the key of **C** until the third bar, where it modulates to **G**, and remains in that key until the second crotchet in the sixth bar, where it returns to the key of **C**.

The accidental sharps, flats, or naturals, are, it is true, the best signs by which we discover a *modulation* to have taken place (as in the above Examples); but it frequently happens that a modulation occurs without these indications appearing in the melody: it is therefore necessary to point out by what means this is effected.

We know that every modulation takes place through the agency of the Dominant; it follows, therefore, that any sounds in a melody which proceed as the intervals of the Dominant chord should proceed, *may* be employed for the purposes of modulation. The notes of modulation which, in a melody, produce the most decided effect on our ear, are those which ascend or descend by half tones.

Modulation by Means of the Intervals of a Melody.

First Rule.

" A note of modulation which ascends a half tone, modulates either

" *To the key which lies a half tone immediately above it (whether major or minor), or*

" *To the relative minor of the above-mentioned major key.*"

In the former case, the Dominant of the key to which we are modulating is found a major 3rd below the note of modulation, and in the latter case a 5th below.

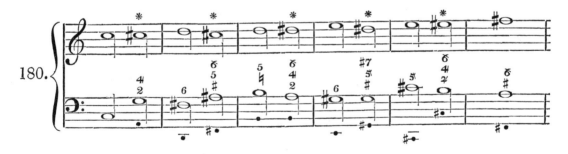

In bars 1, 3, and 5 of the above Example, the note of modulation has been employed to modulate to a major key; and in bars 2 and 4, the same note of modulation modulates to the *relative minor* of the above-mentioned major key.

T 2

Second Rule.

"The note of modulation which *descends* a major half tone, modulates either

"*To the key to which it will be the major 3rd when it has so descended,* or

"*To the relative minor of that key.*

"In the first case, (as in the following Example, at *a,*) the Dominant will be a fundamental 7th below the note of modulation; and in the second case it will be a minor 9th (as at *b*)."

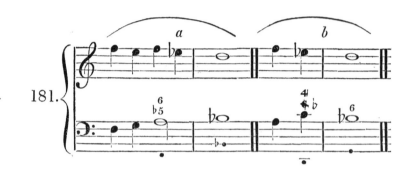

In the second bar of the following Example, the note of modulation modulates to the relative minor of the original key, in which the melody remains until the fourth bar; here the B♭ descending a half tone, modulates to F major.

In the 5th bar, B♮ conducts the harmony back to the original key of C, by the first rule of modulation in melodies.

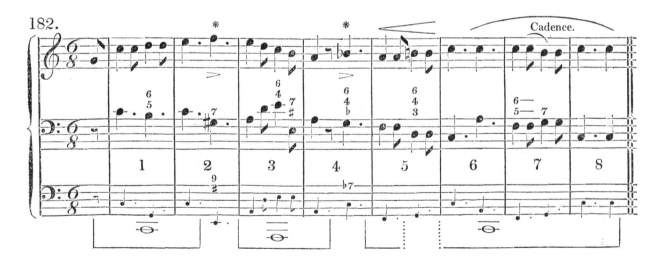

Third Rule.

" The note of modulation which *descends a whole tone* modulates either

" *Direct to the key which lies a whole tone below it* (Example 183, *a*); or,

" *To the relative minor of that key.* (*b*)

" In the former case, the Dominant will be found a fifth below the note of modulation ; in the latter it will be a seventh below it."

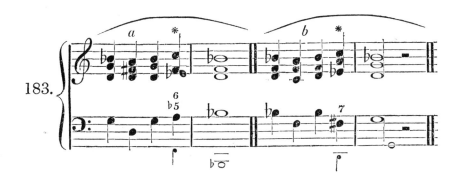

The following air continues in G minor until the end of the second bar, when the note of modulation, C, in the third bar, descending a whole tone, modulates to the relative major of G. In the seventh bar the same note of modulation modulates back to G minor.

In the following Example (at *a*), the notes of modulation descending by whole tones, modulate throughout to major keys.

And (at *b*) the same sounds modulate throughout to the relative minors of the former keys.

Fourth Rule.

"The note of modulation which ascends a whole tone can only modulate

"*To one key, to which it will be a major 3d when it has thus ascended* (Example 186 *a*).

"The Dominant will be found a fifth below the note of modulation," thus :

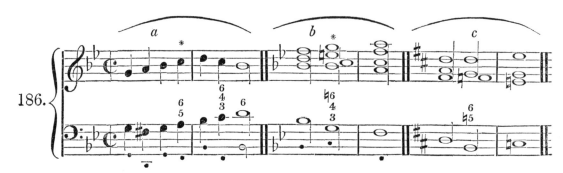

This rule must be employed with some degree of caution, as otherwise we may be easily led too far from the original key. The danger of making mistakes is least to be apprehended when we modulate from a minor to its relative major, as in the foregoing Example (at *a*); or to any key which has one sharp more, or one flat less (as at *b*); but it is not advisable to modulate to a key which has two sharps less, or two flats more (as at *c*).

In the following Example, (187,) the melody remains in the key of G, until the end of the fifth bar. In the sixth bar, the note E ascending a whole tone, modulates to the key of D, and closes the first part in that key.

In the ninth bar, a modulation back to G is effected in the same manner.

In bar thirteen, a modulation takes place to C, after which the Example closes with an irregular cadence.

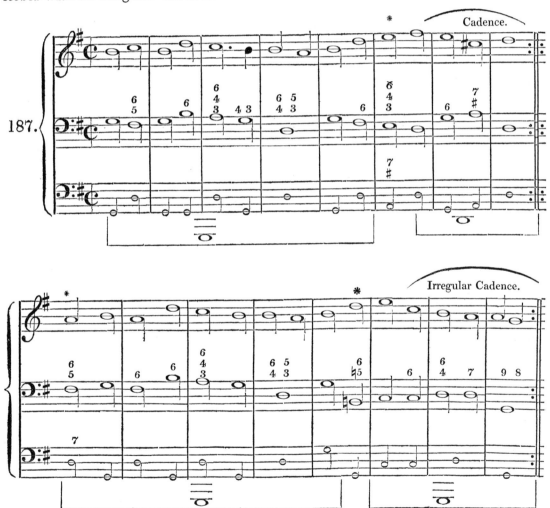

Fifth Rule.

"When any interval is repeated, it may modulate

"*To the key to which it is a fifth.*

"The Dominant of this note of modulation will be found an octave below
it ;" thus,

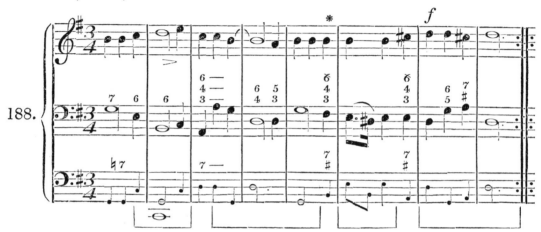

188.

At bar　5 the note B remaining in its place modulates to E minor.

,,　　9　,,　D　　　,,　　　　　,,　　G.

,,　　13　,,　B　　　,,　　　　　,,　　E minor.

The following example exhibits the preceding rules combined :—

At *a*, the note of the melody is repeated, we can therefore modulate to —.

At *b*, the note of the melody ascends *a whole tone*, we can therefore modulate to —.

At *c*, the note of the melody ascends a half tone, therefore we modulate to —.

At *d*, the note of the melody descends a half tone. To where can we modulate?

At *e*, the note of the melody descends a whole tone. To where can we modulate?

Sixth Rule.

" The note of modulation which ascends a perfect fourth (or descends a fifth), modulates direct

" *To a key to which it will be an octave;* or,

" *To a key to which it will be a fifth.*

" In the first case, the Dominant is an octave below the note of modulation; in the latter case, a fifth below. In both cases, the modulation may proceed either to a major or minor key."

In the following Example, the note of modulation modulates to the key to which, when it has ascended, it is an octave.

U

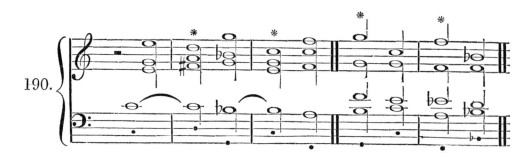

In the following Example, at *a*, the note of modulation proceeds to the key to which, when it has ascended, it becomes a fifth.

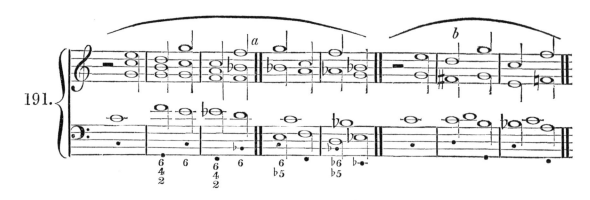

In the above modulations, hidden 5ths and 8ths are generally produced.

In the above Example, at *a*, are hidden fifths between the soprano and alto, and at *b* are hidden octaves between the same parts. In cases of emergency we might allow the 3d of the Dominant to fall, as in the second bar of the following Example, by which the hidden 5ths and 8ths, which at present appear in the 3d bar, are prevented*.

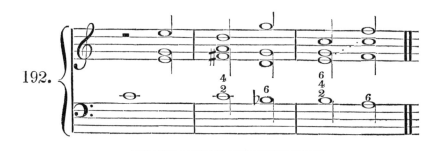

* These however may be considered as allowable, being found in the works of the best composers.

When the melody falls a fifth, we might perhaps prefer the first inversion to the third, because the extreme parts would then proceed by contrary motion, as in bars four and five of Example 191 (*a*); nevertheless, the third inversion should not on that account be rejected, for though the extreme parts do proceed, in consequence, by similar motion, still, as no hidden 5ths and 8ths are thereby occasioned, the effect is not bad. (See the following Example, at *a*).

When, however, the melody ascends a fourth, the first inversion is not quite so good, because hidden 8ths occur between the extreme parts, as at *b*.

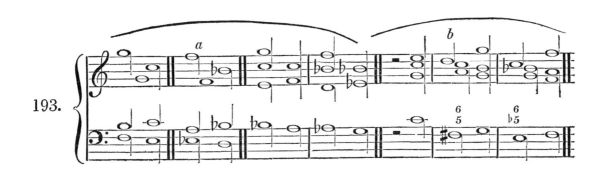

193.

The following is an exercise on the above rule; at *a*, the note of modulation modulates to a key to which it becomes a 5th; and at *b*, to one to which it becomes an 8th.

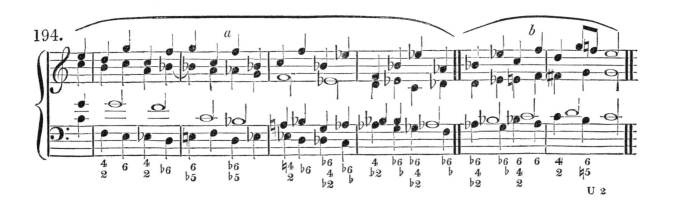

194.

U 2

The following is a melody in which the foregoing rules are exemplified :—

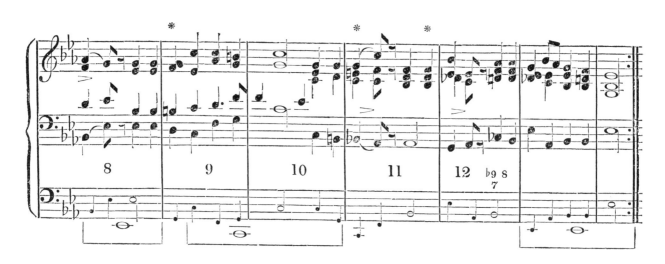

In bar 2, the note F, ascending a fourth, does not modulate, as it remains in the key.

In bar 4, however, where the F falls a fifth, it modulates to B♭.

In bar 9, the note G, ascending a fourth, modulates to C minor.

In bar 11, the same note G, ascending a fourth, modulates to F minor.

In the same bar, the note F, ascending a fourth, makes a protracted modulation to E♭ ; and then falling a fifth, modulates to A♭ in the 12th bar.

The following is an Exercise on the *First Rule ;* the note of modulation, ascending a half tone, proceeds to a minor key.

In bar 5, the note C♯ modulates to B minor; the same occurrence takes place in bar 13 ; and at bar 15 the F♯ modulates to E minor. At *a*, a licence has been taken, by letting the 3d of the Dominant chord fall to the 5th, in order to preserve the harmony in four parts. At *b*, another licence has been taken, allowing the 7ths to ascend.

With such an extraordinary latitude of modulation in melodies, as allowed by the foregoing rules, we cannot be too cautious in keeping the original key continually in view, in order to prevent extraneous modulations taking place ; by which is understood modulating to those keys which lie too remote, and bear no relation to each other.

By studying the preceding rules with attention, the pupil will arrive at a thorough knowledge of the various modes of treating a melody ; it will open to him at one glance a *vast* field of modulation, comprised within the limits of a *short* melody.

New Melodies, arising from those modulations, will be created in the alto, tenor, and bass, which may again be employed as *original* melodies, and treated accordingly.

Chord of the Sharp Sixth.

Whenever we make a modulation by the second inversion, we know that the 5th of the Dominant chord will be the inverted Bass. If we lower that inverted Bass a minor semitone, it will produce the chord of the major 6th.

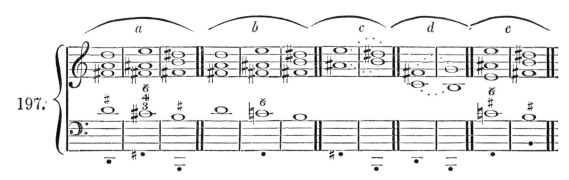

At *a*, the modulation has gone as usual from D to B♮, by the second inversion, *viz.* $\frac{6}{4}$; but at *b*, the inverted Bass has been *lowered* a half tone, by which means the distance between the Bass and the note represented by the 6, is become greater by a half tone ; and that note is therefore called the sharp 6th ; for the natural 6th to C is A, and not A♯.

If we analyze this chord with a sharp 6th (at *b*), we shall find that it contains within it the principal intervals of two distinct fundamental 7ths (see *c, d*). The former would lead the ear to B♮, and the latter to G♮, which when heard thus together, as at *b*, produce on the ear an ambiguous effect.

Every person may convince himself of this fact by striking the chord, as at *b*.

To avoid this, one of the intervals must be removed—but which of them ? The note A♯ cannot be dispensed with, because it is the principal interval in the Dominant chord, *viz.*, its 3d, or leading note. E cannot be removed, because it is the fundamental 7th. The only interval, therefore, which can be dispensed with is the F♯, the octave of the fundamental Bass. Let us take away this interval, and, in order to preserve the four parts complete, double the fundamental 7th, as at *e,* and it will then be correct. When this chord is in the position as at *e,* the 7th in the soprano must *descend,* and that in the tenor *ascend.* Should the 7th be doubled in the alto and tenor in unison, the alto must ascend, and the tenor descend, as at *f* in the following Example.

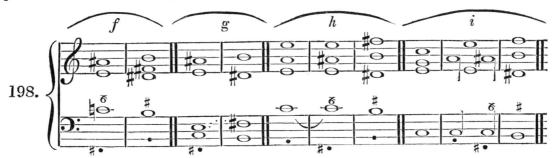

198.

Should the 7th be doubled in octaves, as at *g,* then the alto must descend, and the tenor ascend.

This chord is frequently written as at *h, i,* particularly by the old church writers; and produces thus a very beautiful effect, though it does contain an improper progression of hidden 5ths. The best time to introduce this chord is when we are in a minor key, and wish to modulate to its Dominant; as in the following Ex. :—

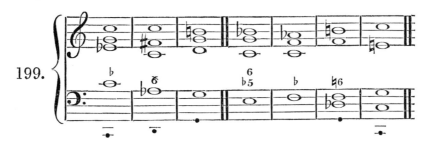

199.

We may nevertheless modulate with this chord to other keys, thus :—

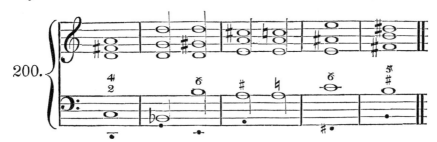

200.

The chord of the sharp 6th has this great advantage, that we can go direct to the key a major semitone below, without a chord of connexion, though a chord of connexion may likewise be introduced with effect.

By way of exercise, we will modulate through the chromatic scale descending, proceeding by *major semitones,* thus :—

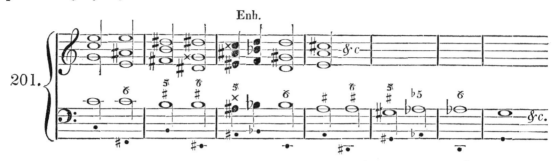

Why did we not modulate in bar three at once to B♭, instead of A♯?

Because B♭ is not a major semitone below B.

Why is the enharmonic change employed in the same bar ?

Because the major semitone below A♯ is G×, which would lead us to keys with too many sharps.

N.B. *Let it be observed,* that the chord which follows the sharp 6th must be *major.*

Chord of the Sharp 6th with the Minor 9th added, which we shall call the Compounded Sharp 6th, or ⁶₅.

It has already been explained that, in order to obtain four parts in the chord of the sharp sixth, the fundamental 7th must be doubled. If, however, instead of doubling the 7th, we add the minor 9th, as in the following Example (at *b*), we shall not only have obtained four parts, but shall have produced a chord which, in the practice of modulation, is of the utmost importance.

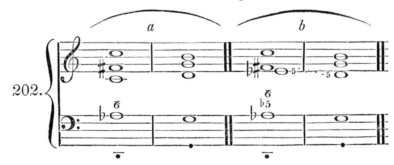

This chord, as will be seen by the fundamental Bass, is merely the second inversion of the fundamental 9th, with the Inverted Bass lowered a half tone.

At (*a*) the 6 as usual.

At (*b*) the 9th is added, and 7th removed.

It must be observed, that as the Bass in this chord is *obliged* to *descend* one degree, and as the 9th (which is now by inversion become the 5th) must also descend, consecutive 5ths will be the consequence.

There are two modes by which this improper progression may be prevented, viz.

1st. By letting the 9th descend to the 7th in the same chord (as at *a* in the following Example), by which means the latter interval becomes doubled, as in Example 198.

2d. By suspending the following 5th by means of the 6th (as at *b, c, d,*). Haydn has thus avoided consecutive 5ths, as will be shewn hereafter:—

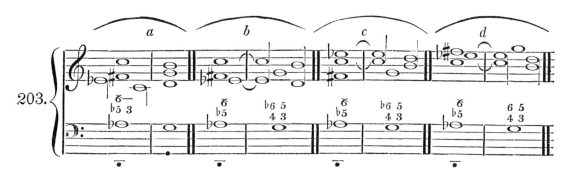

Exercise on the Chord of the Compounded Sharp 6th.

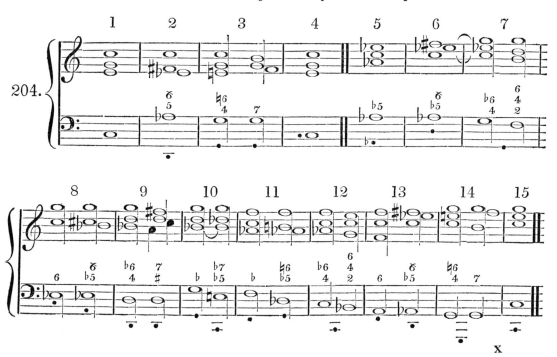

x

At bar 2: in the foregoing Example, the 5th (E♭), instead of descending to the 5th in the third bar, is suspended by the 6th. This 6th, however, is here changed to major, which produces a fine effect.

At bar 7: The 6th (E♭) resolves as usual into D, the 5th of the fundamental Bass. Instead, however, of the modulation closing here, the fundamental 7th (F), is introduced as an inverted Bass, by which the modulation is carried to C minor in bar 8. This mode of proceeding produces a good effect, and is called a Protracted Modulation, to be hereafter noticed.

Minor Melodies resumed from Example 176, *with the introduction of the Chord of the Compounded Sharp Sixth.*

As the following melody commences with the fifth of the scale, this fifth must have a minor chord; but it is immediately afterwards accompanied by a major chord, by which a modulation is effected to G minor.

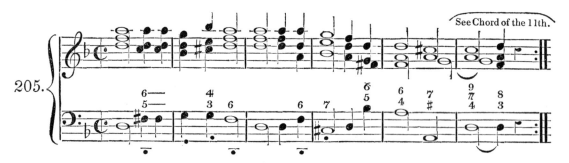

At bar 2, the harmony has modulated back to D minor. At bar 3, the melody is the same as at bar 1; but, in the succeeding bar, the fourth of the scale descending is accompanied by the Dominant, therefore the preceding fifth of the scale must have a minor chord.

The following Example is written partly in extended, and partly in compressed harmonies :—

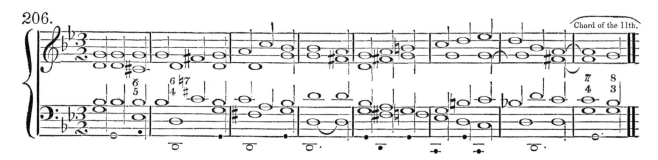

The following is an Exercise in Four Parts :

207.

X 2

At bars 12 and 15 of the foregoing Example, it will be observed that the alto and tenor have crossed each other.

This subject has been already noticed, but we will take advantage of this opportunity to add some further remarks, which before could not have been so well understood.

It must have been observed, that in Compressed Harmonies, the motion of the different parts is very circumscribed.

Let us suppose that there is only a certain quantum of motion to be distributed amongst the whole; if one part engrosses a large portion, the others must suffer.

If one part is monotonous, the others will be more melodious.

As the soprano and bass are the two extreme parts of the harmony, and consequently the most conspicuous, we are frequently tempted to divide between them the chief part of the motion, leaving the others moving within very narrow limits.

It is in such cases that we are led to break through the restraint, at least as far as the two parts within themselves afford the means; thus, by allowing the two inner parts (*i. e.* the alto and tenor) to interchange places, it is evident that we gain an *extension* of the limits of each part, as far as was before allotted to both, enabling us to produce more interesting melodies.

It is only necessary further to observe, as a general rule, that this crossing of the parts should be used with caution, and ought only to be allowed between the inner parts; for if the alto crosses the soprano, or the tenor the bass, it must of course interfere with one of the principal melodies.

By the following Example, which is merely the two first bars of the foregoing, it will be easily perceived what power is given to us of producing variety, even only by thus extending the harmonies and crossing the parts.

The Example exhibits also specimens of the various modes of accompanying the fifth of the scale when it ascends to the 6th, and falls again to the 5th.

At (*a*) the harmonies are compressed.

At (*b*) the inner parts have crossed, producing interesting melodies, which will be more apparent if separately played with the bass, and compared with those at *a*.

At (*c*) the harmonies are extended, and new melodies arise.

At (*d*) new harmonies have been given to the 5th, which ascends to the 6th, and falls again to the 5th.

At (*e*) a partial interchange takes place, and

At (*f*) the two parts change places nearly all through the Example.

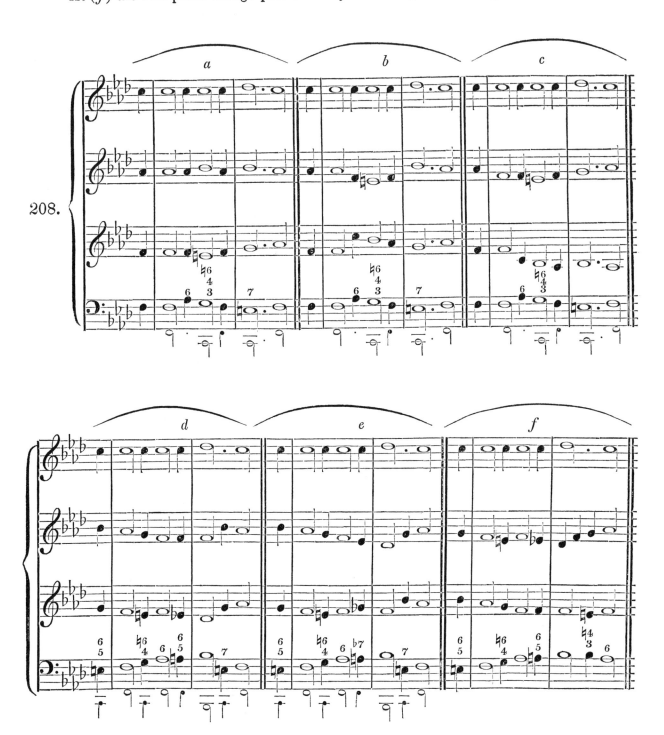

The following is an Exercise on the preceding subject.

209.

Minor Scale.

Some authors write the ascending and descending minor scale differently from what has been given in this work; chiefly to avoid the progression of the sharp 2d between the 6th and 7th of the scale, thus :—

210.

This liberty may be taken in performing the scale, ascending and descending very rapidly, when these sounds are passing notes, as thus:

211.

But in *harmonizing* the scale, it is presumed no change ought to be introduced, because the peculiar beauty and character of the minor scale is derived, in a great measure, from the progression of that very sharp second.

The 6th of the Scale in Major *Keys accompanied by the Dominant.*

By the introduction of the minor 9th, we have been enabled in *minor keys* to accompany the 6th of the scale descending by the Dominant. This we have called the " Fifth Rule for employing Fundamental Basses*." It now becomes necessary to state, that in future this rule may also apply to *major keys ;* in which case the 6th of the scale will be a *major* 9th to the fundamental Bass. This major 9th is *a whole tone* above the 8th (see the following Example at *a*), whereas the minor 9th, as will be recollected, is only *a half tone* above it (as at *b*).

Whenever the 6th of the major scale is thus accompanied by the Dominant, producing the chord of the major 9th, it is to be treated in every respect exactly the same as the minor 9th.

But as this chord of the major 9th may be employed on other occasions as well as when the sixth of the scale descends, it may be observed that the best effect is produced when the 9th is at the top of the chord (as at *a*), and that the first inversion (as at *c*), or the third (as at *e*), should be used in preference to the second (at *d*).

The fourth inversion (as at *f*) should be sparingly used.

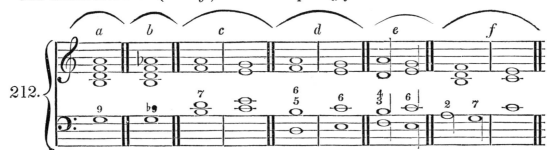

212.

N.B. In writing this chord, carefully avoid placing the 3rd over the 9th : a little observation and experience will shew the propriety of this and the preceding remarks.

---

* See page 133.

The following is an Exercise for the employment of the major 9th.

At *a* and *d,* the 6th of the scale is accompanied by the Dominant, and the chord of the major 9th is in the third inversion.

At *b,* it is in the first inversion, and

At *c,* in the second.

This interval of the major 9th must now be considered as forming part of the Dominant Chord, and we may employ it as a note of modulation in a melody.

As this interval descends a whole tone, we may now make the following addition to the 3d rule of modulation in airs (Example 183) :—

"The note of a melody which descends a whole tone, may modulate to the key of the 5th below the note to which it descends."

In the following Example, bar 3, the note E, descending a whole tone (to D,) modulates to the key of G ; and in

Bar 4, the last crotchet (A), descending a whole tone (to G), modulates back to the key of C.

Method of harmonizing a Melody, when written in the Alto, Tenor, or Bass.

Hitherto our themes for harmonization have been given in the soprano, and we have added the harmonies underneath; but should we think proper to write the theme first in any of the other parts, we must proceed to harmonize it exactly in the same manner as before, merely taking care to dispose the remaining parts of the harmony in their proper places; all the preceding rules being equally applicable in this case.

Suppose we choose that the theme shall be given in the alto, we must first place it in the alto staff, and then write the inverted bass in its proper place ; as in the following Example, at *a*.

Y

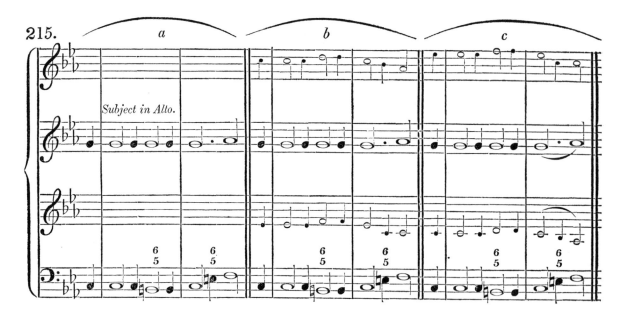

After this there are still two parts wanting, the tenor and soprano, which are added, at *b*, in compressed harmonies, being written as near as possible to the given melody in the alto.

It may also be written in extended harmonies, as at *c*.

By comparing the above two Examples, it will be seen that the soprano and tenor at *b*, have exchanged places at *c*, each being transposed an octave*, whilst the tenor and bass remain unchanged.

We shall not here make any remark on the *counterpoint in the octave*, but direct the attention of the pupil to the variety of melody thus afforded, and the very great difference of effect resulting.

The following is a melody given in the alto, with compressed harmonies.

In bar 3, will be observed the chord of the compound sharp 6th.

In bar 6, a false cadence: (see farther, where that subject is treated upon.)

In bar 14, the soprano has crossed the alto, in order to obtain a good melody and contrary motion.

N.B. Any notes observed in these Examples which do not belong to the chord, come under the general denomination of Passing Notes, particularly explained hereafter.

---

* When we wish to interchange the parts thus, we must be careful that the Bass in the first instance (as at *b*) does not approach the Soprano nearer than an octave.   See page 119.

The following is the same air as the above, and in the same manner written in the alto, but with extended harmony; the soprano and tenor having changed places, the former being written an octave lower, and the latter an octave higher.

The following is the same melody written *in the tenor*. The Example is merely commenced, and may be completed by the pupil:

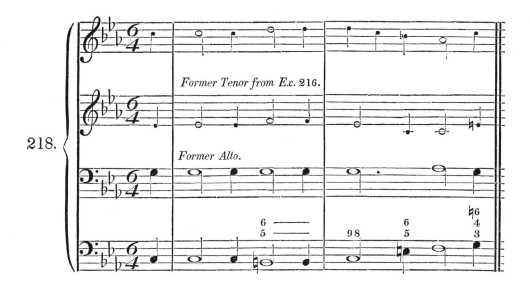

When a melody is written in the bass, it must be treated in exactly the same manner as if it were in the soprano; with this exception only, that the fifth of the scale and the fourth when *descending*, are generally accompanied by the Dominant.

The air being written as in the following Example, at *a*, add the fundamental Basses, as at *b*, and figure the melody, which thus becomes an inverted Bass; and to this add a counter melody in the soprano, as at *c*.

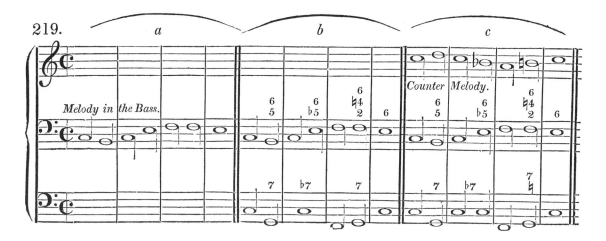

In order to form this counter melody, it is only necessary to observe the rules already given, for selecting an inverted Bass to a melody*. For instance, in the first bar of the above Example, at *c*, the 3d being in the Bass, we have taken the 5th for the melody.

In the second bar, the 3d is again in the Bass, but we have taken the 7th in the melody.

In the third bar, the 7th is in the Bass, and the 3d in the melody†.

The following Exercise consists of the same air as the one in the preceding, with the harmony added. The fundamental Bass is figured with all the dissonances allowed by each progression, any of which may, of course, be introduced at pleasure.

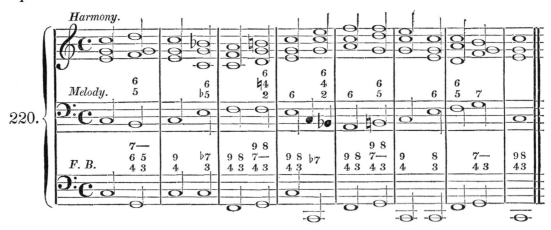

The following Melodies in the Bass are intended for Exercise on the preceding rules.

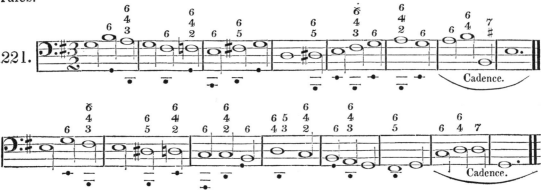

* See page 100 and following.

† The frequent employment of contrary and oblique motion is here recommended. See farther, where this subject is treated upon.

In the following theme in the Bass the harmony is extended, except in the 6th bar, where it is compressed for the purpose of preserving a good melody:

In harmonizing the above Bass melody, it will be perceived that the rules of modulation in airs, commencing at page 137, have been put in practice.

In bar 4, the note of modulation (C) falling a whole tone modulates to B♭.

In bar 5, the last quaver (D) ascending a half tone modulates to E♭.

In bar 6, the second note (E♭) falling a half tone modulates to B♭.

In the following Example (at *a*) is given an instance of the application of the latter part of the *second* rule of modulation (page 140), producing the chord of the sharp second, which necessarily resolves on the chord of the $\frac{6}{4}$.

As this latter chord partakes much of the nature of the discord of the $\frac{6}{4}$ by suspension, the effect is unsatisfactory.

The employment of this rule of modulation, therefore, in a Bass melody should be avoided ; unless this chord of the $\frac{6}{4}$ is immediately succeeded by such intervals, as at *c*, where that chord has been treated as a discord and resolved accordingly ; or as at *b*, where the note of modulation (which is here the 9th) falls into its fundamental bass, *&c.*

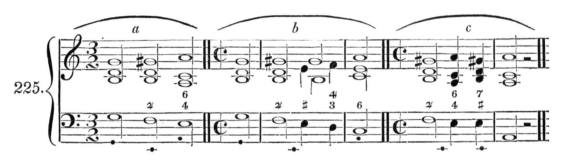

225.

In the following Example are shewn two applications of the sixth rule of modulation, " where the melody ascends a fourth."

As these are the *true* fundamental progressions which point out the peculiar *character of the Bass,* they ought to be treated as *Fundamental Basses* (see *a*), and not as *intervals* of a chord (see *b*), the latter producing a crude and inharmonious effect.

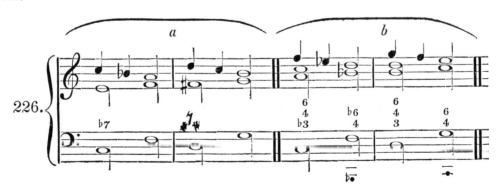

226.

The following is a melody given in the Bass, to which a soprano is added.

The Bass Melodies in the succeeding Examples are given as Exercises to be completed in four parts. In the first Example the *fundamental* Bass is pointed out, that the pupil himself may figure the inversions. In the second, the Bass melody is *figured*, and the pupil will find the fundamental Basses.

* See Deceptive Modulation.

Z

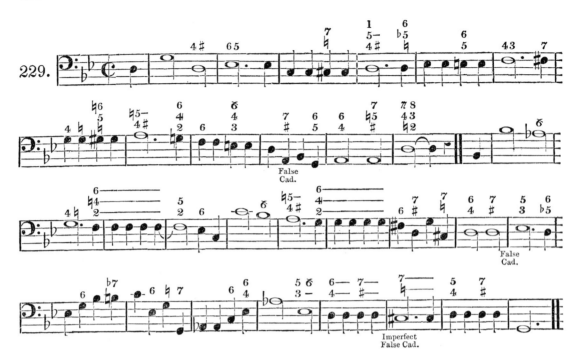

It will be observed, that whenever any note of a Bass melody is treated as the sharp 6th, the *first* part of the *third* rule of modulation is employed*. In this case, however, instead of the note of modulation descending a *whole* tone, it descends only a *half* tone, as in bars 13, 17, and 26 in the above Example 229.

The following is an Exercise on a Bass melody which is only partially figured:

----

* See page 141.

The two following Exercises are entirely without figures*:

231.

232.

Passing Notes.

A melody may either be *simple* or *embellished*. A simple melody is formed from the intervals of the chords only; thus, the melodies which have been hitherto harmonized are all simple. When any notes are introduced into a melody which do not belong to the chords from which that melody is constructed, the air or melody is said to be embellished; and the notes so introduced are called *Passing Notes*†.

In the following Ex. at *a*, the intervals of the melody ascend and descend by thirds.

Between these intervals may be introduced *Passing Notes,* as represented by dots at *b*.

At *c*, these Passing Notes are exhibited as they are generally written. The time of the note in the original melody being divided into two portions, the *latter* of which is occupied by the Passing Note. In order to distinguish the *essential* notes of the simple melody, we shall continue for a time to mark them as in this instance at *c*.

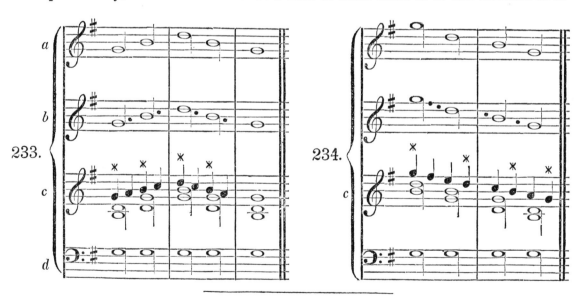

233.

234.

---

* For further practice on this part of the subject, the Pupil is referred to No. 75, and succeeding Numbers, in the Book of Exercises. † They are also by some authors called *Transient Notes.*

Z 2

The Passing Notes in the above Example, 233, are said to be UNACCENTED, because they are introduced AFTER the essential notes of the harmony.

When a Passing Note, however, is struck *before* the essential note of the harmony, it is said to be *accented*. In this latter case, the *Passing Note* occupies the *first* portion of the time belonging to the original note of the melody, as in Example 234, *c*, where the F is an UNACCENTED Passing Note; and the E, C, and A *accented*.

In the following Example, at *a*, is a simple melody, proceeding chiefly by 3rds, as affording the best opportunity for the introduction of Passing Notes.

At *b*, are introduced some UNACCENTED Passing Notes, which produce a very graceful melody, and give to particular passages a marked peculiarity of character.

At *d*, is the inverted Bass in its *simple state*.

At *c*, the same Bass, with Passing Notes introduced.

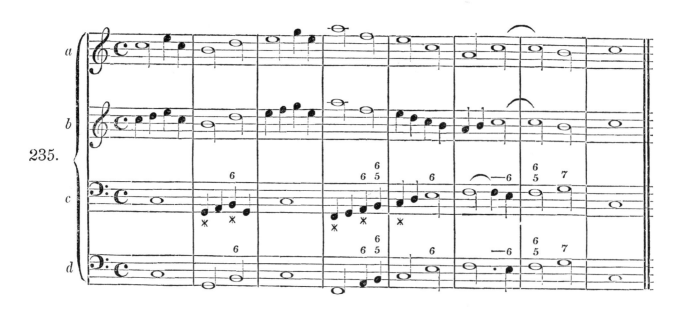

Let us now take the above melody with the Passing Notes as at *b*, and harmonize it in four parts, with extended harmonies; retaining the *same* fundamental Basses, with very little alteration of the *inverted* Bass. It will be observed that the peculiar character in one part is found afterwards imitated in another, repeated in a third, &c. &c.; the same sentiment, as it were, pervading the whole.

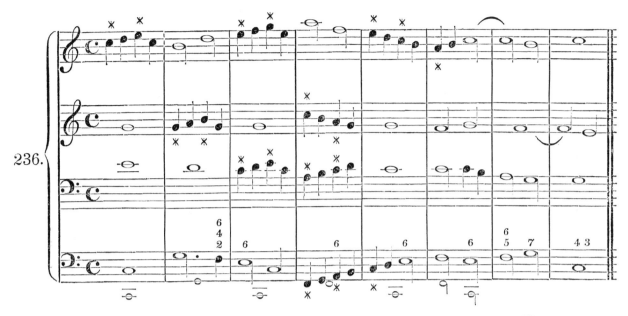

236.

The melody in the *Soprano,* at bar 1, is embellished by the Passing Notes, and imitated in bar 2 by the *Alto.* At bar 3, the *Tenor* has the same passage, accompanied by the *Soprano* in thirds, which may be called *Compound* Passing Notes*.

The *Tenor,* at bar 4, is imitated at 5 by the *Soprano* proceeding by contrary motion.

The *Bass,* at bar 5, is imitated by the *Soprano* at bar 6.

We find that the UNACCENTED Passing Notes are *less* dissonant than the *accented,* as they are not heard until *after* the chord which accompanies the melody has been struck ; whereas, the *accented* Passing Notes are struck *with* the chord itself, producing all the effect of a *dissonance unprepared.* Let us compare the different effects—

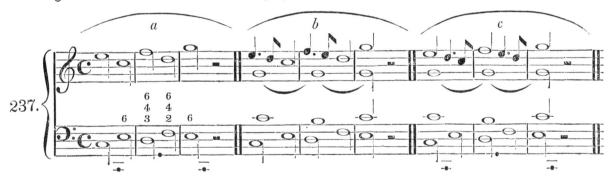

237.

At *a,* is a simple melody with its Bass.

At *b,* UNACCENTED Passing Notes are introduced in the melody.

At *c, accented* Passing Notes.

---

* This compound progression of Passing Notes can only take place when two parts move together by 3rds or 6ths.

In the following Example, Passing Notes are introduced both in the Soprano and Bass.

238.

At *a*, unaccented Passing Notes in the Soprano and Bass.

At *b*, unaccented Passing Notes are introduced in the Soprano, and the passage is answered, or imitated in the Bass, with *accented* Passing Notes, by contrary motion.

At *c*, the Bass proceeds with *unaccented* Passing Notes, and is answered by the Soprano with *accented*, by contrary motion.

In the following Example other inverted Basses have been chosen, and the melody which appeared in the *Bass* in the above Example at *c*, is here transferred to the *Alto*.

239.

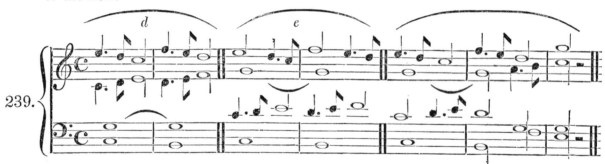

At *e*, the Tenor and Alto having changed places, the Passing Notes are introduced alternately in the Soprano and Tenor, and Tenor and Alto.

It may be observed that the *accented* Passing Notes produce a better effect when in the Soprano (as above at *e*), than in the Bass (as at *b*); the latter, however, is equally correct. Observe that all the different effects in the above two Examples are derived from the simple melody, at *a*, Ex. 233, by the introduction of Passing Notes.

Should the melody proceed by an interval of a second, and this second be a whole tone, a Passing Note between will be a minor semitone. This Passing Note, when unaccented, should not be employed where the note of the melody to which it belongs is a *Major* 3rd to the fundamental bass. The following Example is the Diatonic Scale of C, with Passing Notes:

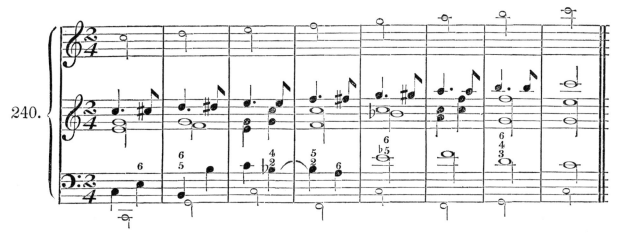

240.

To shew how Passing Notes in a melody ascending by half tones, may be converted into notes of modulation, let us take the soprano part of the above Ex. as a melody, and harmonize it according to the first rule of modulation: it will then appear thus:

241.

The following is a short Exercise on the introduction of Passing Notes by half tones.

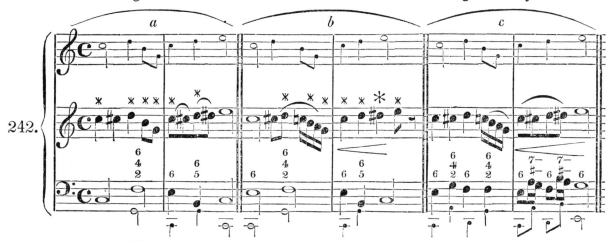

242.

At *a*, it will be observed that all the Passing Notes are *unaccented*.

At *b*, they are *accented*.

At *c*, they are treated as notes of modulation.

The following melody affords an opportunity of introducing Passing Notes by whole tones and semitones, and will serve as a specimen of the application of the preceding rules.

At *a*, is exhibited the melody unembellished.

At *b*, the same air with Passing Notes.

N.B. In the fourth bar the Tenor crosses the Alto, in order to prevent hidden 5ths between the Soprano and Alto.

---

* Chord of the 11th, see Ex. 264.

Auxiliary Notes.

These notes are employed as substitutes, where the melody does not afford an opportunity for the introduction of *passing* notes. They may be written *above* or *below* the notes of the melody, and may be either *accented* or *unaccented*.

244.

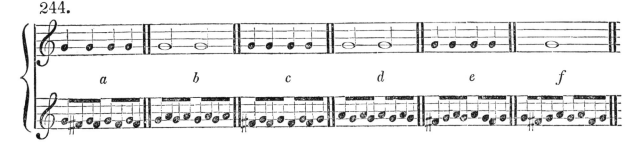

At *a,* auxiliary notes below.

(N.B. These ought always to be a *half* tone below the note of the melody.)

At *b,* auxiliary notes above.

(N.B. These may be either a *whole* tone or a *half* tone, as the note next above in the melody happens to be.)

At *a* and *b,* the auxiliary notes are *unaccented.*

At *c* and *d, accented.*

At *e,* accented notes above and below intermixed.

At *f,* all are introduced.

Imitation.

By the introduction of passing notes, we have not only obtained a smooth and graceful melody in the different parts, but have been enabled to communicate to any progression of a simple melody a more marked character, so as to render it more easily to be distinguished when re-appearing in any other part of the harmony.

Any *short progression of notes* (whether or not arising from the introduction of passing or auxiliary notes) we shall call *a passage.* When such a passage is followed by a similar one in any other of the four parts, it is said to be imitated; this imitation may take place in the unison, 2d, 3d, or in any interval of the scale.

The following Example of Imitation (which, for the purpose of simplicity, is founded on one single chord) will serve also to shew the utility of auxiliary notes in giving a marked character to those parts where passing notes could *not* be introduced.

2 A

245.

At *a*, is a simple melody, formed out of two intervals of the chord which accompanies it. This melody, proceeding by thirds, admits of passing notes, and
it is by the introduction of these passing notes that the passage at *b* is formed.

This passage we are desirous of imitating in the *Alto*, but we find in that part (at *c*),
only a repetition of the *same* note, which does not admit of passing notes; however, by
having recourse to the auxiliary notes, an imitation is produced in similar motion, as at *d*.

Suppose it were our object to introduce the imitation in the *Tenor* instead of
the Alto; we find in that part (*e*) only one note (a minim); but as we are at liberty,
if we think proper, to divide that minim into quavers (as at *f*), the auxiliary notes may
be employed, and the imitation effected, as at *g*, which, for the sake of variety, is
written in contrary motion (with respect to the passage at *b*), merely by commencing
with the auxiliary note above. N.B. It will be perceived that this imitation would
have been in similar motion had we commenced with the auxiliary note below.

At *h*, the imitation is introduced in the Bass in similar motion.

It has been shewn (see Example 236) that compound *passing notes* can be used where any two parts proceed in thirds or sixths. Compound auxiliary notes may be employed in the same manner. Thus, in the above Example, we find that the Tenor and Alto are thirds to each other; auxiliary notes can, therefore, be introduced in both parts at the same time (see *i*). The same occurs in the Tenor and Bass at *k*.

From the above it is evident, that even a *single* note, by the application of auxiliary notes, may become a subject for imitation, as in the following Example, which is merely the ascending scale harmonized; a single interval only of the first chord is taken to form a passage, which is subsequently imitated alternately in the other parts.

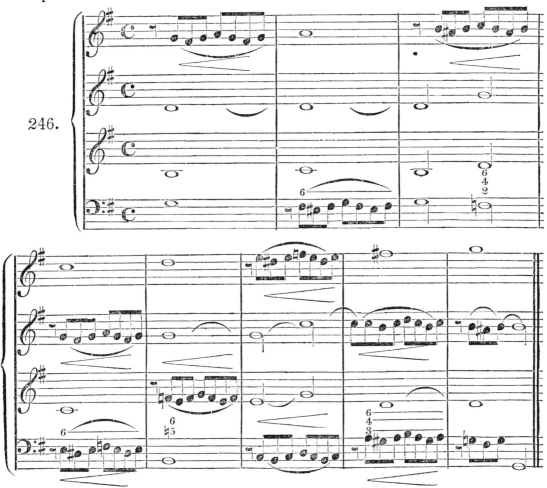

246.

When the intervals of a melody are far removed from each other, passing and auxiliary notes may also be employed with excellent effect; in which circumstances we shall call them *extended*.

2 A 2

Extended Passing and Auxiliary Notes.

In the following Example at I., is a simple melody, calculated to display these notes of embellishment, as exhibited at II. and III.

247.

At *a*, all are extended passing notes.

At *b*, ... extended auxiliary notes *below*.

At *c*, ... extended auxiliary notes *above*.

At *d*, ... common passing notes.

N.B. These notes of embellishment, when thus employed, may, as in former cases, be either accented or unaccented. In the above Example they are all *unaccented*.

The following Example will enable us to perceive how upon a simple melody (as at I.), all the preceding notes of embellishment may be introduced.

At *a,* are employed accented auxiliary notes *above.*

At *b,* . . . . accented extended passing notes.

Extended passing and auxiliary notes may follow each other in immediate succession, thus—

At *c,* the second note is an extended passing note *unaccented,* and the third note is an extended auxiliary note *accented.*

At *d,* the same as at *c,* intermixed (at *e*), with simple passing notes accented.

At *f,* two extended auxiliary notes follow each other in immediate succession.

At *g,* a passage from Haydn's " Creation," in which the composer has employed extended auxiliary notes accented.

In the following Exercise (being the descending scale) all the various notes of embellishment are introduced in the Bass.

249.

The two Basses, at *a* and *b*, which are written upon the *same* fundamental harmony, but *differently* embellished, are calculated to shew us at one view the various effects that may be produced by a judicious employment of passing and auxiliary notes.

At *a*, are introduced simple *passing notes* accented and unaccented.

At *b*, extended passing and auxiliary notes.

N.B. In order to introduce those at *b*, we must suppose the Bass to have been written originally as at *c*, which is produced by the employment of secondary harmonies hereafter explained.

Secondary Harmony.

Harmony in *four* parts may sometimes be made to produce an effect nearly equal to *five* or *six* parts*, by letting some of the intervals of the chord be heard in more than one part at the same time. This will be better explained by an Example.

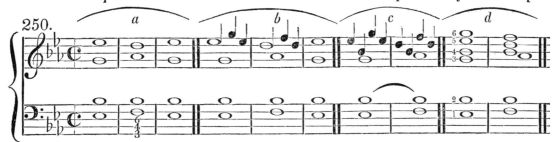

At *a*, the harmony is in four parts.

At *b*, in consequence of the Soprano proceeding in the first bar to G, and in the second bar to F, the effect of five parts is produced.

At *c*, the harmony appears in six parts, which will be clear if we examine it as written at *d*, which represents all the sounds; and although they are not heard all at the same time, yet they will, in a great measure, produce that effect upon the ear.

In order to prevent impurities occurring in the harmony on such occasions, it is only necessary to let the interval of the secondary harmony, which thus *doubles another*, proceed by contrary or oblique motion, with the *original* interval.

The following Example is the Ascending Diatonic Scale in the Bass.

At *e*, it is harmonized simply in four parts.

At *f*, secondary harmony is introduced in the Soprano; and at *g*, in the Alto.

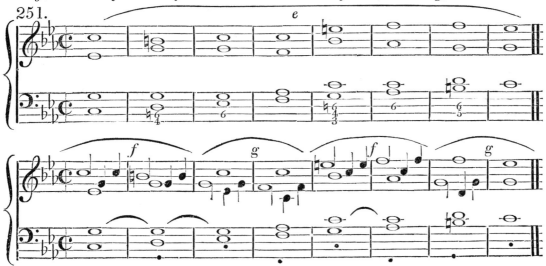

* Writing in more than four parts will be treated upon elsewhere.

In consequence of the change of melody produced at f in the preceding Example, by the employment of secondary harmony below, we are enabled to introduce extended *auxiliary* notes, as in the following Example at h and i.

By employing the secondary harmony *above*, instead of *below*, extended *passing* notes may be introduced, as at k.

The secondary harmony appears at h in the Soprano, and at i it is in the Alto.

In Example 253, at l, it is in the *Alto* and *Tenor*, and at m in the *Bass*.

At *n,* in the following Example, the Ascending Diatonic Scale is in the Bass, with the same secondary harmonies as in the first four bars at *m* (in the preceding Example), to which are now added passing and auxiliary notes.

At *o,* the scale is continued in the *Alto* instead of the *Bass,* the secondary harmony proceeding in the same order as in the Bass at *m,* from bar 4. The passing and auxiliary notes, which are here introduced, produce an imitation between the Bass, at *n,* and the Alto, at *o.*

Dissonances with Secondary Harmony.

In employing secondary harmony, we have seen that a consonance may proceed to any other note of the chord; therefore a dissonance (which always stands in place of a consonance) may, in like manner, proceed to any interval of the harmony before its final resolution.

In the following Example, at *a,* we have introduced the secondary harmony in the Tenor, and at *b* in the Soprano, without dissonances. But it appears from the progression of the fundamental Bass at *a,* that we may introduce the dissonance of the 4th, and at *b* the dissonance of the 9th.

2 B

At *c* and *d* these dissonances are employed, and are made to proceed to some other note of the harmony before being resolved.

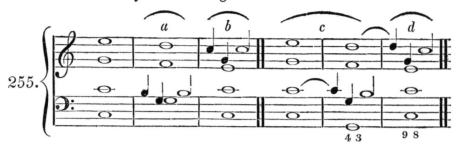

In the above Example the dissonance, before its final resolution, descends to an interval of the chord, but it may also be allowed to descend to an extended auxiliary note below, as in the following Example at III.

At **IV.** simple auxiliary and passing notes are employed in the other parts, and proceed at the same time in conjunction with these secondary harmonies, which may take place whether dissonances are introduced or not.

At I. appears the harmony with dissonances. At II. the dissonance, before its resolution, proceeds to one of the secondary harmonies. At III. are employed extended auxiliary notes. At IV. simple auxiliary notes intermixed, and in conjunction with extended*.

As the preceding Examples, it is presumed, will sufficiently illustrate all that has been said upon this subject, it is unnecessary to give further rules for the employment of these various embellishments; the best advice which can be given is, to examine the works of the most classical composers, and observe how they have treated them on different occasions.

In exercising upon this subject, it is strongly recomended that the harmony be first written in four parts, before a single dissonance, passing note, or secondary harmony be introduced. A strict adherence to this rule will prevent many errors.

In order to enable the Pupil still more easily to distinguish the various passing and auxiliary notes whenever he may meet with them, we will take a simple melody, such as we have hitherto used for exercises, and arrange it for the *piano-forte*, introducing the above embellishments, together with the usual marks of expression, rests, dots, &c., to give it character and effect†.

It must be previously observed, that when writing for the piano-forte, we are frequently obliged (in order to produce a bold and majestic effect) to double notes of the harmony; in which case the rules respecting consecutive octaves are not always observed. Octaves also are frequently played by the left hand, which must not be considered as consecutive octaves, being merely introduced to give force to the Bass. The rule relative to consecutive 5ths, however, must be strictly attended to.

In the following Example (at *a*) is the simple melody, and (at *d*) the fundamental bass, with the part arranged for the *piano-forte* between them (*b c*). Now let us examine the melody, at *b*, and shew by what marks of expression and ornament it has been formed from the essential notes at *a*.

At bar 1: The second minim of the melody at *a*, has been reduced to a crotchet, and the time completed by a rest, &c., by which the air acquires a greater degree of energy. A spirited effect is also produced by the rapid progress of the semiquaver ascending to the next note in the succeeding bar. This effect will be very perceptible when we compare that passage with the simple melody at *a*.

At bar 3 (upon the latter half) is introduced an extended auxiliary note.

At bar 4: Whilst the melody (or right hand) reposes, a passage is introduced for the left hand, serving to keep up the interest, and smoothly gliding from the dominant to its tonic.

---

* Why the auxiliary note E♯ (in bar 7) and at A♯ (in bar 9) cannot be introduced, has been explained at the bottom of page 174.   † This frequently gives to a composition the appearance of intricacy, when in reality it consists of merely the simple materials already explained.

In the following Example the foregoing melody is preserved in its simple state, and a variation constructed out of the inner parts of the harmony.

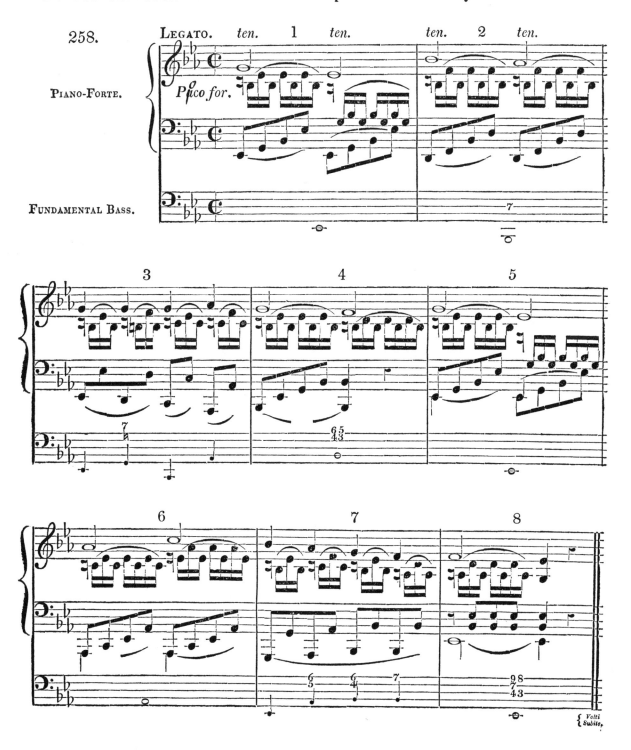

In order to give more interest to the Bass, secondary harmonies have been introduced into that part, the melody being in this Example exceedingly simple, it will appear on examination that the *whole* of the chord has been generally employed, broken into quavers. In bar 9, the notes for the right hand are written on the Bass staff, to avoid the use of ledger lines.

The following is a variation, in which passing notes are introduced in the melody, to be played by the right hand in octaves. The inner parts, with the addition of secondary harmonies, are played by the left hand.

A spirited effect is produced in the following variation, by the occasional introduction of *extended passing*, and *auxiliary* notes, which are given to the right and left hand alternately.

The following is a short specimen of another variation of the same melody in which the passing and auxiliary notes are given to the right hand in octaves, whilst the left hand plays the harmony in broken chords.

This should be completed by the Pupil, who ought not only to exert his ingenuity in constructing other variations on this same melody in different styles, but also endeavour to treat other melodies in a similar manner.

Nothing perhaps will be more likely to give him a complete knowledge of the use and importance of these notes of embellishment, than industriously exercising as above recommended in constructing variations upon a simple theme.

It would lead us far beyond the limits necessarily prescribed to this work, were we to enter more fully into this very fertile and interesting subject of writing for the piano-forte; however, as opportunities offer, we shall so arrange the subsequent exercises, that, instead of merely shewing the plain chords, they shall at the same time convey useful hints respecting the different modes of applying the instructions to compositions for the piano-forte*.

---

* The author is preparing for publication a little work, expressly for those who are desirous of employing their theoretical knowledge in compositions for the piano-forte. In this work specimens will be given of the earliest writers for that instrument, to the present day.

Ascending Dissonances, or Retardation.

If, in the progression of the chord of the fundamental 7th, instead of letting the 3d ascend *directly* to the octave, we should continue it upon the succeeding bass, it will become a dissonance (*viz.*, the 7th), which must *afterwards* ascend into the octave. This is called an Ascending Dissonance, and as it thus *retards* the succeeding consonance, we shall call it a Retardation, as in the following Example, at *a.*

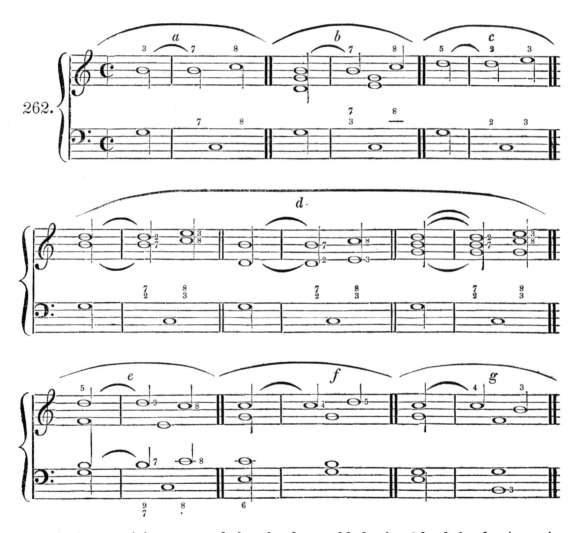

At *b*, the remaining notes of the chord are added, the 3d of the dominant is carried forward into the chord of the tonic, and forms thus the chord of major 7th (usually called the *Sharp 7th*).

If, in the progression of the dominant chord in an *ascending* melody, the 5th is continued on the tonic, it will form the dissonance of the 2d ascending into the 3d (as at *c*). If the dissonances at *a* and *c* are employed in conjunction, they will produce the chord of the $\frac{7}{2}$ (as at *d*).

When the melody *descends*, the note which is at *c* a dissonance by *retardation* (the 2d into the 3d) will become a dissonance by *suspension* (the 9th into the 8th), as at *e*. To ascertain, therefore, whether this dissonance is a 2d or a 9th, it is necessary to examine its progression. Should the dissonance *ascend*, it will be a 2d ; should it *descend*, it will be a 9th.

Having disposed of the two principal dissonances by retardation, let us proceed to the last, *viz.*, the 4th into the 5th. This dissonance is not so satisfactory to the ear as the two preceding ; which is occasioned by a certain ambiguity in the effect (see *f*), for, as we cannot decide whether the 4th is a *retardation* or a *suspension*, until it has either ascended or descended, it will be doubtful, in the meanwhile, whether the dissonance and its resolution are not heard together, as at *g*.

To avoid this ambiguity, we shall raise the dissonance a half tone, as in the following Example (at *a*), by which its ascending resolution is immediately anticipated, and all doubts respecting its identity are removed.

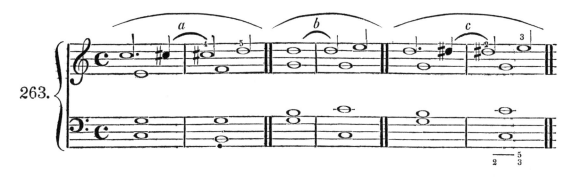

263.

In the same manner the 2d may also be raised a semitone, by which means a similar ambiguity is avoided ; for the dissonance of the 2d, when not employed in conjunction with the 4th by *suspension**, may be mistaken for the 9th until its resolution has taken place, and in the meanwhile the harmony will appear deprived of its principal interval, *viz.* the 3d (as at *b*) ; but by raising the 2d a half tone (as at *c*) this uncertainty is removed, as it cannot then be considered any longer as the 9th.

---

* Which would produce the chord of the 11th. See Example 267, *b*.

2 C 2

The same rule which has been given in employing dissonances by *suspension*, *viz.*, " That the dissonance and the note suspended shall not appear at the same time," must also be observed when we employ *retardation ;* thus, as the C♯, in the second bar of the following Example, retards the D (being the 4th into the 5th), the D which appears in the tenor (and which is the 5th), cannot be admitted.

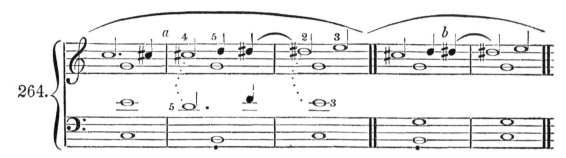

The same error which occurs in the second bar, appears also in the bar which follows, where the 3d of the chord is found in the tenor, whilst the same interval is retarded in the soprano : both these errors are avoided at *b*.

The following is an Exercise on the Diatonic Scale, in three* parts, with ascending dissonances, intermixed with passing and auxiliary notes.

---

* The subject of writing in more or less than *four* parts will be treated upon separately.

The preceding Exercise written in four parts.

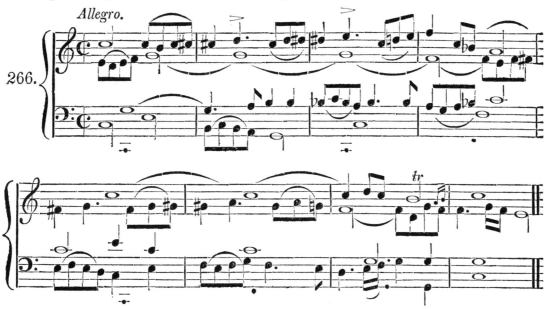

That the Pupil may the better understand how these dissonances (intermixed with passing and auxiliary notes), have been introduced, he is recommended first to write the simple harmony of the scale in an extended position, as it is here exhibited, and afterwards to add the dissonances and notes of embellishment, according to the rules given.

In the above Example it will be perceived that the diatonic scale, after commencing in the soprano, is continued in that part for only three bars; after which the alto takes it up for the following three bars, by which an imitation between these two parts is effected. The soprano resumes the diatonic scale for the last two bars.

Chord of the Eleventh.

When *all* the intervals of the chord of the fundamental 7th are continued upon the succeeding tonic bass, the dissonances of suspension and retardation will be united.

At *a*, in the following Example, are two suspensions (the 9th resolved into the 8th, and the 4th resolved into the 3d); and one retardation (the 7th into the 8th).

At *b*: two retardations (the 7th into the 8th, and the 2d into the 3d); and one suspension (the 4th into the 3d).

At *c*: are two suspensions and two retardations.

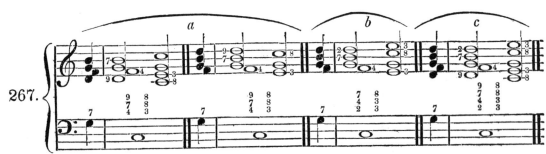

267.

By placing *under* the dominant chord, at *a*, its tonic (as at *b*) in the following Example, the intervals will change their names; that is, the original 3d will become a 7th, the original 7th an 11th, &c., and it is from the latter interval that the chord on which we are now treating derives its name.

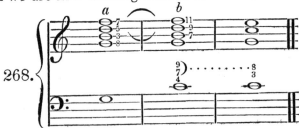

268.

N.B. The interval of the 11th is always figured with a 4; figures beyond 9 being seldom or never employed in harmony.

In the following Example, the diatonic scale, it will be observed, is accompanied by the usual fundamental basses and harmonies, but the tonic* (or generator) being placed on a staff below, the chord of the 11th is produced at *a*.

269.

If we compare Examples 267 and 269, we shall find that the chord of the 11th has two distinct characters; first, as *prepared*, and secondly, as *unprepared*.

* Here we see that the vibration of a string produces the chord of the 11th.

The chord of the dominant, as we know, ought to resolve upon its tonic; instead of which, in Example 267, the whole chord of the dominant is continued over the tonic, and thus its intervals are in their progress suspended and retarded.

In the *second* case, the chord of the dominant is at once placed over the tonic bass, without having been previously heard, producing a mere progression of the chord of the fundamental 7th, accompanied by its tonic, instead of its *own* fundamental bass, which latter is entirely omitted.

In order to distinguish those two characters, it is only necessary to ascertain whether this chord of the 11th has been preceded by the harmony of the dominant; should this *have been* the case, then it is *prepared*, and falls on the accented part of the bar; should this *not* have been the case, it is *unprepared*, and will be (as already observed) a mere progression of the dominant chord, accompanied by the tonic, instead of it *own* bass.

At I. In the following Example, the melody is harmonized as usual.

At II. The chord of the 11th is introduced, unprepared at *b*, and prepared at *c*.

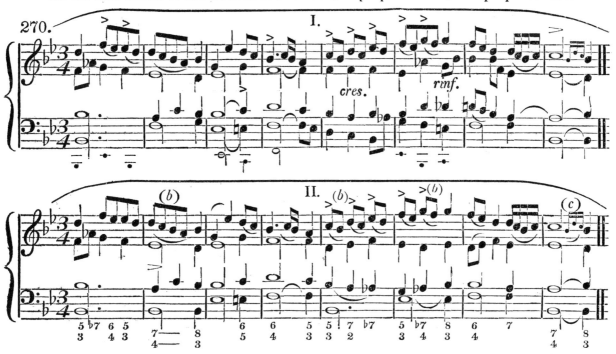

In the chord of the 11th, the fundamental 7th may ascend, as in the above Example, II., bars 5 and 6.

When the chord of the 11th is introduced, *without preparation*, it ought to be preceded by the fundamental chord of its tonic, into which it subsequently resolves.

In this case also the usual dissonances, allowed by the progression of the fundamental bass, may be added.

In the following Example are introduced (at *a*) the 6th into the 5th, and (at *b*) the 4th into the 3d.

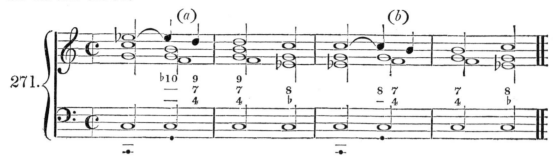

In the following Ex. the chord of the 11th appears (at *a*) *unprepared*, with the 6th into the 5th ; (at *b*) *unprepared*, with the 4th into the 3d ; and (at *c*) *prepared*.

At *d*, the chord of the 11th is introduced upon a false cadence, which should be compared with the chord as written in bar 6.

Chord of the Thirteenth.

The construction of the chord of the 13th is similar to that of the 11th ; for, by placing the whole chord of the dominant with the *major* or *minor* 9th over its tonic, the chord of the 13th will be produced.

In the following Example (at *a*) the chord of the *major* 9th, and (at *b*) the chord of the *minor* 9th is placed over its tonic.

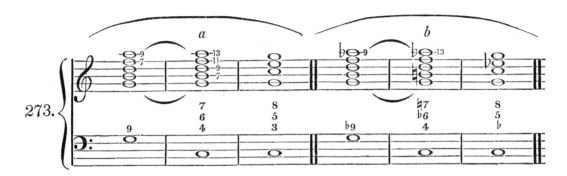

N. B. It will be perceived, that by thus placing the chord of the 9th over its tonic, the interval of the 9th will be changed into the 13th, from which the chord derives its name.

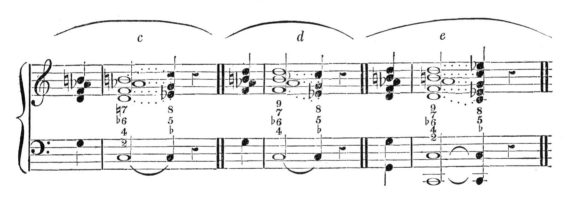

In the above Example, at *c*, are two suspensions, *viz.*, $\frac{6}{4}$, and two retardations, $\frac{7}{2}$.

At *d*, three suspensions, *viz.*, $\frac{9}{6}$, and one retardation, *viz.*, the 7th

At *e*, three suspensions, $\frac{9}{6}$, and two retardations, $\frac{7}{2}$.

Should the chord of the 13th be preceded by the chord of the dominant, it will be prepared.   (In the preceding Example it is always prepared.)

Should it *not* be preceded by the dominant, it will be (as we have said of the chord of the 11th) *unprepared,* and may be thus treated precisely as the latter chord.

2 D

In the following Example, which is the Minor Diatonic Scale with its attending harmonies, the chord of the 13th is unprepared.

The dissonances of the 6th or 4th may also be added, as in Example 271.

The following Example (which is arranged for the piano-forte) exhibits the chords of the 11th and 13th in a variety of forms.

2 D 2

In the preceding Example

At *a*: The chord of the 13th appears in four and sometimes in five parts, un-prepared.

At *b*: In five parts, unprepared, with the suspension of the 4th added.

At *c*: It is prepared.

At *d*: Is the chord of the compounded sharp 6th, upon which immediately follows (at *c*) the chord of the 13th, prepared.

At *e*: Is the chord of the 11th, unprepared.

At *f*: The chord of the 11th unprepared, with the suspension of the 4th added.

At *g*: The chord of the 13th is shewn as arising from the chord of the *major* 9th. On the following crotchet it is changed into the chord of the 11th, after which the chord of the 13th re-appears (at *h*) arising from the *minor* 9th.

At *i*: Is the chord of the 13th unprepared, with the dissonance of the 6th added. N.B. The 6th in this chord will be found much more poignant in its effect than the 4th at *b*.

In conclusion we shall observe, that the 4th and 7th are the principal intervals in the chord of the 11th; and the 4th, 6th, and 7th, the principal intervals in that of the 13th; none of these can be dispensed with, but either of the remaining intervals of the chord may be used or omitted at pleasure.

Variety of Final and other Cadences.

Before the reader proceeds, he is strongly recommended to peruse once again the commencement of this subject, as it appears from page 82 to 85, of which this may be considered as a continuation.

In order to avoid monotony in final and other cadences, some are occasionally introduced which are less perfect than those already described; for example: The chord of the *subdominant* is sometimes *omitted*, the $\frac{6}{4}$ or $\frac{5}{4}$ being retained upon the dominant, as in the following Example, at I.

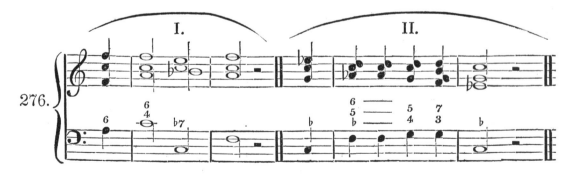

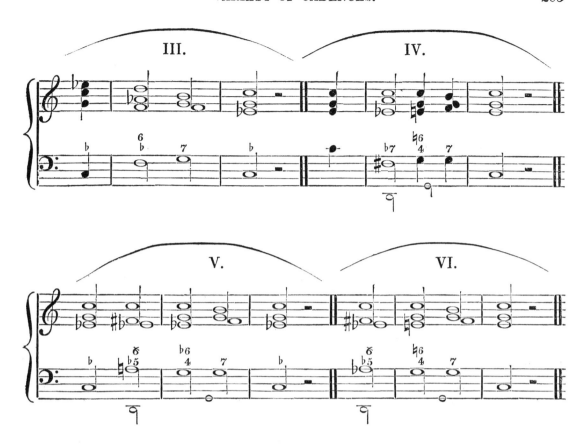

At II. We find the $\frac{6}{4}$ is omitted, and the *subdominant* with the added 6th re-tained.

At III. The 6th only appears upon the subdominant.

Sometimes the cadence is written as at IV., with the first inversion of the minor 9th (*i. e.*, the diminished 7th).

Or as at V., employing the second inversion of the same chord.

Or again, as at VI., with the compound sharp sixth $\flat\frac{6}{5}$.

It will be perceived, by referring to the fundamental basses that the last three cadences are founded upon a *protracted* modulation*.

It frequently happens that a cadence is made in some other key different to that in which we may happen to be at the time; in which case we shall call it an

---

* Hereafter to be noticed.

Irregular Cadence.

In the preceding Example

At VII. We are in the key of D *major;* but the cadence is made in the key of the *dominant* (A).

At VIII. We are in the key of F *minor;* but make a cadence in the relative major (A♭).

At IX. We are in the key of A♭; but our cadence is in the relative minor (F).

At X. We are in the key of D *minor*, and have made a cadence in the relative *major* (F).

At XI. The key is D *minor*, and the cadence is in A *minor*.

At XII. The key is again D *minor;* but the cadence is made *in B♭.*

It occurs frequently, that, instead of proceeding direct from the tonic to the subdominant, a minor chord is first introduced, whose bass (when we are in a *major* key) is a MINOR 3rd below the tonic. See XIII. (*a*).

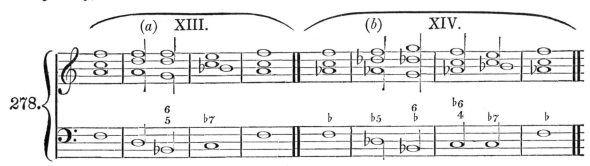

On the contrary, when we are in a *minor* key, this bass must be a MAJOR 3rd below the tonic and the chord major. See XIV. (*b*).

When a cadence is made in a minor key, the added 6th may be written *minor,* instead of major. See XV. (*c*).

At XVI. (*d*) the added minor 6th is doubled, and the 5th of the chord omitted.

N.B. As this chord of the minor 6th is calculated to express feelings of the most poignant grief and sorrow, it should be sparingly used.

In the following Example of Modulation, most of the preceding cadences are introduced, and referred to by the numbers placed above.

2 E

Imperfect Cadence.

The final cadence, after frequent repetition, will necessarily lose much of its effect; because, the ear being accustomed to its regular indications, will anticipate its arrival, and a certain degree of indifference will arise. Instead, therefore, of letting the chord of the $\frac{6}{4}$ resolve upon the *fundamental* chord of the 7th, the 3rd inversion of the chord of the 7th may be introduced, by which the ear will be disappointed in its expectation, and a higher degree of interest excited.

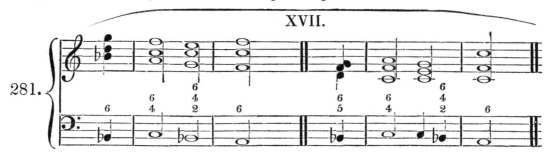

False Cadence.

However, as the ear may at length become accustomed to this description of disappointment, and be prepared for such an occurence, another kind of deception may be put into practice. For example, we may lead the ear quietly as far as the fundamental 7th, after which no disappointment could be apprehended, and the final cadence would appear as necessarily to follow; but, instead of resolving the chord of this fundamental 7th upon its tonic, another chord may be suddenly introduced, which has the effect of immediately recalling the languid attention of the hearer; and though no interruption is given to the proper progression of the principal intervals of the dominant chord (for they resolve as usual into consonances), yet, the bass not being the one expected, produces a pleasing disappointment, well calculated for the purpose above explained, and this we shall call a False Cadence.

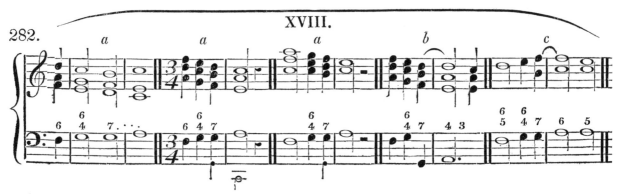

In the preceding Example, at *a*, the dominant, instead of proceeding to its tonic, ascends a *whole* tone to A, which must be a minor chord; and it is necessary to be observed, that the bass, in a false cadence, ascending a *whole* tone, can only be employed in a *major key.* At *b* and *c*, dissonances are introduced.

Should the preceding false cadence, by frequent repetition, likewise begin to lose its effect, we may let the bass of the dominant ascend a *half* tone, instead of a whole tone, as in the following Example, at *a*.

In this case, the concluding chord of the false cadence must be major; thus,

" When we are in a major key, the false cadence may be produced by the bass ascending either a *half* or *whole* tone ;" but,

" When we are in a *minor* key, the bass can ascend *only* a *half tone*" (*b*).

A false cadence may be introduced, without being preceded by either the subdominant, or by the $\frac{6}{4}$ (*c*).

After the introduction of a false cadence, two modes of proceeding present themselves:

First, We may at once make a final cadence in the key to which it was our original intention to proceed ;

Or, *Secondly,* We may be supposed to have really *modulated* to the key to which we made only a false cadence ; in this case, we may first modulate back to *that* dominant which preceded the false cadence, by means of the sharp sixth (♯), as at *a* in the following Example, the $♭\frac{♯}{5}$ (*b*), or diminished 7th (*c*), and from thence back to the original key.

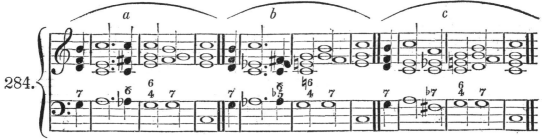

In the following Example of Modulation, the preceding cadences are introduced.

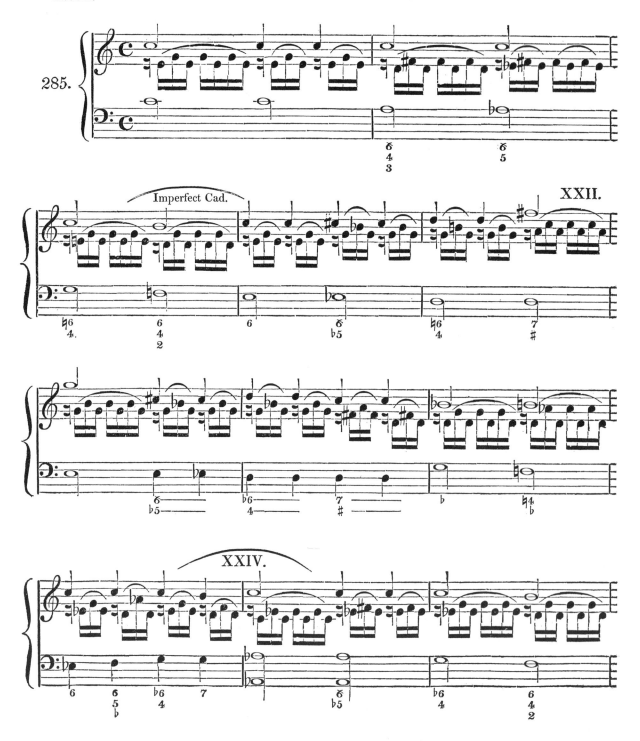

Interrupted or Broken Cadence.

Instead of introducing a final, or false cadence, we may make a sudden stop after the dominant, placing a *rest* instead of the tonic, as in the following Example (*a*), after which we may proceed as pointed out at *b*, or as already recommended in Example 284.

Irregular False Cadence.

In the preceding examples of false cadences, the intervals of the dominant chord proceeded uniformly into *consonances ;* a false cadence may, however, be constructed *so*, that these intervals (although their progression remain the same) *shall not* proceed into consonances.

We may recollect that, in the former false cadences, the bass *ascended* a whole or half tone, direct to its fundamental bass. In the following Example the bass *descends* a major semitone ; not indeed into a fundamental bass, but into the first inversion of the minor 9th.

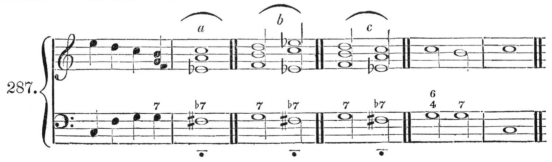

In the preceding Example,

At *a*: The principal intervals of the dominant chord of G ascend and descend as usual, but not into consonances: the *third* proceeds to the fundamental 7th, and the *seventh* to the minor 9th. We shall, therefore, call it an *Irregular* False Cadence.

At *b*: The 5th ascends, by which the 9th is doubled.

At *c*: The 3rd is permitted to *descend*, in order that the following chord may be more complete.

N.B. The best mode of writing this chord is as at *a*.

Suspended Cadence.

If, instead of proceeding with the dominant chord immediately to the tonic, we should first make a few protracted modulations, and then close, the cadence will be suspended.

Great Cadence.

In the perfect final cadence, the tonic is always preceded by the *dominant*. In the great cadence, on the contrary, the tonic is preceded by the *subdominant*.

This cadence is usually employed in solemn and sacred music, to the word *Amen!* It produces a grand and elevated effect, and is calculated to create in the mind a feeling of reverence and awe.

Equivocal Modulation.

In order to form a clear and distinct idea of the principles on which these modulations are established, a few preliminary remarks will perhaps be necessary. It has frequently been observed, that the two principal intervals of the dominant 7th, in their progression, insensibly lead the ear towards the chord of its tonic ; the 7th having a tendency to *descend* and the third to *ascend.* This incessant inclination of these two intervals to proceed *thus,* will be found on investigation to be occasioned principally (if not entirely) by the 3rd in the chord being major, for, were we to make the 3rd minor, this inclination would immediately cease, as will be evident on performing the following Example.

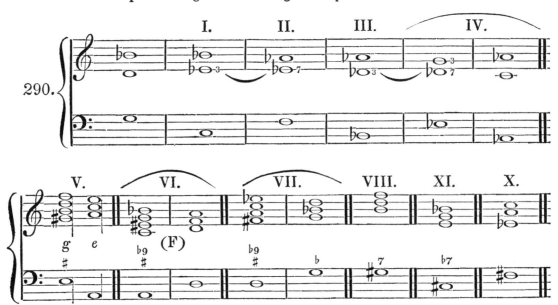

The chords at I., II., III., having *minor* 3rds, no expectation is excited in the mind that these 3rds *ought to ascend,* although each chord contains a fundamental 7th ; the ear (as it were) remains passive, and without the smallest reluctance permits *these* 3rds to be changed in the course of their progression into 7ths. At IV., however, the case is very different, for the 3rd (G) being *major,* the ear immediately expects this 3rd to ascend, and the chord of the tonic (A♭) to follow : thus the chord of the minor 9th at (V.), having a *major* 3rd, must necessarily proceed to its tonic (A); at VI. to D minor; and at VII. to G minor. Now let us recollect, that this important interval forms a major 3rd with the fundamental bass *only,* and with no other interval. If, therefore, the fundamental bass be taken away, no major 3rd will be found in the chord to guide or direct our ear. See VIII., IX., X. We are left, as it were, in complete uncertainty as to where the chord will proceed ; for the remaining intervals of the chord (after the fundamental bass has been removed) are *all minor* 3rds, no one of which possesses any peculiar power or quality to guide the ear. But, if we *lower* any one of these four intervals of the chords at VIII., IX., X., a half tone, it will produce a *major* 3rd, giving thereby a decided direction to the course of the modulation (which was before equivocal). Now as the interval *thus* lowered will be the dominant of the key to which we modulate, and as each of these four intervals may alternately be lowered a half tone, it follows that an equivocal chord may be converted into *four different* dominants, and may consequently modulate to four different keys. The three remaining intervals of the chord undergo no alteration, except what may be occasioned by an enharmonic change, which may perhaps be found necessary when once the dominant is established.

At 1 : is the chord of the diminished 7th. It has no decided character but what it receives from the fundamental bass, which has been placed under it, by which the modulation goes to D minor.

The C♯, in the inverted bass at 2, is at 3 *lowered* a semitone to C♮, and thus E (which at 2 was a *minor* 3rd), is changed to a *major* 3rd ; and as the C♮ is the dominant to the key of F, we modulate to that key at 4.

N.B. All the rest of the intervals remain as before.

Here we see that by only *lowering one* interval of the chord of the dimished 7th, we are enabled to modulate to F instead of D minor.

At 5 : The chord appears again as originally written at 1, but at 6 the E is *lowered* a half tone to E♭ (forming thus a *major* 3rd with G), and as E♭ is the dominant to A♭, we modulate (at 7) to that key, instead of D *minor*.

N.B. All the intervals remain as before, except C♯, which must be

2 F

changed enharmonically to D♭; because the fundamental 7th to E♭ is D♭, and not C♯.

At 8 : The chord appears again written as at 1.   The G is *lowered* at 9 a half tone to G♭; and as G♭ is dominant to C♭, we modulate (at 10) to *that* key instead of *D minor*.

N.B. Two intervals must here be changed enharmonically, *viz.*, E to F♭, and C♯ to D♭.   The reason is obvious.

At 11 : *No* change of modulation has taken place, for, by lowering (at 12) the B♭ to A, we produce the *same* fundamental bass as at 1: the only difference is, that, as the minor 9th is removed, we have modulated to a *major*, instead of a minor key.

N.B.   Any inversion of the minor 9th may be thus employed, as well as the diminished 7th, instances of which are given in the following Example.

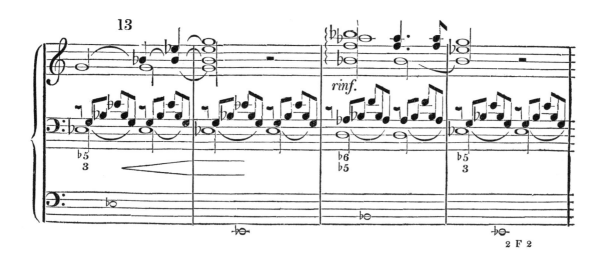

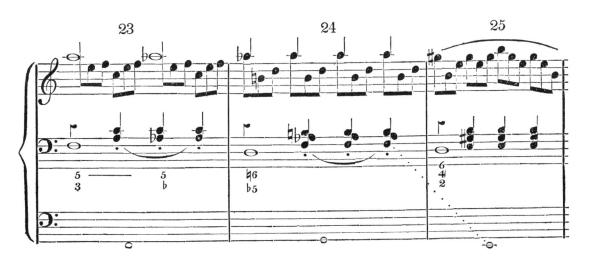

Modulation

In the preceding Example—

At 2 : A demonstration is made to modulate to D *minor*, by the *third inversion*
of the minor 9th ; but by lowering G (the inverted bass) at 3, a half tone
to F♯, a modulation is effected to B♮ *minor* (at 4).

At 5 : A demonstration is made to modulate to A *minor*, by the first inversion
of the minor 9th ; but B♮ being *lowered* (at 6) a half tone to B♭, the
modulation goes (at 7) to E♭.

At 8 : We make a demonstration to modulate to F *minor*, by the *second* inversion of the minor 9th ; but, the B♭ (at 9) being lowered to A, the
modulation proceeds (at 10) to D *minor*.

At 11 : The demonstration is made to C *minor ;* but (at 12) B♮ is *lowered* to B♭,
and we modulate (at 13) to E♭.

Although the ear cannot recognise any change having taken place
between the chords at 14 and 15, when played on the piano-forte ; yet,
if we examine the fundamental basses of these two bars, it will be
evident, that in order to modulate to G minor (at 16) this alteration of
the chord became necessary ; for, as the dominant to G is D, and
not F, we could not have modulated directly from the chord at 13 to
G minor at 16 : it would have been ungrammatical, as modulating
without a dominant.

At 20 : We make a demonstration to modulate to B♮ : changing this determina-
tion, however, by lowering the A♯ to A♮ (at 21), we make a demonstration to modulate to D : here, however, the course is again changed,
by resuming the dominant F♯ (at 20), and we seem to modulate once
more to B♮ ; instead of which, however, we lower the C♯ (at 21) to
C♮, and modulate (at 13) to F.

The preceding Exercise, which is written for the piano-forte, not only abounds
in *secondary harmonies, extended, passing,* and *auxiliary* notes, but is likewise calculated to point out some of those contrivances in a composition, by which a
series of modulations or progressions may be made pleasing and interesting ;
For example : From the commencement to the end of bar 12, the right hand plays
variations, founded on secondary harmony, interspersed with *extended, passing,*
and *auxiliary* notes, whilst the left hand accompanies this variation by the simple
chords.   In order to produce still more variety, the right hand, from bar 13 to 25,
plays a simple melody, without the least embellishment, whilst the left plays a
variation, founded on the intervals of the chord.   At bar 26, the right hand again

commences a variation, the left hand accompanying as before. The Example concludes with a cadence, commencing at bar 28, in which the *minor* 6th has been introduced.

Equivocal Modulation by the Compounded Sharp Sixth $_{\flat 5}^{6}$.

This chord is another powerful agent, which may be employed with great effect in producing an equivocal modulation.

If we lower the bass of any inversion of the chord of the minor 9th a *minor semitone*, the chord of the $_{\flat 5}^{6}$ will be produced, after which we can modulate as already explained in Examples 202 to 204.

N.B. We must be careful not to mistake *this* chord for one of those just described in Example 291 ; because the note which was there lowered became a *dominant*; whereas, in the present case, it becomes a false 5th, and (being the bass) is the second inversion of the dominant chord.

In the following Example (at bar 2), is the first inversion of the minor 9th. The bass being thus lowered (at 3) a semitone, the $_{5}^{6}$ is produced, and thus instead of modulating to *A minor*, we modulate (at 4) to *F♯ major*.

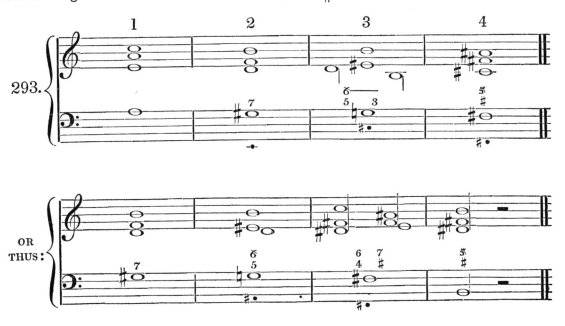

The following Example will shew the application of this method of treating the chord, which will be found particularly effective when introduced immediately after the imperfect false cadence.

At 2: An irregular false cadence having taken place upon the first inversion of the minor 9th, this inverted bass F♯ is lowered a half tone in bar 3, to F♮, producing thus the $\frac{6}{5}$. Here we ought to modulate to E, instead of which, however, we make that E a dominant, apparently with the intention of proceeding to A (for at 4 a regular cadence commences in that key); but instead of proceeding to the tonic, the dominant chord at 5 falls again at 6 a major half tone, as it did at 2, and thus produces once more an *irregular false cadence* on the chord of the diminished 7th. The same process is observed through each succeeding four bars of the Example, until we arrive again at the key from which we set out.

Deceptive Modulation—in which the *Fundamental Seventh* resolves into the *Octave*.

It cannot be too frequently impressed upon the mind of the learner, that the chord of the Fundamental 7th has a natural tendency to guide the ear to the *chord of its tonic only*. When, therefore, either of the principal intervals of the dominant chord (*viz.*, the fundamental 7th or 3rd), do not proceed thus, though they may resolve into consonances, a kind of deception is practised.

In the following Example, at 1, the 7th of (G) the fundamental bass descends as usual, but instead of proceeding to the third of its tonic (C), it falls, at 2, into the octave of the following dominant chord.

The 3rd, instead of *ascending* into the octave, *remains in its place*, and becomes a 5th.

The 5th likewise remains in its place and becomes the 7th; and the bass, instead of proceeding to its tonic (C), ascends a minor semitone, and forms the major 3rd*: thus we modulate to *A minor* instead of *C*.

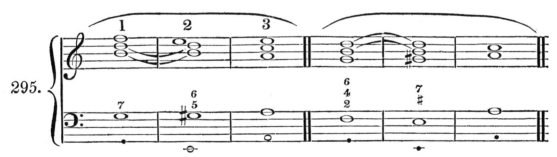

295.

N.B. All the inversions of the fundamental 7th may be here employed; the most effective, however, are the *first* and *third*.

The effect which these deceptive modulations produce, will be better understood by the following short Example of Recitative.

---

* This must, however, be understood as referring only to the *inverted* bass, because the fundamental bass falls on this occasion on a *minor* 3rd.

Deceptive Modulation—in which the *Fundamental Seventh* resolves into the *Fifth*.

In the following Example, the dominant (G), instead of proceeding to its tonic (C), ascends a whole tone, and becomes (as in the foregoing Examples) the dominant of another key, which latter we prefer to be minor, as being the relative minor to the subdominant of the expected key C.

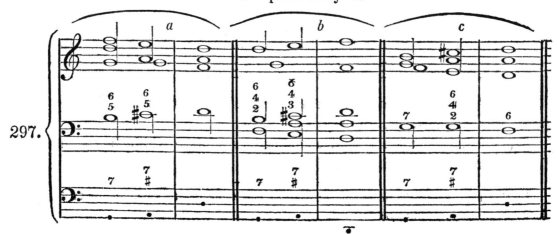

In this deceptive modulation the 7th descends on the 5th of the *new dominant;* the 3rd ascends *into the 3rd* in the inverted bass, and the octave remaining in its place, prepares the 7th in the chord of the new dominant. The different inversions of the above chords are exhibited at *b* and *c.*

The following Example is an Exercise on the preceding.

Observe, that the subject of the two first bars in the *tenor,* is imitated in bars 3 and 4 by the *bass;* in bars 5 and 6 by the *alto;* in bars 6 and 7 again by the *tenor;* and in bars 8 and 9 by the *soprano.*

Protracted Modulation.

If the 3rd of the dominant chord, instead of *ascending* to the 8th, continues to fall a minor half tone on the 7th of the following dominant, it will produce alternately the $\frac{6}{4}$ and $\frac{6}{5}$, and form thus a continued chain of *unresolved* dominant chords, by which the expected tonic is omitted, and the *final close* of the modulation deferred, or protracted, as in the following Example.

At *b*: Dissonances are introduced, by which the imitation which naturally arises out of these modulations is more apparent.

The following is a protracted modulation with the addition of the chord of the minor 9th.

At *a*: A modulation, such as has been exhibited in Ex. 293 (*b*), is here introduced.

At *b*: Appears the *imperfect false cadence*, as shewn in Example 294.

The following Example shews another kind of protracted modulation, by which the inverted bass is enabled to descend by semitones through the whole octave.

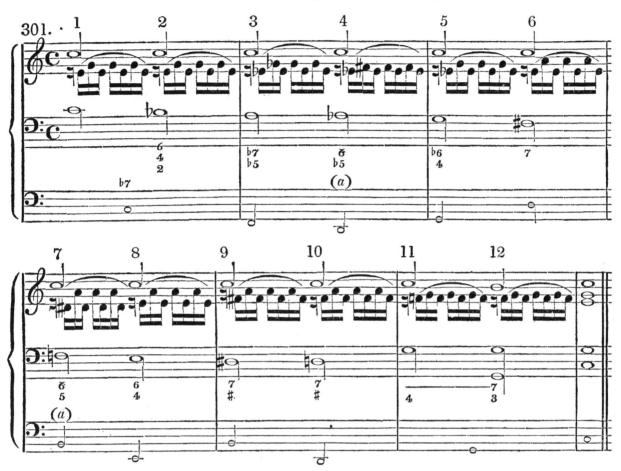

At 3 : Is the first inversion of the minor 9th, changed at 4 to the chord of the compounded sharp sixth by the inverted bass being lowered a semitone*.

At 5 : The resolution of the chord of the $\frac{6}{4}$ has been omitted, but we proceed as if it had taken place thus :

At 6 : The chord of the diminished 7th.

At 7 : The chord of the compounded sharp sixth.

At 8 : The resolution of the $\frac{6}{4}$ again omitted.

At 9 : The first inversion of the minor 9th.

At 10 : The 9th of the preceding chord changed to a 7th.   See Example 303.

---

* See Example 293.

In the following Example the fundamental 7th is changed to a minor 9th, by which the inverted bass continues to *ascend* by half tones.

The above modulation bears a strong resemblance to Example 295. *Here*, however, the 7th is not resolved into the octave, but changed into a 9th, which occurs again at II. and III.; and in this manner we are enabled to modulate through the whole ascending chromatic scale.

In the preceding Example the fundamental 7th was changed into a minor 9th; in the following Example, on the contrary, the 9th is changed into a 7th, by which the inverted basses continue to *descend* by half tones.

The following Example will shew how the several inversions of the minor 9th may be employed with effect.

The first five bars contain only the chord of the minor 9th. The bass commences with the interval of the-9th, and passes from thence to the 7th, 5th, and 3rd successively, the rest of the parts interchange places; during which the *alto* proceeds from the 7th to the 9th; the *tenor* from the 5th to the 7th; and the *soprano* from the 3rd to the 5th. The same occurs frequently in the course of the Example. From the commencement to the end of the fifth bar, we are led to expect the arrival of the key of C minor; however, the 3rd (B♮) in that bar having been lowered a half tone to B♭, in the sixth bar, we modulate in the seventh bar to E♭*. From thence to the twelfth bar is continued the chord of the minor 9th of F, and thus a demonstration is made to modulate to B♭ minor, but, by the introduction of the ♭$\frac{6}{5}$ in the thirteenth bar †, we modulate to G, and from thence to C minor.

Modified, or Secondary Basses.

The only fundamental basses which have hitherto been employed in harmonizing melodies, are the tonic, dominant, and subdominant. We have seen that from these *three* basses, with their harmonies, inversions, occasional introduction of modulation, dissonances, passing and auxiliary notes, we have been enabled to proceed thus far with sufficient variety. Let us now, however, make an attempt to discover other basses than these hitherto employed, and thus procure a still greater diversity of effect.

It has already been stated, that the natural scale consists of *three sounds only*; that our modern diatonic scale is compounded of two of these scales; that, were we to continue the succession of these scales of three sounds, we should continue to modulate *ad infinitum*; that, in order to avoid this, we are necessitated to break off at the sixth sound, and modulate back to the original key, by which consecutive fifths and octaves are produced.

Let us now, instead of *breaking off* at the *sixth* sound, continue the scale, without paying any regard whatever to the semitones which should occur between each of the subsequent scales of three sounds. If we continue to repeat the figures 8, 5, 3, in succession, over the intervals of this scale, and write the fundamental basses as indicated by these figures, we shall find, that (after the first two scales) the intervals which follow, instead of being accompanied by the tonic, dominant, and sub-

---

* See Example 291.   † See Example 293.

dominant, will be accompanied by other basses; the chords of which (except those arising from the three original) are either minor or imperfect*.

If we divide the above continued scale into scales of three sounds, and place under each its generator, or tonic, it will produce a progression of harmony, whose basses continually ascend by fourths, or descend by fifths.

305.

In accompanying the scale as above, it is evident that we have deviated (commencing with the third bar) from the path pointed out by nature, and consequently the harmony produced is often obscure and crude. Yet this very obscurity we shall endeavour to turn to advantage, and by introducing it judiciously amongst the harmonies of the three original basses, produce still more light and shade than heretofore. Having premised thus much, let us enter into an examination of each interval of the diatonic scale, and see how the chords, as exhibited in the above Example, may be employed in our future Exercises.

The *first sound of the scale* we know may be accompanied by *two* basses, *viz.*, the *tonic*, which is an 8th below, and the *subdominant*, which is a 5th below†. Now, if we take the note which is a minor 3rd below (as at *a* in the following Example), we shall procure a new bass (which is neither one of the original

---

* An imperfect common chord has its 3rd and 5th minor; thus,

The imperfect common chord of B is B, D, F.

——————————————————— D — D, F, A♭.

† Third rule of accompanying the scale, page 38.

three belonging to the scale, nor a dominant by which we can modulate), and which, for distinction, we shall call a modified or secondary bass.

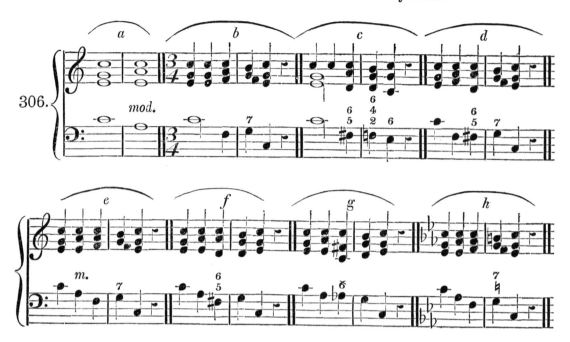

306.

In order to shew the application of these basses, and enable the pupil to form a just idea of their effect, let him compare the accompaniments to the melody at *b, c, d,* in the above Example with those at *e, f, g.*

At *b* : The *first of the scale* has been accompanied according to the third rule of employing fundamental basses*.

At *c* : According to the second rule of modulating in a melody†.

At *d* : Both are united.

At *e* : Modified bass, with third rule of accompanying the scale.

At *f* :   ,,   with second rule of modulation in a melody.

At *g* :   ,,   followed by the chord of the sharp 6th.

At *h* : When the key is minor, the modified bass to the first of the scale has a major chord.

The *second of the scale,* as we know, has only one original fundamental bass, which is a fifth below, and thus admits of two modified, *viz.,* one an *octave,* and the other a *third* below (see *a* in the following Example).

---

* See page 38.   † See page 140.

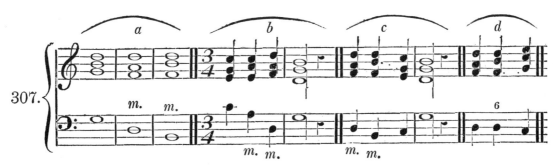

It is necessary to remark, that the modified bass, which is an octave below, produces a better effect than the other, and should therefore have the preference; the reason is this,—the chord produced by the modified bass, a 3rd below, is an *imperfect common* chord, having a minor 3rd and false 5th. The false 5th and octave of this chord, when heard together, produce the same effect upon the ear as the two principal intervals of the fundamental 7th (to the first inversion of which the imperfect common chord in its effect bears a strong resemblance). But, as the false 5th in *ascending* (d), and the octave in *descending* (e), have the same effect as if the fundamental 7th had ascended and the 3rd had descended, the ear feels a certain degree of dissatisfaction, particularly when this chord is employed *fundamentally* (c); when inverted (d), the defect is not so very perceptible, owing to the octave not being doubled.

The *third of the scale*, having but one original fundamental bass, may be accompanied by two modified basses, *viz.*, a 5th and 8th below: the *first of these*, being the chord of the relative minor to the original key, *produces the best effect*, as in the following Example, at *a*.

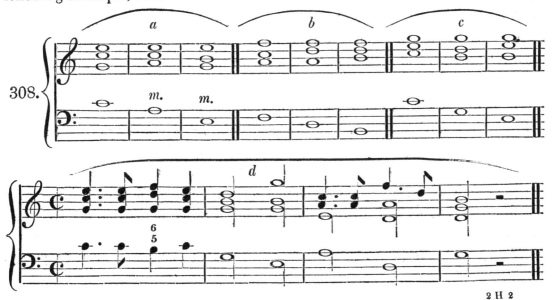

The *fourth of the scale* may have two modified basses, *viz.*, a 3rd and 5th below (*b*). The *former* is preferable, the latter being the imperfect common chord.

The *fifth of the scale* has but one modified bass, *viz.*, a 3rd below (*c*).
An application of the preceding modified basses will be found at *d*.

The *sixth of the scale* has two modified basses, *viz.*, a 5th and 8th below (as in the following Example at *a*), both of which are good.

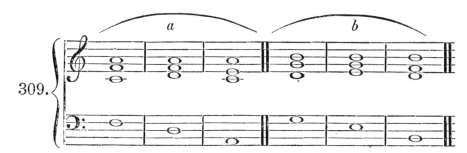

309.

The *seventh of the scale* has two modified basses, *viz.*, a 5th and 8th below. The first is preferable, as the latter produces the imperfect common chord.

It is necessary to remark, that the introduction of modified basses demands great care and circumspection, as in employing them more mistakes are likely to occur than on any other occasion; these, however, will be prevented by a little attention to the following observations :—

1*st*, Employ the modified basses very sparingly; for, as melody is derived from the harmony of the original fundamental basses, *they* should be more frequently employed than any other: they originate with nature, and, therefore, are the most satisfactory and pleasing. On the contrary, by introducing too many modified basses, the beauty of natural harmony accompanying a simple melody is frequently obscured, and crudities arise which we should endeavour to avoid.

2*dly, Very seldom employ* the imperfect common chord *fundamentally :* to the first inversion of that chord, however, no objections can be made.

3*dly,* Those modified basses, which produce the relative minors of the *tonic* and *subdominant,* should be employed in preference to any other, particularly when introduced as *fundamental basses ;* they are on these occasions exceedingly effective.

4*thly,* No modified basses should on any account be introduced until the melody has first been harmonized with the three original basses, employing the five rules, and rules of modulation, as occasion may require ; after having *done so,* we should carefully examine where the modified basses may, with most propriety, be introduced.

In order to shew the application of these basses, and give some idea of their effect, the simple melody at I. in the following Example (written within the compass of a 6th) is variously harmonized.

Harmonized with the *original* basses, interspersed with a few modulations.

With *other* modulations.

Modified basses employed, interspersed with modulations.

Harmonized almost throughout with modified basses.

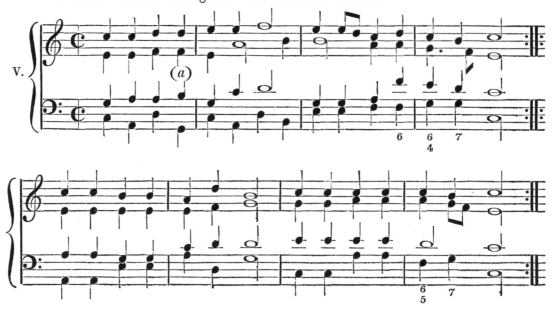

At (*a*) III. Is a deceptive modulation, the fundamental 7th resolving into the
      8th.

At (*a*) V. The 3rd of the dominant chord is permitted to *descend:* this licence
      is often indulged in by composers, to obtain a fuller harmony.

Sequences of Sevenths.

It must have been observed, that hitherto we have treated only of such 7ths as required no preparation, *viz.*, fundamental or dominant 7ths; we shall now introduce 7ths which require to be prepared.

In referring to Example 305, we shall find that the generator or tonic, being placed under each scale of three sounds, produces a continued progression of basses, ascending 4ths (or descending 5ths); which uniformity of progression we shall call *a Sequence;* and when such basses are accompanied by common chords (as in the above-mentioned Example) we shall denominate them—*Sequences of Common Chords.* Now, as the above progression of the bass ascending a 4th (or descending a 5th) is the same as from a dominant to its tonic, 7ths may be added; and when they are added, we shall call the progression—*a Sequence of Sevenths*.*

When these 7ths are added to *minor* or *imperfect* common chords, the effect produced will be extremely dissonant, unless the 7ths are prepared. In order that the pupil may clearly understand the nature of a sequence, let us write a progression of basses, descending a 5th, and ascending a 4th, or *vice versâ*, as at *a*, and then add the simple melody as at *b* in the following Example.

* In this progression of sequences a most admirable symmetry is observable. It was the great source from which the ancient composers drew their subjects for fugue, and the ground upon which they chiefly constructed their church compositions.

If, instead of permitting the 3rds of the basses, in the preceeding Example, at *a b*, to ascend, we let them remain in their places (as at *c*), they will produce a succession of 7ths prepared by the 3rds. At *c*, the 7th appears only alternately; but if we add another part, as at *d*, we shall have an uninterrupted chain of 7ths, as at *e*, where it will be perceived, that, in consequence of the uniform progression of the bass, we are enabled to treat the 3rds of the new part which was added at *d*, exactly in the same manner as those at *c*.

These sequences of 7ths seem to partake in a great measure of the character of *unresolved* retardations,—see *f*, where the retardation of the 7th has been regularly resolved upwards.

If we write the preceding Exercise in four parts, as in the following Example at *a*, each chord will be accompanied alternately by a 5th or 8th: that is,—the 8th remains in its place, and, by the progression of the bass, is changed into a 5th, similar to a progression of fundamental 7ths.

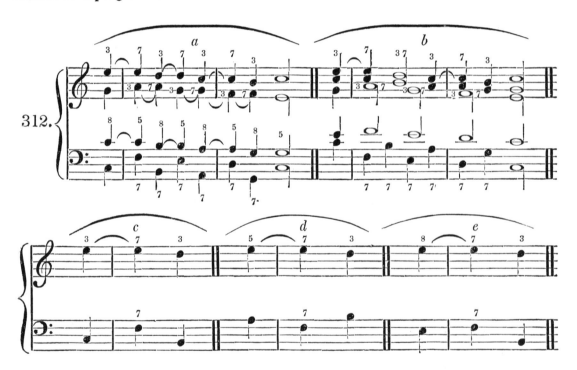

At *b*, this Exercise appears in five parts; and the interchange of the 5th and 8th takes place between the second soprano and tenor alternately.

Observe that the preparation of the 7th may be effected by any interval of the common chord. At (*c*) the 7th is prepared by the 3rd; at (*d*) by the 5th; and at (*e*) by the 8th.

Characteristic difference between the chord of the Fundamental 7th, and that of the 7th in Sequence.

The chord of the fundamental 7th is produced by nature *.	The chord of the 7th in sequence is produced by art.
It stands between *consonances* and *dissonances*, as it requires *no* preparation, but must be resolved.	It is a dissonant chord, and must be prepared.
By its means all modulations are effected.	It prevents modulation.

In every other respect both chords are exactly alike.

The 7th by sequences has its inversions like the Fundamental·7th.

313.

At *a*: First inversions.   At *b*: Second inversions.   At *c*: Third inversions.

In the above Example, sequences of 7ths and common chords succeed each other alternately, which produces a much better effect than an uninterrupted succession of 7ths.

Intermixture of the Fundamental 7ths with 7ths in Sequence.

When the 7th in sequence is a half tone higher than the fundamental 7th, the chord will be a major chord (*a*).

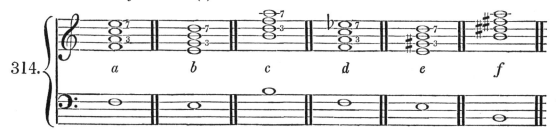

314.

When the 7th in sequence is a whole tone below the octave (like the fundamental 7th), the chord will be either minor as at *b*, or imperfect as at *c*.

---

* See Example 63.

If, therefore, in the first case, (at *a*) the 7th be lowered a half tone, as at *d;* or the chord changed from minor to major, as at *e;* or from imperfect to perfect, as at *f;* the chord of the fundamental 7th will be produced.

If, during the progression of sequences of 7ths, we change any one of the chords to a dominant chord, a modulation will immediately be effected to the *succeeding tonic*, upon which a close, though not a final one, may take place; or, if we choose we may, upon this *last tonic*, commence a progression of sequences, and continue as before.

Observe that, in a progression of sequences, no sharp or flat can be introduced which does not belong to the key in which the progression takes place; for a modulation to another key would be the immediate consequence, as will be seen by the following Example :—

The sequences continue to the third chord (inclusive); the fourth chord, having been made major, modulates to the key of A minor at the 5th chord, after which we close with a cadence.

These progressions of sequences may be intermixed effectively with a progression of dominants, thus—

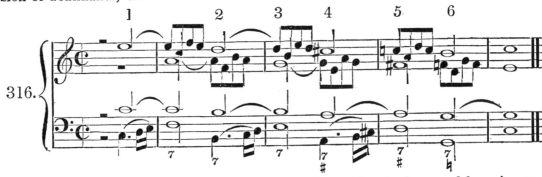

In the preceding Example, the same progression of the fundamental bass is continued throughout; but, after the first three, instead of *sequences*, we have employed *dominant chords*, by which a protracted modulation is effected at 4, 5, 6.

The following Example will shew how admirably these sequences, when inter-mixed with dominant chords, are adapted for imitation and variety of effect.

317.

In the preceding Example, at 1, 2, the soprano commences a short subject, selected from the two first chords of these sequences; and, in order to give this subject more character, two notes of secondary harmony have been introduced.

At 2, the alto commences the imitation, which is continued to 6; here the tenor takes up the subject, with a slight variation, and pursues it as far as 10, where it is resumed by the alto, and subsequently imitated by all the parts alternately.

The bass, at 1, 2, also commences a short subject, founded on the two first fundamental basses, with their first inversions. This subject is answered at 11 by the tenor, and at 14 again, slightly, by the bass; which part, at 15, takes up and continues the subject of the soprano to 19.

The sequences continue as far as 7, consequently we remain in the *original* key.

At 8, commences a *protracted* modulation*, which ends in the key of E♮; for, at 11, the modulation is arrested in its progress by the introduction of sequences, which continue to 14.

From 15, a mixture of protracted and deceptive modulations† leads us back to the original key.

In order to ascertain whether a bass melody, about to be harmonized, will admit of sequences, it is only necessary to examine whether it contains any of the following progressions.

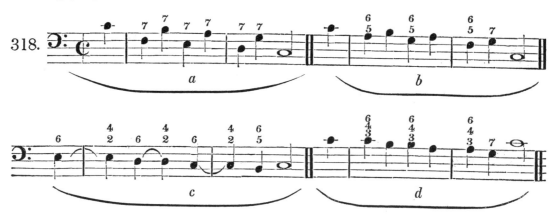

At *a* : Is the progression of the fundamental bass itself.

At *b* : The progression of its 3rd.

At *c* : The progression of the 7th; and as that interval must be always prepared, it is easily distinguished from any other, by *two notes* of the same deno-

---

* See page 227   † See page 225.

mination being tied together. The first of these notes is the preparation of the 7th, the second is the 7th itself, and the note which follows is its resolution.

Although the progression of the 5th is similar to that of the 7th (see *d*); yet the effect is not so good, and therefore it ought to be sparingly employed.

Let us suppose that we were required to harmonize the following bass melody :—

It is evident, from the progression of the intervals of the above theme, that the greater part of them may be considered in three points of view :—

First, They may be treated as a progression of sequences as follows :—

Secondly, As a progression of dominant 7ths, and thus modulate :—

Thirdly, As partaking of both :—

In the following Example, at *a*, the bass melody of Example 319 will be found harmonized throughout with sequences, except where the progression of its intervals rendered it impracticable.

The following is the same melody and harmony as the foregoing, with the addition of passing and auxiliary notes and secondary harmonies, by which the imitation between the several parts, naturally arising out of a progression of sequences, will be more clearly perceived.

N.B. The 5ths, at *c*, between the soprano and tenor by contrary motion, are allowable*.

*See Example 327 (*f*).

Those basses, which in the preceding Example were treated as *sequences*, are in the following Example treated sometimes as *dominants:* the rules of " modulation by the intervals of a melody* " have likewise been employed; and thus an effect is produced, so very different from that in the preceding Example, that one would scarcely imagine both to have emanated from the *same* bass melody.

The Student will find much improvement in a careful examination and comparison of these two Examples.

N.B. In the second bar a deceptive modulation takes place†.

Lastly, The melody, in Example 320, *which has been extracted* from the bass melody of Example 319, is, in the following Example, re-harmonized with *other basses,* according to the five rules of employing fundamental basses, and " modulation by the intervals of a melody."

---

* Page 137 to 149.   † See Example 298.

By comparing the bass and harmonies in this Example with those of the two preceding, we shall perceive what a variety may thus be created; and those who are inclined to study composition, will, even in these few Examples, find ample matter.   The preceding specimens will sufficiently show how 7ths in

(a) See Licensed Resolution of Dissonances, Ex. 382.   (b) See Ex. 255.   (c) Ex. 223, f.   (d) Ex. 268.

sequence may be employed with effect; their introduction not only prevents frequent modulation (thus impressing the present key more strongly on the mind), but also adds strength and vigour to the texture of the harmony. They contribute, moreover, materially to cement and interweave the several sections of which periods are constructed*, thus forming a still more connected chain throughout the whole composition.

Sequences of 6ths, 6 5 and 7 6.

From the progression of fundamental sequences of common chords, at *a*, arise those at *b* and *c*.

* See Periods, Example 345.

In employing the progressions of the preceding Ex., it may perhaps be better to let the 6th appear on the accented part of the bar (as at *b*), because the 5th in that situation produces in some measure the effect of consecutive 5ths: this observation, however, has only reference to what is called the strict style of writing *.

By omitting the common chord in the progression at *c*, a sequence of the chord of the 6th will be produced (as at *d*), the effect of which, when judiciously employed, is very good.

From the descending progression of 6ths at *e*, is derived that at *f*, which indeed is nothing else than the dissonance of the 9th resolving into the 8th; in this case, however, the interval of the 9th (which is the 7th to the present bass) must appear in the soprano: were we to give it to the alto, as at *g*, consecutive 5ths would be produced; for the intervening dissonance does not obviate the improper progression. This is shewn at *gg*, where the dissonance is omitted; should we, however, consider the proper fundamental bass to this progression to be, as written at *h*, then the 7 6 arises from a sequence of 7ths, and these two intervals may appear in the alto.

It may be observed, that a sequence of 6ths is better calculated for a harmony of three parts than four; because, in avoiding the consecutive 5ths at *l*, the tenor is obliged (as at *i*, *k*) to proceed by great intervals, which disturbs that smooth and graceful progression for which sequences of 6ths are distinguished.

How admirably Haydn has treated a progression of sequences of this description will be seen from the following specimen, extracted from one of his quartetts.

324.
HAYDN.

The following Example, which is written for the piano-forte, exhibits all the preceding sequences in their various forms, ascending and descending.   They are

---

* See Strict and Free Style.

written chiefly in three parts; and still more clearly to show their effect when
written thus, a contrast is produced, by writing the harmony on every other occasion as full as possible.

325.

* See Example 304.

Three Motions in Harmony.

When two or more parts proceed together in ascending or descending, they are said to proceed by similar motion (as at *a*):

326.

When one part ascends or descends, whilst another remains in its place, an *oblique* motion will be produced (*b*). When one part ascends while another descends, they proceed by *contrary* motion (*c*). These different motions or progressions may be more or less combined :—for example : two parts may proceed by *similar* or *contrary* motion, and a third part remain in its place. At *d*, the soprano and alto proceed by similar motion, and by the bass remaining in its place, they produce collectively the *similar* and *oblique*. At *e*, the soprano and bass proceed by *contrary* motion ; but, the alto remaining in its place, they produce collectively the *contrary* and *oblique*. At *f*, the soprano and alto descend by *similar* motion, whilst in like manner the bass and tenor ascend, producing collectively the *similar* and *contrary* ; and at *g*, the *oblique* has been added. At *h*, all these various motions have been exemplified by the progression of the chord of the fundamental 7th to its tonic.

Consecutive 5ths and 8ths.

It has already been shewn how these forbidden progressions in some measure may be avoided*; we shall now dilate somewhat more on this subject, and introduce specimens from the works of the most classical authors, to show how they have proceeded on these occasions. One *general* rule, however, by which these troublesome progressions may be got rid of, is, to employ contrary or oblique motion. In the following Example,

At *a*: Consecutive 5ths and 8ths.

At *b*: Prevented by contrary motion.

At *c*: Consecutive 5ths and 8ths.

At *d*: The 8ths are prevented by *contrary*, and the 5ths by *oblique* motion.

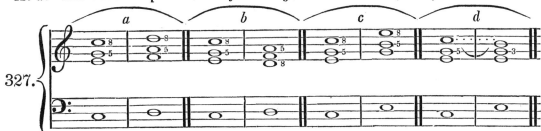

5ths and 8ths may follow each other in the *same* parts, provided they proceed by *contrary* motion.

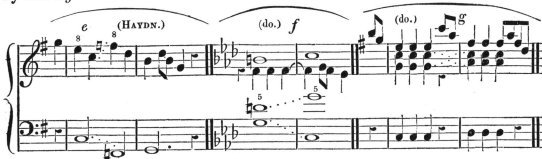

At *e*: Are 8ths between the treble and bass.

At *f*: 5ths between the tenor and bass.

At *g*: As here written, there appear consecutive 5ths between the tenor and bass, but the composer makes the second violin and tenor *cross* each other, and thus the 5ths are prevented†.

---

* Page 22.   † Page 32.

Hidden 5ths and 8ths.

When two parts, proceeding together by similar motion, terminate their progression by 8ths, they are said to produce *hidden* consecutive 8ths (as at *a*) ; for if the space between these two intervals be filled up (as at *b*), consecutive 8ths will be evident; but, as these notes are not introduced, such consecutive 8ths are therefore purely *imaginary :* they may easily be prevented by contrary motion (as at *c*).

The same observation may be applied to hidden 5ths (*d*).

Such hidden 5ths or 8ths as are produced by both parts proceeding by *skips* (as at *e*), are worse than the preceding, and should be cautiously avoided.

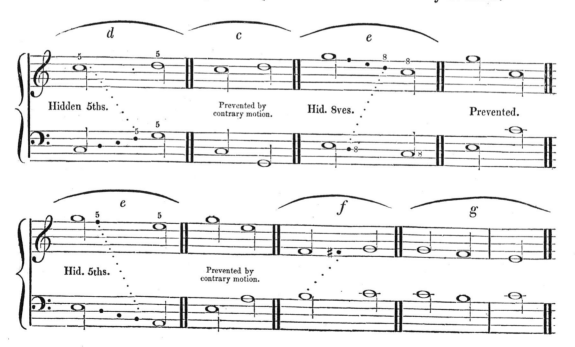

The *minor* or false 5th should (strictly speaking) not be allowed to *precede* the major 5th, because a hidden perfect 5th is found between them (*f*)*; but the *major* 5th *may precede* the minor 5th (*g*). Hidden 5ths and 8ths are generally allowable, and it will be found that the works of the best and most classical authors abound in them; between the *extreme* parts, however, it is at all times advisable to avoid them. Yet, even *here*, we find Haydn and others have had no scruple in using them (see *a*).

The consecutive 5ths which are produced by the progression of the chord of the $\frac{6}{5}$ at *a*, are at *b* prevented by *suspensions*. Cherubini, however, in one of his late church compositions, has permitted those consecutive 5ths, as exhibited at (*c*), to appear more than once†.

Consecutive 5ths (when produced by passing notes) are permitted, because passing notes do not form an essential part of the harmony‡.

* This rule is not much attended to by modern composers. † See page 153.

‡ See Sulzer's *Allgemeine Theorie der Schönen Künste*, page 758.

2 L

Improper progressions cannot be prevented by diversifying, or (as it is usually called) breaking the chord; for, whether the intervals of the chord are varied as at (*a*), or struck together as at (*b*), their effect, with reference to their improper progression, will remain the same.

Nor can consecutive 5ths or 8ths be prevented by the introduction of rests (*c*).

As a progression of 3rds is allowed, why may not a progression of 5ths or 8ths be allowed also?—NATURE HERSELF APPEARS TO REJECT THEM!

We find that the harmony arising from the vibration of a string produces consecutive 3rds, but neither consecutive 5ths or 8ths.* Nature has here been most decided: she points out to us an uniform uninterrupted chain of harmony, so closely interwoven that not the least break is discoverable. *Hidden*, or, in other words, *imaginary* 5ths and 8ths do present themselves, but no *real* consecutives. Neither shall we find that two intervals of the same name, except 3rds, follow each other directly; and *even those* are of different species; for, the first of them (which is produced on the second of the scale) is *major*.

The continual interchange of intervals which takes place in the harmony of the scale, arising from nature, points out to us the origin of that beautiful variety and regularity, so indispensable in a musical composition. In one word, it is the fountain from which flows the first stream of pure harmony, and the stream ought to be kept as pure in its course as the source from which it springs.

The necessity, therefore, for the rule, that "consecutive 5ths and 8ths are to be avoided," is self-evident, and we may rest assured that, when these improper progressions have been permitted to take place, it has been at the sacrifice of a better melody and harmony.

---

* See page 50.

INTRODUCTION TO THE CONSTRUCTION OF MELODIES.

On the different measures of Time, Rhythm, &c. &c.

Hitherto the pupil has harmonized only such melodies as were written for him; it shall now be shown how he himself may construct melodies.

The first step towards the accomplishment of this object will be to make him acquainted with the formation of a bar, and the various descriptions of time in which a composition may be written.

In order clearly to understand what is meant by different measures of time, let us suppose the notes in the following Example performed with an equal degree of strength throughout; in this case they will convey no particular meaning or expression, except what is produced by their rising and falling; they are (if we may be allowed to use a metaphor) *inanimate;* and though *harmony, modulations, dissonances,* &c., might contribute much towards calling them into life, yet one powerful ingredient would still be wanting, viz., *a proportion* or form.

332.

In order to obtain this *rhythmical* form, let us divide the above series of notes into portions of two notes each, as in the following Example.

333.

These divisions we shall call bars, which are distinctly separated by lines drawn across the staff. This process gives us eight bars. Were we, during the performance, to count them—one, two, three, &c., to eight, we should unconsciously lay a stress upon the *first* note of each bar, but not on the second; this we shall call ACCENT; and it is the commencement of rhythm.

From the *first* division of two notes in each bar is deduced the rule that, " when a bar contains two portions of equal value, (whether they be semibreves, minims, or crotchets,) the *first* half is accented, and the *second* half *unaccented.*

2 L 2

This measure of time we shall, for the present, mark by the figure 2, at the beginning of the staff; thus: $^2/_1$ for two semibreves in a bar; $^2/_2$ for two minims; and $^2/_4$ for two crotchets*, and as each bar consists of *two* notes of equal value (or their equivalent) we shall call it *equal* or *common time*†.

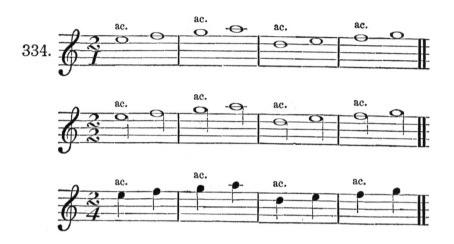

Two bars of the above may be united to form *one* bar; which will produce a measure of time of four; thus: $^4/_1$, $^4/_2$, $^4/_4$, $^4/_8$.

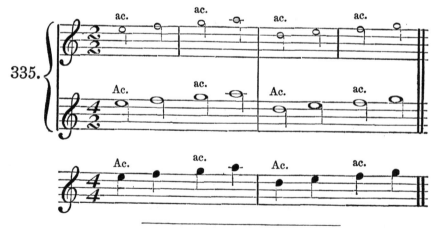

---

* The upper figure expresses the number, and the lower figure the value (as to time) of each note in a bar.

† In modern compositions, this measure of time is generally marked thus, ₵: it would, however, be advisable to adopt the above simple mode, as it is better calculated to show the real difference between the $^2/_4$ here mentioned, and the $^2/_4$ hereafter shown.

As each bar of the *latter* arises from an union of two of the *former*, it follows that each bar of the latter must necessarily have also *two accents*, viz. on the *first* and *third* portions; with this difference, however, that the *second* accent (marked here with a small *a*) is not so strongly accentuated as the *first*.

The time arising from four notes of equal value is called *long common time.*

N.B.—Let this distinction between the measure of $^2/_2$ and $^4/_4$ be carefully kept in mind.

If that *equal* measure or division of time which was first described, be destroyed by doubling the value of the *first* portion, (as at *a* in the following Example,) or by reducing that of the *second* portion to one half of the value, (as at *b*), a new measure of time will arise, consisting of three notes of equal value (as to time) in each bar; this is called triple, or unequal time, and is marked thus: $^3/_2$ $^3/_4$ $^3/_8$.

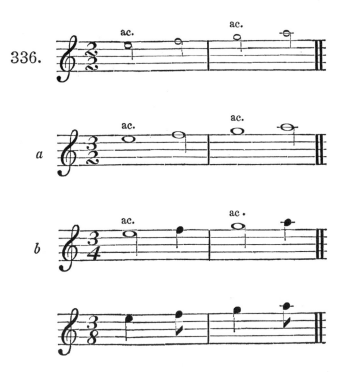

As the above triple time arises out of the measure of $^2/_2$, as described at **Ex. 334,** it should consequently have but *one* accent, viz., on the first portion of each bar.

It is, however, necessary to observe, that another kind of triple time is in use, arising out of an original grouping of *three notes* of equal value, between which notes the accent is sometimes equally divided.

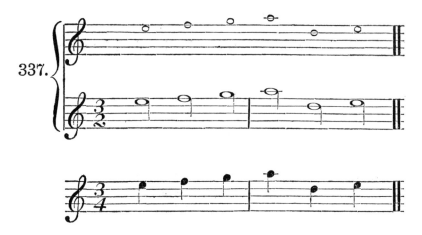

The characteristic difference between these two species of triple time is sufficiently strong, not to be easily mistaken: for instance, it will be clearly seen that the triple time at (c) in the following Example, is derived from the measure of 2 at (b); whilst that at (d) is derived from an original grouping of three notes of equal value. The accent of the former measure of time admits of no doubt, whilst that of the latter is equivocal.

If in a bar of 2, one half its value be added after each note, a new measure of time will again be produced, called compound common time, marked thus: $6/4$, $6/8$.

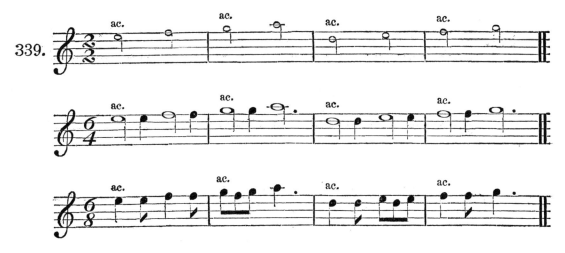

As this division of time arises out of the measure of 2, it ought consequently to have but *one* accent, and we shall call it short compound common time.

When two bars of triple time, arising out of the measure of 2, are united, *long* compound common time will be produced.

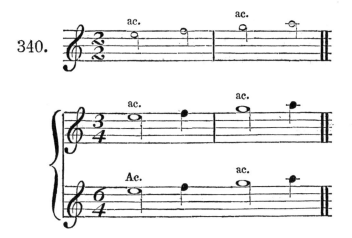

As this time arises out of the measure of 4, each bar must of course have but *two* accentuations, as in Ex. 335. This *long* compound common time, arising out of 4, is sometimes mistaken for that arising from 2. The difference, however, will be immediately perceived on comparing the *short* compound common time at (*b*), with the long at (*c*)＊ in the following Example.

By adding the bars of short $6/4$ together, we produce $12/8$; and as this measure of time arises from $4/4$, it follows that *two* accents must take place in each bar.

＊ See also Ex. 348.

By adding one-half of its value, to each note of 3 in a bar, compound triple time, $9/8$ is produced.

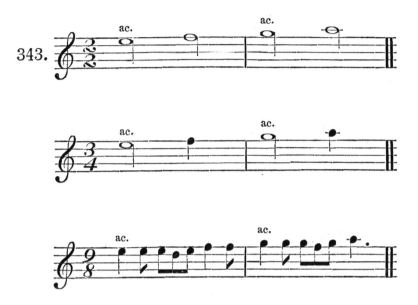

Whether the accent is to fall on the *first* part of the bar or to be equally divided, will of course depend on the *original* measure of time from which this compound time is derived.

The following Example (344) will exhibit, in a still stronger point of view, the variety of effects which may be produced by merely altering the *rhythmical* form of a simple melody. In this it will be perceived that, without deviating from the *original* progression of the notes, all the subsequent variety of effects has been produced by either changing the measure of time; by shortening or lengthening the value of some of the notes, by employing dots, rests, &c. &c. As one example often tends more to elucidate a subject, than pages of explanation, the following may serve as a slight specimen of the importance of rhythm; and to show how much it influences the effect of a musical composition, a description has been attempted of the various feelings and passions supposed to be pourtrayed by the different alterations of the rhythmical form of the melody. Rhythm, indeed, may be considered as the soul of music, and demands our utmost attention.

On the Construction of Periods, or Musical Phrases.

In the preceding Examples it has been shown that, by dividing a succession of notes into certain portions, bars are produced. Proceeding thus with a succession of bars, we shall produce *musical periods*, or *phrases*. A union of several of these periods forms a composition. As the most natural measure of time arises out of an even number of bars, *viz.* $\frac{2}{2}$, $\frac{4}{4}$*; those periods which consist of 2, 4, 8, 10, or any even number of bars, are the most natural and

---

* See Example 334.

2 M 2

pleasing ; we shall therefore call them *regular periods*. The conclusion of a period, in music, is similar in effect to a full stop in language ; every period should therefore end with a cadence.

The following Example is a period consisting of four bars, including the final cadence.

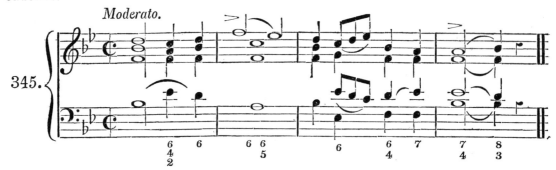

As at the close of this period the ear is brought to a state of perfect rest by the final cadence, we shall call it a "*perfect period*."

It is not absolutely necessary that all periods should end in the same key in which they commenced.

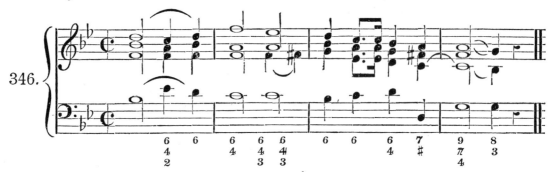

Here the period commences in the key B♭, and ends in its relative minor : it will however be understood, as a matter of course, that the melody cannot end *thus*; something must follow, in order to return to the original key.

After having commenced a period of eight bars, we perceive, on approaching the fourth bar, that we are imperceptibly attracted towards the harmony of the dominant, and a desire is experienced, at that point, to come to a certain degree of repose. If, therefore, in the fourth bar of a period of eight bars, we come to the harmony of the dominant*, whether by *progression*, or *modulation*, we shall call it a half period ; to proceed by modulation, however, is preferable. The period

---

* Although the harmony of the dominant is here the most natural, yet for the sake of variety, a modulation to the relative minor, or its dominant, subdominant, &c., ought not to be objected to, as will be shown presently.

in the following Example consists of eight bars, divided by the half period effected by modulation at (a).

Had the harmony of the third and fourth bars of the above Example been written as at (b), the half period would have been formed by progression.

Where the melody is written in long common, or long compound time, the period will generally be found to consist of four bars only: in that case the half period will of course fall on the second bar.

A period, or half period, may also be divided into smaller portions called "Sections," which may either proceed by *progression*, or *modulation*. When a section of modulation is introduced on the accented part of the bar, we shall call it an *accented section of modulation*; and when introduced upon an *unaccented* part of the bar, an *unaccented* section of *modulation*; the effect of the latter, when contrasted with that of the former, will be found much more soft and insinuating.

These matters will probably be more clearly comprehended by examining the following melody with attention.

1*st,* It comprises sixteen bars, divided into two parts of eight bars each. Each of these parts consists of a whole period. The first is divided by a half period, effected at (*a*), by a modulation to the dominant. At (*b*), are *accented* sections of modulation, and at (*c*) they are *unaccented*.

Had the same melody been written and harmonized as in the following Example, the sections, together with the half period, would have been by *progression* instead of *modulation.*

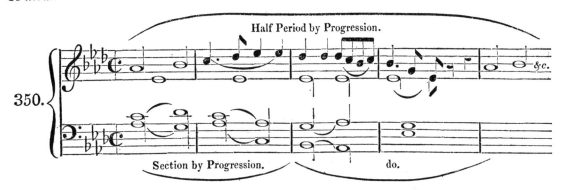

350.

The notes constituting the final cadence, may of themselves be treated as a period, as in the following Example; but, as the effect produced by such short periods (particularly when written in immediate succession, and without modulation) is exceedingly monotonous and puerile, they should be avoided.

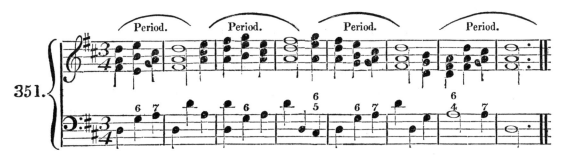

351.

By the introduction of modulation, however, even such short periods may be made pleasing and interesting.

352.

By a careful examination of the above, we shall find, 1*st,* That the monotony produced by the second period in Ex. 351 is here avoided by a modulation to E minor.   *2dly,* That the last four bars which in Ex. 351 appear as *two periods,* are here united into *one,* by the introduction of the modulation to B minor in the sixth bar.

It will be perceived that the modulations by which a union is effected between the several periods in the preceding Example take place upon the unaccented parts of the bar; if, however, the rhythm of these bars be altered, a new and more striking effect will be given to the whole subject, thus :—

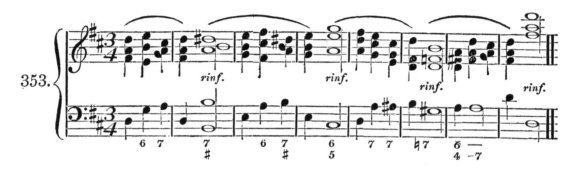

353.

That the rhythm here is neither so natural nor so flowing as in Ex. 351, is evident; nevertheless, when introduced with judgment, it will produce an excellent effect.

N. B. It is not necessary that the cadence which closes a period should always be so complete as those in the preceding Examples; a mere *progression* of the chord of the Fundamental 7th, to its tonic, will often be found quite sufficient to satisfy the ear, and conduct it to a certain degree of rest.

The national air of "God save the King" contains two periods; the first of which has six, and the last eight bars. They are divided into sections of **two** bars each.

354.

The following Example contains a period of six bars, divided into sections of three bars each.

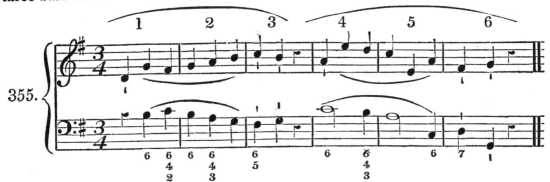

355.

It has been stated, that those periods which consist of an *equal* number of bars are the most natural and pleasing; some authors, however, in order to produce peculiar effects, do not scruple to depart from this general principle.

The period in the following Example consists of nine bars; the first four bars of which form the half period, and the second portion contains five bars.

356.

HAYDN.

This odd number of bars, when first heard, produces a very singular effect: the seventh bar in this period appearing to be uncalled for, and as if it were interpolated. It is, however, only necessary to play this charming melody a few times over, to convince us that the *added* bar is, in fact, a very great beauty.

The following Example shews how very effectively Mozart has introduced periods consisting of three and five bars.

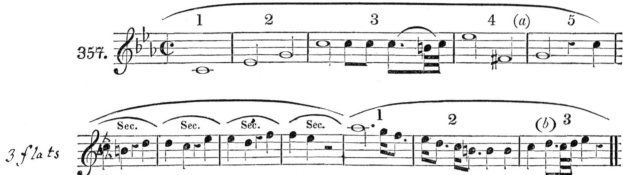

357.

3 flats

The first five bars constitute a half period. The period which follows contains *four* bars divided into sections, and the last period consists only of *three* bars. Had the above specimen been written as in the following Example, we should have had each portion equally divided, that is,—the first half period would have contained *four* bars instead of five, and the last period *four* bars instead of three; but then, that spirited and energetic effect which the unequal division of the bars at (*a* and *b*) is calculated to produce, would have been totally sacrificed. (See *c* and *d*.)

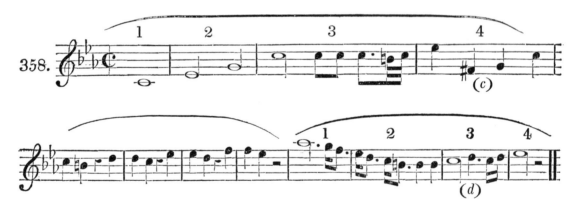

358.

N. B. Those periods which consist of an *unequal* number of bars, we shall call "*irregular periods.*"

It is not necessary that a period should always commence with the accented part of the bar; on the contrary, it may commence with a *part,* or the whole, of the unaccented measure; in which case the value of the notes at the end of the period, when united with those at the beginning, must constitute a whole bar.

The periods in the following Example commence at (*a* and *b*) with the whole; at (*c*), with three eighths; and at (*d*), with one-half of the unaccented part of the bar.

We often find that two periods in immediate succession are constructed, so that the *last* bar of the one immediately preceding is also the *first* bar of the one succeeding.

Although the interweaving of periods in this manner is sometimes very effective, it can only be considered as a license, and ought not to be indulged in too frequently.

---

* Ending of the first period and commencement of the second.

When the expected final close of a period is interrupted by either an imperfect, or any of the false cadences, we shall call it "*an irregular period.*"

How to Construct Melodies.

The pupil may now construct melodies himself, by proceeding thus:—Having determined on the key and the time in which he intends to write, (the former of which we shall suppose to be the key of C major, and the latter, short common time, $^2/_2$,) let him divide the staff into eight bars; on the *first* and *last* of which let him place the tonic, and on the *fourth* bar the dominant*. This simple arrangement may be considered as the first sketch or outline of a whole period, divided in the middle by the half period.

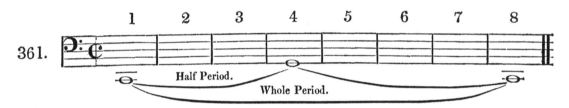

The unoccupied bars may now be filled up with different fundamental basses, as in the following Example.

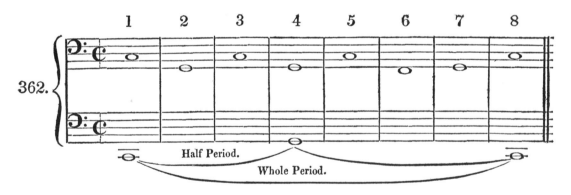

The pupil is here supposed to have chosen the dominant for the second bar, and the tonic for the third, thus arriving at the half period by *progression ;* from hence he sets out again with the tonic, succeeded by the sub-dominant and dominant.

* See note in page 268,

Having now selected his fundamental basses, let him extract from these his inverted basses, which will produce a melody in the bass*.

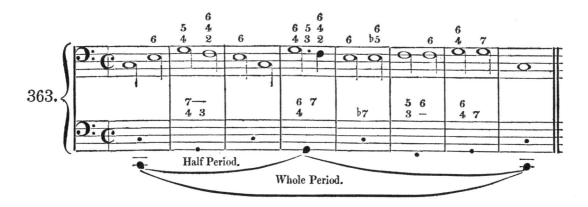

From these inverted basses, or bass melody, must be extracted a counter-melody for the soprano, or treble †.

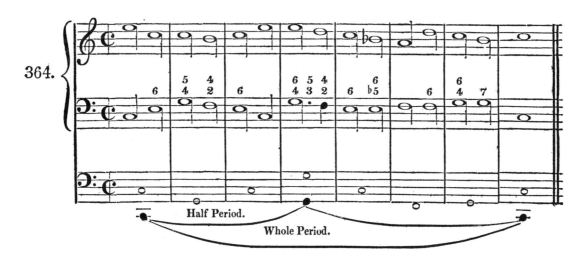

To which let him now write the alto and tenor, and he will have a simple melody harmonized in four parts, to which may be added, if necessary, dissonances

---

* The pupil will be greatly assisted in selecting his inverted basses, by again perusing what has been said upon that subject, commencing at page 99.

† See Ex. 219.

and passing notes, according to the instructions already given ~~from~~ *at* page 62 to 171.

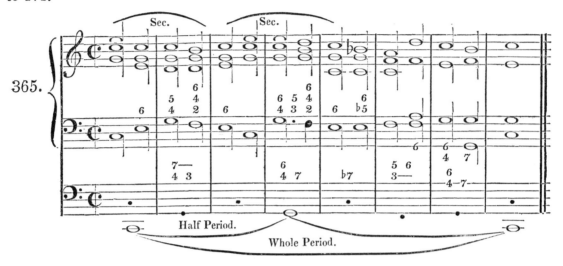

Although the above specimen is, for the sake of simplicity, constructed in common time $2/2$, yet, that it may be changed with very good effect into any other measure is evident, according to the principles laid down from Ex. 332 to 343.

In the following Example the same melody has been altered into short compound common time $6/4$*. No change in the harmony has taken place (except that of its being extended), as will be seen by examining the fundamental and inverted basses.

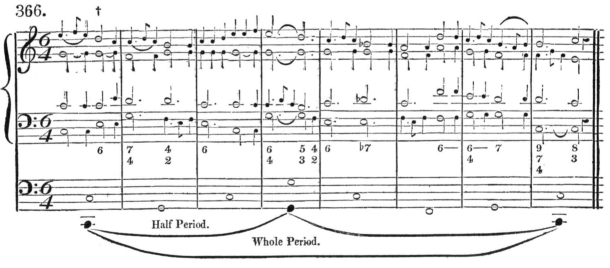

* See Ex. 339.   † Accented passing note, see Ex. 238 (c).

In the following Ex. the *original* melody (at Ex. 365), is harmonized in the minor mode. Dissonances are added, with passing and auxiliary notes, and the harmony is extended. At (*a*), the 2nd inversion has been chosen instead of the fundamental bass.

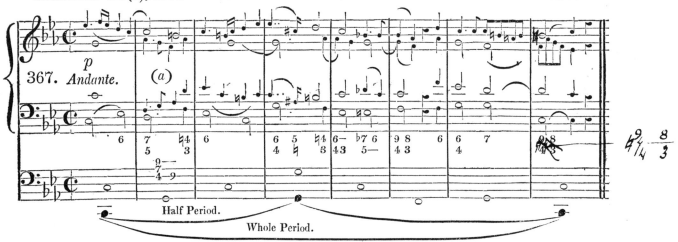

The same melody as in the preceding Example is written for the piano-forte, in the style of variations.

In the second bar of the following Example, a slight alteration has been made in the *inverted bass*, by which the *soprano* is affected. The passing and auxiliary notes are here introduced chiefly in the bass. The pupil is recommended to compare the simple inverted bass at (*a*), with the florid one at (*b*), either of which may be used.

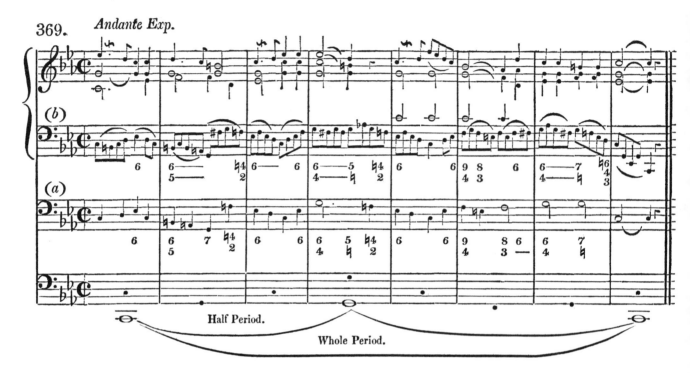

The following Example exhibits the former melody, written in *long* common time*.

* See Ex. 335.

The melody of Example 367, is, in the following Example, divided and dispersed between all the parts, shewing how imitation may thus be effected, without any alteration whatever in the original fundamental harmony.

From 1 to 4, the melody appears in the 2nd violin*; at 5 and 6, in the tenor; at 7, in the 2nd violin; and at 8, 9, and 10, in the 1st violin. The two first bars of the melody (as they appear in the 2nd violin), are imitated by the bass in bars 3 and 4.

The student is requested to examine this specimen with care and attention, as he will find it not only *improving*, but very *interesting*.

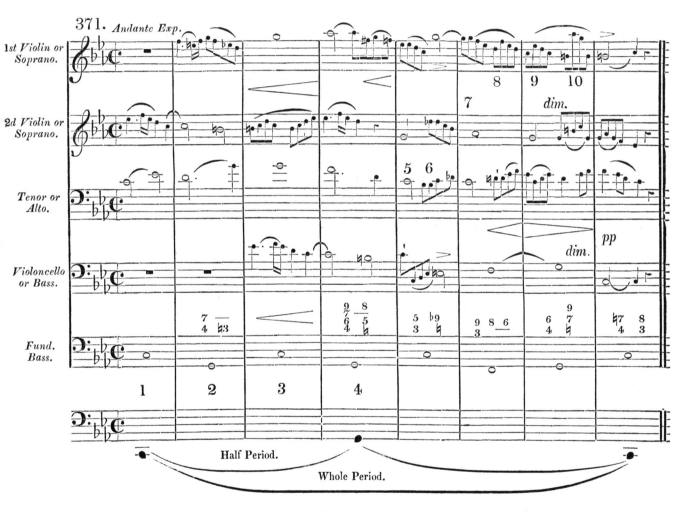

* The above Example, it will be perceived is arranged for two violins, tenor, and violoncello; the student will, however, observe, that this arrangement does not in the least affect the harmony, which may be performed by two sopranos, tenor, and bass.

2 O

It is presumed that the pupil, by this time, will have formed a tolerably just idea how a period may be constructed, and when once constructed, how variety may subsequently be produced, by either altering the inverted basses, employing different passing and auxiliary notes, dissonances, &c., and lastly by changing the rhythm, or measure of time, in which the melody was originally written.

Let him recollect, *that all the different effects which have been produced during the last nine Examples, have arisen solely out of the sketch or outline in Ex. 362, and that no other fundamental basses, or inversions, have been employed during that time, but those found in Ex. 364*; and when he also reflects that many *other* bass melodies may yet be extracted from the same fundamental basses, and that these melodies *again* will produce correspondent melodies in the soprano and inner parts,—he will easily perceive that, in the preceding examples (however *simple* the original materials), the subject is very far from being exhausted, and that much, *much* more may yet be done with it! This fact ought to stimulate the pupil to exert his own ingenuity in discovering *other* bass melodies, from the *same* fundamental basses; and should he in the beginning find some trifling difficulty in succeeding according to his wishes, a very little practice will convince him that this difficulty exists more in *imagination* than in *reality*.

If, then, so much variety can be produced from the simple materials exhibited in Ex. 362, what may not be produced when the first outline (Ex. 361) is filled up with different progressions of fundamental basses.

The following Example exhibits at one view a variety of specimens of filling up the original outline with different fundamental basses and inversions.

At II, we arrive at a half period by modulation, from which we proceed by a modulation to C, and from hence to D minor.

N.B. A and D, in bars 1 and 2 are modified basses.

At III, a half period by modulation; preceded in the second bar by a modulation to the relative minor.

At IV, a half period by modulation; preceded by a false cadence at bar 3.

At V, a half period by progression; after which a modulation to the relative minor takes place.

---

* Except in one single instance, where the second inversion is chosen instead of the fundamental bass, and which is scarcely worth noticing.

At VI, a half period by modulation: this modulation has previously been effected at bar 2.

VII, needs no explanation.

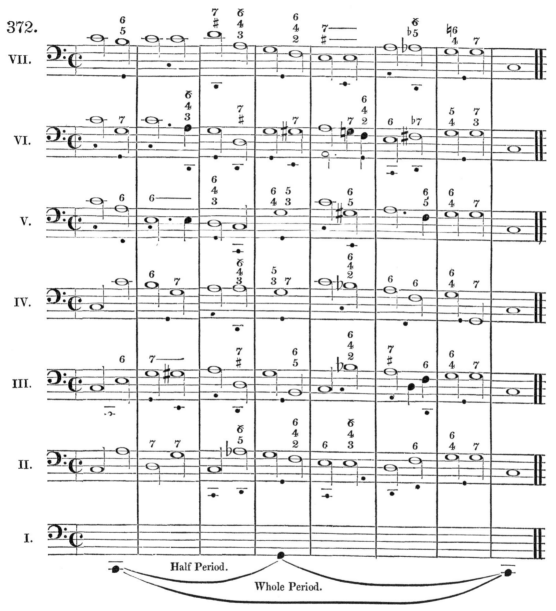

The pupil may take any of the above bass melodies, and proceed as already shown in the preceding Example.

In the following Example (373) the *dominant* of the relative minor has been selected to conclude the *half period*. At **I.** we arrive there by *progression;* a modulation to the tonic of the relative minor having previously taken place in the second bar.   At II. we arrive at the half period by modulation.

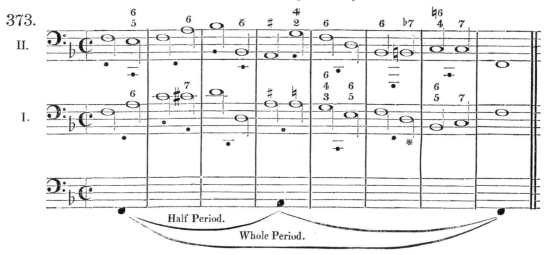

Here follows an example where the half period ends with the relative minor of the sub-dominant.

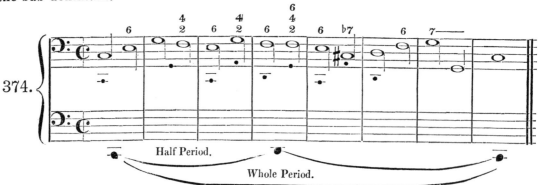

In the following sketch the half period ends with the relative minor.

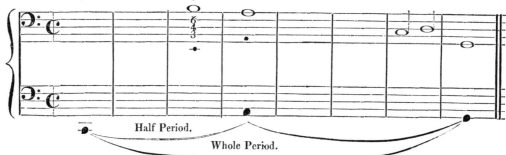

Heretofore, our sketches have consisted of one period or part only; the following Example exhibits such as consist of two parts.

* See Example 278 (a).

In sketching the outlines of the first period, it will be perceived, that nothing decisive has been settled with respect to the key in which the half period is to end ; that arrangement shall hereafter be left to the judgment and taste of the pupil himself: for the present, we shall only point out how he may proceed on such occasions.

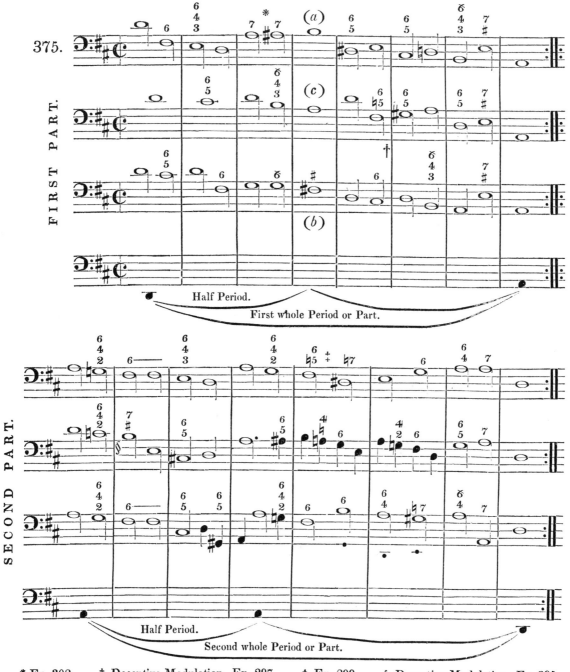

*Ex. 302.   † Deceptive Modulation, Ex. 297.   ‡ Ex. 299.   § Deceptive Modulation, Ex. 295.

At (*a*) we have modulated to the relative minor;

At (*b*)   to the dominant of the relative minor;

At (*c*)   to the dominant of the original key;

which latter will produce rather a monotonous effect, as the *same* modulation occurs again in the eighth bar.

In the *second part*, the half period is made to fall upon the *dominant* of the *original* key : this arrangement became absolutely necessary, in consequence of the several modulations which were introduced after the first half period, and by which the ear was imperceptibly led away from the original key. The dominant, however, in the 12th bar, is calculated to recall to our recollection the original key; and thus our ear is gradually prepared for its re-introduction.

Hitherto our periods have consisted of eight bars only; but by the introduction of the false cadence at (*a*), and the irregular false cadence at (*b*), the final close on the eighth bar has been avoided, by which these periods are lengthened to ten bars.

376.

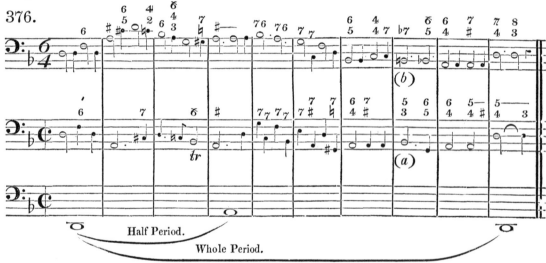

The following questions very naturally present themselves at this time, *viz.*, *suppose I commence in a certain key, in what key shall I conclude my first period*, and *commence my second, &c.?*—In answer to these questions, we shall proceed to give the following suggestions as general rules. Let us suppose that the melody is to consist of sixteen bars, divided into two parts of eight bars each :

If the key is C major, we can end the *first part*—

1*st.* In the tonic, C.   2*nd.* In the dominant, G.   3*rd.* In the relative minor, A.   4*th.* In the dominant of the relative minor, E.

Should the *key be minor*, (suppose C minor), we can end the first part—

1*st.* In the tonic, C.   2*nd.* In the dominant, G.   3*rd.* In G minor, (the 5th of the original key). 4*th.* In the relative major of the original key E ♭.

FIRST CASE.

Suppose the key is *major*, and the *first* part ends in the *tonic?*

> Then the half period may end
> 1st. With the dominant by modulation, ... G.
> 2nd.   sub-dominant by modulation, ... F.
> 3rd.   relative minor of the sub-dominant, D.
> 4th.   relative minor of the original key, . A.

The *first* part having been thus disposed of, the *second* part may commence with,

The *dominant*, G, at once, or with a modulation to it.

> The *half period* may end
> 1st. With the relative minor, ... A.
> 2nd. Dominant of the relative minor, . . E major.
> 3rd. Dominant of the original key, ... G.

Again:

The *second part* may commence with the *dominant* of the relative minor, (E major).

> In that case the half period may end
> 1st. With the relative minor . . . A.
> 2nd. Dominant of the original key, G.

Again:

The *second part* may commence with the dominant of the relative minor of the *sub-dominant*, A major.

> Here let the pupil choose the key of the half period himself.

SECOND CASE.

When the first part ends in the dominant, G.

> The half period may end
> 1st. In the dominant, proceeding there by progression.
> 2nd. In the relative minor.

The first part having been thus disposed of, the second may commence

1st. With the dominant, G.
2nd. With a modulation to the relative minor.

> Here let the pupil again choose the key of the half period himself.

THIRD CASE.

When the first part ends with the relative minor.

> The half period may end
> 1st. With the dominant, G : proceeding there either by progression or modulation.
> 2nd. With the sub-dominant, F.
> 3rd. With the dominant, G.

The second part may commence

1st. With the relative minor, A.
2nd. With a modulation to the sub-dominant.
3rd. With the dominant of the relative minor, E major.
4th. Modulation to the relative minor.

> The *half period* may end as the judgment of the pupil directs.

A melody which originally consists of only eight bars, may be extended to 10, 12, 16, or a greater number, by repeating some sections of 2, 4, 6, or any other even number of bars.

The following Example is a melody, consisting of eight bars. At (*b*) it is extended to ten, by twice repeating the last crotchet of the fourth bar, with the three crotchets immediately following—At (*c*), the same melody is extended to sixteen bars, by repeating the last six bars found at (*b*).

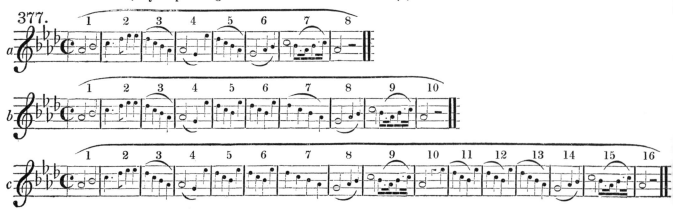

All these additional bars, however, are not intended to be introduced in the soprano only ; some of them are also to appear alternately in the *alto, tenor,* or *bass :* and as these parts will in consequence be obliged to interchange places, a series of imitations will be produced.

In order to show the practical utility of this extension, and how these re-iterated sections (which in the last Example occasioned rather a monotonous effect) are here employed to produce imitations, let us harmonize the preceding melody in four parts.

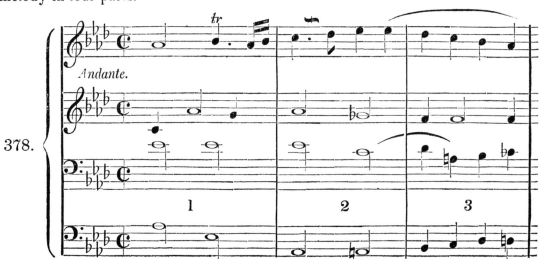

The letters *a, b, c,* have been added to the soprano, alto, and bass, in order that the interchanging of the parts in the above Example, by which the imitations are effected, may be more easily perceived.

At 5, the section for imitation (marked *a*) appears in the *soprano* as originally written. At 6, it is imitated by the *alto* an octave lower, and at 7,

2 P

by the *bass.* Whilst the *alto* and *bass* thus successively imitate the *soprano,* the latter, at the same time, at 6, imitates the *bass* (*b*), and then the alto (*c*).

At 7, the tenor also partially imitates the *bass* (*b*). From 10 to 16, the parts continue to imitate each other with still more variety ; for the sections in the *soprano* and *bass,* at 5, appear at 11 in the *tenor* and *bass,* and are imitated at 12, by the *soprano* and *alto.* And whilst at 13 the sections *a, b,* appear once more in the *bass* and *tenor* (but inverted)*, the *soprano* at the same time again imitates the *alto* (*c*) an octave higher. Observe also that the melody in the *tenor,* from 7 to 10 inclusive, has, at 13, been transferred to the *alto.*

It will be observed that hitherto the imitation has always commenced upon the *same* measure of the bar as the subject itself: in the following Example, however, the case is different ; for, although the subjects for imitation (which here appear in the soprano and *alto*) do commence on the *second* crotchet of the unaccented part of the bar, as in the preceding Example, yet they are *not* answered by the *tenor* and *bass* on the *same* measure, as heretofore, but on the *second* crotchet of the *accented* part of the bar. Thus a mixt rhythm is introduced, by which a new and still more striking effect is produced.

* By which the two original parts in bar 5 proceed by what is called "double counterpoint" in the octave. See Ex. 150.

The parts which appear in the soprano and alto at I, are here transferred to the tenor and bass, by which a mutual interchange of all the parts is effected.

The alto and tenor, at II, have here interchanged places; the former being written an octave *lower*, and the latter an octave *higher*. The soprano and bass remain unchanged.

There is not perhaps a more fertile subject, and one which might be more dilated upon, than that upon which we have just been treating.   If, however, the student possesses a little perseverance and industry, it will be found that enough has been said to enable him to pursue his object with pleasure and benefit.

In the meantime he is requested to examine and compare the preceding specimens with care and attention (commencing from Ex. 377) ; and here he will see how few materials * are sometimes requisite to enable us, by a little ingenuity, to produce variety and pleasing effects.   This truth will be still more illustrated and confirmed when we commence analyzing the compositions of some of our best and most classical authors, which we shall do presently : preparatory to this, it will be necessary to give a few hints with respect to what is called the strict and free styles of writing.

In the *truly* strict style, four sorts of notes only, (that is, with respect to their duration) are allowed ; for example : if the longest be a semibreve, then the shortest will be a quaver, the latter of which can be employed only as a passing note.

All dissonances, in which is included the fundamental 7th, require to be prepared upon the *unaccented,* and struck upon the *accented* part of the bar.   No *octaves* or *5ths* on the *accented* part of a bar as exhibited in Ex. 323 (*k*), are permitted, nor may they be thus prevented.   The note of *preparation* must not be of less duration than the *dissonance ;* and to add still more to the seriousness of the style, these dissonances must be *suspensions*†.   Consecutive major thirds, whether proceeding diatonically, or by skips, as well as all extraneous modulations, or progressions‡, are prohibited.

---

* From these few notes are derived all the foregoing imitations and effects :

See Example 377, bar 5.

† Progressions of sequences are therefore particularly suited to the strict style.   See Ex. 315 to 322.

‡ See Examples 85, 86.

In the following Example at (1) the note C in the alto is succeeded immediately by C♯ in the inverted bass; this is called "a false relation between two parts," and is forbidden. A false relation is exhibited at (2) between G in the tenor, and G♯ in the bass; and at (3) between the soprano and inverted bass.

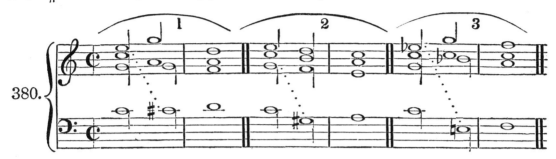

These are a few of the leading features characterizing the truly *strict* style; which style of writing, however, is now generally considered as antiquated, and almost entirely laid aside.

In the *free* style many licences are permitted which would be quite inadmissible in the style just described. For instance: dissonances may be introduced upon the accented or unaccented part of the bar, prepared or unprepared.

These dissonances, when introduced thus, are sometimes written as at (*a*) but performed as at (*b*), and are called appoggiaturas.

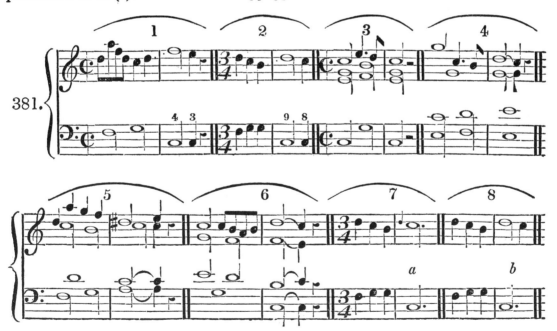

It has already been explained, that dissonances should resolve upon the same fundamental bass on which they are heard*.

In the free style however, dissonances, instead of resolving upon the *same* bass, may resolve upon another bass, provided that the intervals of the resolved discords form either the common chord, fundamental 7th, or 9th, with that bass; so that, in point of fact, the bass on which the dissonance *should* have resolved is altogether omitted, and another substituted. This will be better understood if we peruse the following Example, where, at I, the dissonances resolve as usual, and at II, they have been resolved upon a *new bass*. This may be called a *licensed resolution of dissonances*, and employed with great effect on various occasions.

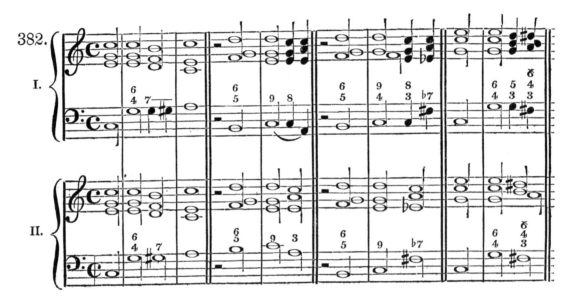

ANALYZATION.

It is both instructive and amusing to trace the gradual, and almost imperceptible change which has taken place in the compositions of eminent writers since the time of Corelli to the present; and how, with nearly the *same materials*, one author has constructed works so very different, with regard to their general style and effect, from that of others, that one would scarcely believe they had ema-

---

* Page 69.

nated from the same source. With the peculiarities and excellencies of the works of these great masters, then, the student should make himself acquainted, and as this can only be accomplished by analyzing them*, we shall detail the method to be pursued on this occasion; and in order that we may preserve regularity and method in this branch of the study, let us divide our materials into the following parts:

> The Key, whether major or minor.
> The Time.
> Fundamental Basses.
> Modulation and Fundamental 7ths.
> Dissonances.
> Passing Notes, Auxiliary Notes, and Secondary Harmony.
> Periods.
> Sections and Imitation.

Each of these several parts shall be explained as we proceed.

The composition which has been selected for analyzation is the first concerto of Corelli, and commences in the key of D major.

Q. How do we know that it is that key?

A. Because D major has two sharps.

Q. But as the relative minor B requires also two sharps, might it not be the latter?

A. No,—because the first chord then should have been B minor, being the key chord †; besides, between the 7th and 8th of the scale, a semitone must be found. Had the key been B minor, the note A♮ being the 7th of the scale of that key, could not have been admitted: it must have been A♯.‡ This not being the case, the key is decidedly D major.

The time is long common time §.

Let us now proceed to find the fundamental basses, that the ground upon which the superstructure of the present work rests may be clearly established.

---

* The pupil will be much assisted in this study by perusing the work called "Practical and Theoretical Studies," being a selection from the compositions of Corelli, Handel, Haydn, Mozart, Beethoven, Clementi, &c., arranged for the piano-forte, and analyzed by the author of this work.

† See Ex. 173.

‡ See Ex. 157.

§ See Ex. 335.

The

The composition commences with the common chord of D ; D, therefore, is the fundamental bass, which we place under the chord.

N.B. The notes E and G, in the first and second violins are accented passing notes*.

If we examine the notes of the four parts (2), we find that they collectively produce the chord of A : the note A therefore we place as fundamental bass under that chord.

C, in the bass, being the 3rd of the chord, consequently produces the first inversion ; *viz.* the chord of the 6th.

N.B. The note B, in the first violin, is an accented passing note.

At (3) the chord B minor arises from a modified bass† on the first of the scale, which is here used fundamentally ‡. The second chord at (3), we find to be the chord of the fundamental 7th, to E. The seventh is in the first violin ; the 5th, in the second violin ; the 8th in the tenor, and the 3rd in the bass, producing the chord of the $\frac{6}{5}$: the note E, therefore, as fundamental bass, is likewise placed under the harmony, as exhibited in the Example.

---

* See Ex. 234.   † See Ex. 306.   ‡ See remarks on modified basses, " 3rdly," page 236.

N. B. The note A, in the bass, is an unaccented passing note.   E, in the same part, as well as E and B in the first violin, are notes arising out of secondary harmony*.

Continuing thus to proceed upon the same principle,   D will be the fundamental bass at (5), E the fundamental bass at (7), and F♯ at (9).

The inverted bass E, at (10), arises from a *modified* bass, and is an imperfect common chord†.   From 29 to 35, the harmony arises out of a progression of sequences of 5 6‡.   That they are sequences, may be inferred from the uninterrupted and regular ascending progression of the 1st and 2nd violin by imitation.

N. B. The notes G and B in the bass (23), are unaccented auxiliary notes, and C, at (24), an accented auxiliary note.

The harmony from 49 to 52, arises from a progression of sequences of 7ths: this may be proved by the regular and uniform ascending 4ths, and descending

---

* See Ex. 250.   † See Ex. 307, also page 236 " 2ndly."   ‡ See Ex. 323.

2 Q

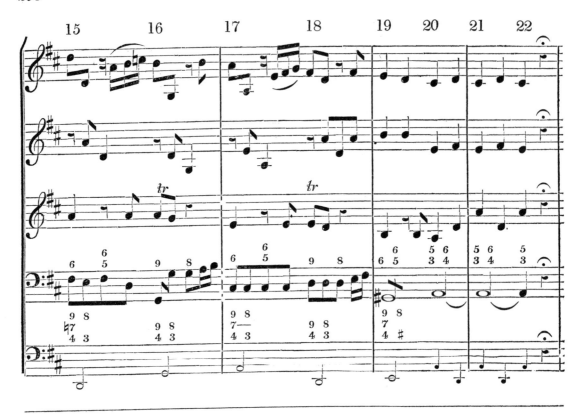

5ths of the fundamental bass, which progression, when divested of its *auxiliary* notes, will appear thus:*

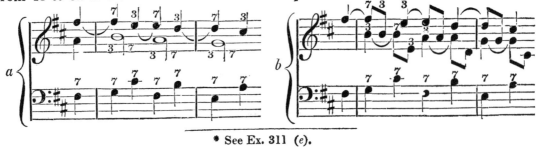

Now, if we add the harmony which the *progression of these* fundamental basses will admit of (*a*), and then compare that harmony with the 1st and 2nd violin in the original, the similarity will immediately appear; for it is only necessary to suppose that the quaver rest in the first violin stands in place of the 7th, and that this 7th previous to its resolution, (according to secondary harmonies,) has proceeded to a part of its chord (*b*), and the legitimacy of the fundamental basses and sequences from 48 to 52 is established.   See also Example 255.

* See Ex. 311 (*e*).

The student may now continue to find the fundamental basses as already shown, and place them under the harmony, as exhibited in the Example.

Let us now proceed to examine the modulations which have been introduced.

The movement commences in the key of D, in which it continues until (3), when a modulation to the dominant takes place, indicated by G♯ in the inverted bass, which ascends a half tone to (*a*),* E being a note of secondary harmony.

At 5, a modulation to D, which is indicated by G♮ in the inverted bass† at 4. At 6, a modulation to G is indicated by C♮ in the first violin. At 8, a modulation to A, and at 10, to the relative minor, both of which are indicated by the inverted bass. From 12 to 17, various modulations have been introduced, which require no further explanation, as the student will easily discover them himself.

---

* See Ex. 180.   † See Ex. 181.

Dissonances.*

As the fundamental bass from 3 to 4, 5 to 6, 7 to 8, &c., ascends by 4ths, or falls by 5ths, we are enabled to introduce the dissonances of the 9th or 4th.

Q. What dissonance has the composer employed?　　*A.* The 9th.

Q. How, and where is it prepared?　　*A.* It is prepared at 3 by the 5th, in the second violin, where it resolves into the octave.

A question naturally presents itself here: Why did not the composer introduce the 9th and 4th *alternately,* as the progression of the fundamental bass admitted of both these dissonances?—thus:

* See Ex. 95, 101.

It would have obviated that monotony which must naturally arise by employing the *same* dissonance so frequently, and consecutively.

Or, by employing both dissonances together thus:

It would certainly have produced more variety and interest. In that case, however, the imitations which appear between the first and second violin, from 5 to 17, must necessarily have been omitted.

N.B. The process of examining the motion of the fundamental bass, as regards the introduction of dissonances, may thus be continued to the end of the composition

That the composer should have figured the bass at 32 with the dissonance of the 9th, without subsequently introducing that dissonance, may seem strange. This

seeming omission will be explained, when we arrive at Imitation: at present, we must consider the *quaver rest* in the second violin to stand in the place of the *dissonance*, as pointed out by the small notes, and which has already been explained, when treating on fundamental basses. The same occurrence takes place at 33, 49, 50, 51, &c. At 33, the 9th has been prepared by the 3rd; at 34, by the 5th, but resolved into the 3rd*. At 11, the fundamental bass having ascended a 5th†, the dissonances of the $\frac{6}{4}$ have been introduced.

Q. How and where have these dissonances been prepared?

A. The 4th has been prepared in the second violin by the 8th, and the 5th in the first violin by the 3rd.

Periods.

From 1 to 4, comprises a half period by modulation‡. From 5 to 6, 7 to 8, 9 to 10, are sections of modulations§. The period consisting of 6 bars concludes at 12 in the relative minor of the original key. From 13 to 20, are sections of modulation similar to the preceding: from 13 to 22 a half period by modulation.

---

* See Ex. 182 (*b*).   † See Ex. 101.   ‡ See Ex. 347, 348.   § See Ex. 348 (*c*).

Here in order to give more dignity and consequence to the half period, the author adds an odd bar, by which it is made to contain five bars.

From 23 to 37, is a *half period*, divided into *sections* by modulation, and progression. From 24 to 25, 26 to 27, are sections of modulation. From 30 to 31, 32 to 33, &c., are short sections by progression, ending at 37 with a half period by progression. From 39 to 42, a short period ending in F♯ minor. From 43 to 48, &c., sections of modulation; from hence to 53, sections by progression.

Imitation*.

The subject at 5 and 6, in the first violin, is repeated at 7, 8, 9, and 10, by the *same instrument* each time a whole tone higher†. Instead of which, had 7, 8, been written in the *second violin*, and 9, 10, in the tenor, it would have produced imitation, and been less monotonous.

At 23, the first violin commences a short subject on the *accented* part of the bar,

---

* See Ex. 245.   † A similar progression of sequences, ascending whole tones, will be found in Handel's Hallelujah chorus, to the words "King of kings."

which is imitated or answered by the second violin, on the *unaccented* part of the bar, in the unison. This *strict* imitation continues uninterruptedly until we arrive at 30; where the imitation, as far as rhythm is concerned, still continues ; but the *intervals* are different in their progression from those of the first violin. Here, that the imitation might be pursued in rhythmical order, it became necessary to suppress the dissonances at 32 and 33, of which mention has already been made*. The imitation from 42 to 48, is similar to that already described from 23 to 34.

It may seem strange that the 3rd of the dominant in the first violin (at 41), instead of proceeding to its 8th, should have ascended a 9th ; but this was necessary, in order that that part (*viz.* the 1st violin) might commence the subject of imitation. It will be perceived that the 3rd of the tonic chord at 42 has been omitted ; such omissions, however, are very frequently to be discovered in the works of ancient composers, particularly when closing in minor keys.

The parts cross each other sometimes very unwarrantably: at 1, and 39, the 2nd violin and tenor, without any ostensible cause, appear above the first violin.

---

* See bottom of page 301.

Why has the author permitted the tenor to appear above the first violin at 59?—Had that part been written an octave lower, it would have been in its proper situation. To prevent the consecutive 5ths in the resolution of the chord of the diminished 7th, between the second violin and tenor at 56, and between the first violin and tenor at 58 (the 9th of the fundamental bass being in both cases above the 5th), the author has caused the tenor to fall to the 5th of the following bass, instead of the 8th. Had the dissonance of the 4th not been introduced, the 5th might have ascended to the 3rd*.

It will be perceived that the fundamental basses have in the commencement been figured with *all* the dissonances which their progressions would admit of. The pupil is advised to figure the rest himself, and he will then see how much more may be added to the harmony.

As music may be considered a language capable of pourtraying all the passions and feelings of which the human mind is susceptible, and as a composition which lays any claims to excellence ought to possess the power of awakening in us at

---

* See Ex. 159.

2 R

least some of those feelings, we shall proceed to make a few general remarks upon the effect produced by the composition just analyzed, with reference to that object.

The introduction, in its effect, is noble and majestic. The first violin performs a melody pourtraying kindness and affability; the steady and measured pace of the bass proclaims dignity and self-possession.

The second violin and tenor play of course mere subordinate parts; for whilst the former appears humbly to echo the sentiments of his superior, the latter is making exertions to attract notice by his little sections of dissonances. Thus the introduction continues to proceed with a degree of seriousness verging on solemnity, until we arrive at 23: here, however, the scene changes; the allegro, which now commences, is gay and playful; the second violins appear to mock the first violin, whilst the bass, having as it were dismissed all state and formality, seems to make amends for the restraint which he had imposed upon himself, and gives way to playfulness and good-humour. This, when contrasted with its former solemnity and sobriety of pace, appears truly comic.

The effect of the passage in the bass, as it continues to ascend, leads us to imagine that, during its progress, it increases in velocity. The tenor, who during

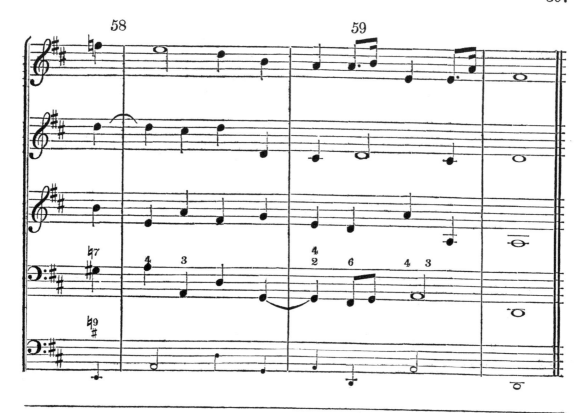

four bars, had been a silent spectator, joins the party at 31, and thus they proceed together in a manner calculated to pourtray a high feeling of joy and extacy, until they arrive at the half-period at 37. Here the parties appear to be brought, for an instant, to a state of reflection; the adagio movement, preceded by the pause, certainly produces that effect upon the mind. This reflection, however, is not of long duration; the former scenes of merriment and joy are resumed at 42, and continue, without interruption, to 53.

We shall now take, for our subject of analyzation, an adagio, selected from one of *Haydn's* quartets.

It is an elegant and highly-finished composition; and, like all the productions of this great master, contains abundant matter for the contemplation of the student. Simplicity and variety are so happily blended, that we scarcely know which to admire most. In order that the student may be better enabled to understand the beauties and excellencies of this composition, we shall, preparatory to our entering upon the particulars of each portion, first explain the general plan and contrivance of the whole.

2 R 2

It will be found to comprise three subjects: the first, a graceful cantabile movement, contains a period of eight bars, divided by the half period at 4. This
subject, with a little alteration, is repeated from 9, an octave higher, and ends
with a cadence at 16. Upon this last bar commences a series of sections by
modulation, on which is constructed, and afterwards continued, the second subject,
commencing with the bass at 16. This subject contains two bars, and is divided

into two portions; the second portion of which, 17, is given to the first violin. By this contrivance, a sort of conversation is maintained between these two parts as far as 20.

Here these parts interchange subjects, after which the conversation ceases at 22.

The first violin now proceeds alone, with passages which are constructed in

such a manner, that we are still enabled to recognize, though but faintly, the subject of the bass, as well as that of the first violin †.

* See Example 173 : also 210, 211.

† The legitimacy of the suspension of the 3rd at 17, 19, and 21, in the tenor, whilst the 3rd itself appears in the 1st violin, is questionable. This oversight (if we may be allowed to use that term when applied to the works of so great a composer) is corrected at 41 and 43.

At 25 the third subject commences, and after various modulations, closes with a cadence in the dominant of the original key, at 33. Here the author, instead of reiterating the first subject, most judiciously introduces one which, though bearing (with respect to its rhythmical form) a strong resemblance to the first, is in fact only calculated to recall it to our recollection. By this admirable contrivance, all extraneous or new matter is excluded, and unity and variety are

preserved ; for, as a mere repetition of the original subject in the dominant would have produced monotony, so an entirely new subject would have had the effect of injuring the simplicity of the whole. This subject continues to 40, where it closes with a cadence.

Here, the second subject is resumed by the bass and the first violin in the dominant of the original key, and ends at 44, where a series of imitations in all the

parts commences, and is continued to 47. It will be observed, that the passage here selected by the composer for imitation, does not contain any *new* matter; it is, in fact, only the last half bar of the second subject at 43.

Thus the unity of the whole is preserved without any sacrifice of variety.

As the passages of the 1st and 2nd violin which follow the imitations from 47 to 48, are written upon the dominant harmony of the original key, an expectation

s

of the approach of that key is excited preparatory to its re-introduction, which takes place at 49*; at the close of which the first portion of the second subject is again resumed between the first violin and the bass, with this difference however, that the *1st violin* commences that subject instead of the *bass,* which now replies to it in the dominant.

* See bars 1 to 8.

At 55, the third subject, which continues for eleven bars, is again introduced, with some alteration in its general construction: upon which follows once more, and for the last time, the first subject.

A series of imitations, founded on the passage of the first violin at 22, commences between the first violin, tenor, and bass, and thus continues until the whole is concluded. This may be considered as the *general plan* of the com-

position : let us now enter more minutely into the examination of its various parts.
The key is C major.—A false cadence occurs between 2 and 3, after which a
modulation to D minor takes place, indicated by C♯* in the 1st violin†.   At 3

* See Ex. 180.   † It may here appear that the fundamental 7th in the alto has ascended into
the 5th, instead of resolving into the 3rd; the author, however, does not in the present instance consider
this chord as that of the fundamental 7th, but the first inversion of the imperfect common chord, see Ex.
307 (d): the same occurrence will be found to take place frequently in the works of this author, and of others.

follow two sequences of 6ths, after which a modulation to the original key is effected. At 5, the first bar of the subject is repeated, but differently harmonized; for that which at 2 was only a progression to A minor, is here become a modulation*.

At 7 a modulation to F has taken place, after which we proceed by an

* See Ex. 183.

irregular cadence* to the original key, and thus close a period of eight bars, the half period of which is by progression.

From 9 to 12, the first half period is repeated, with nearly the same harmony as the preceding. At 13, a modified bass on the fourth of the scale is employed fundamentally†. Here a demonstration is made to modulate to D minor, which

* See Ex. 277.   † See Ex. 308 (b).

modulation is, however, prevented by the false cadence at 14 ; a modulation to F is then introduced, succeeded by the chord of the compounded sharp sixth ♭$^{6}_{3}$, the resolution of which is suspended*, and a final cadence once more closes the former period. Upon the last bar (16) of this period the second subject commences with the bass, founded on the following simple melody,  which is made characteristic and interesting by the introduction of extended auxiliary notes at 16, and by the simple passing and auxiliary notes at 17. From 16 a modulation takes place to G, and from thence to D minor; here the author proceeds, for the sake of variety, to the dominant of the last key, by progression; the same occurrence takes place from 20 to 21, where the first violin and bass interchange subjects.

At 24, a modulation is effected to the original key; the note A, in the second half of that bar, is a modified bass on the first of the scale, and G♯ in the second violin, a passing note †.

At 25 the third subject commences upon the chord of the dominant 7th, whilst in the act of modulating to G. G♯ at (27), in the first violin, is an ascending dissonance, viz. a retardation of the 5th by the 4th‡. At 28 a modulation to G minor takes place, and at 29 to E♭. In the same bar a modulation to G, (the dominant of the original key) commences with the compounded sharp sixth ♭$^{6}_{3}$, the resolution of which is suspended from 30 to 32 §, and closes at 33 with a final cadence. It may now be said that the composition is virtually finished; for that which follows (if we except the first subject, altered as it appears from 33 to 40) is in substance a repetition, in various forms and imitations, of that which has already been noticed, and with which it is presumed the student is now sufficiently acquainted. We shall, therefore, proceed, in conclusion, to make a few general remarks on each of the three principal subjects, and endeavour to discover the feelings which they are calculated to excite.

The melody, harmony, and modulation of the first subject from 1 to 8 is soothing and placid; it pourtrays the peaceful and happy state of a united family, gliding along the stream of life without care or anxiety. This kind and affectionate feeling is particularly observable in the first eight bars, when contrasted with the eight bars which immediately follow; for the latter, being written an octave higher, exhibit a slight degree of excitement, which is increased from 13, by the

---

* See Ex. 196 (b). † See Ex. 240. ‡ See Ex. 263. § See Ex. 204.

rapid succession of modulations ending with the chord of the compounded sharp sixth $\flat\substack{6\\5}$. This excitement seems to increase as we proceed with the second subject from 16 to 24. Here it pourtrays a conversation between two persons at variance, whilst the accompaniments of the second violin and tenor express anxiety. From 22 the first violin seems triumphantly to proceed alone, having, as it were, subdued its antagonist, the bass, which now joins in the accompaniment of the 2nd violin and tenor. Here (at 25) commences the third subject, which, even from its rhythmical form alone, is calculated to pourtray agitation, fear, distress, anguish, palpitation of the heart, and as it were a gasping for breath.

At 28 where the modulation to E♭ commences, the mind seems to be gradually wrought up to the extreme of agony bordering on despair: at 30 it appears to be relieved from those dreadful feelings, and gradually to resume its original and peaceful state in the soothing and gentle strain of harmony which follows at 33.

The preceding specimens of analyzation will suffice to show how the student may proceed on similar occasions.

———

In conclusion, the author makes the few following observations, which he hopes will be useful to him in his future progress :—

It frequently happens, that although the learner sets out with the most determined resolution to study a work of science with care and attention, yet that during his progress he unconsciously accelerates his pace, and overlooks many of those nice points of connection which are indispensable to the proper understanding of the whole. This imprudent haste may often be traced to over-anxiety in the pursuit of knowledge ; to too much confidence in the student in his own quickness of perception, or to natural impatience. But to whatever cause this error may be attributed, the pupil cannot be too cautious in avoiding it. If he has been really desirous of acquiring a perfect knowledge of the work before him, he has no doubt exercised upon the rules as they progressively presented themselves to him ; and if he has done so, he must have observed,—

1st, That from the commencement to the end they are so closely interwoven, and constitute collectively such a chain of causes and effects, that they could not be studied in a desultory or disjointed manner.

2dly, He must have perceived, as he proceeded thus step by step, new and interesting matter continually presenting itself to his attention, expanding his views, and encouraging him to proceed.

3dly, That he himself has made discoveries, without even travelling out of his way in search of them.

Should the learner have thus proceeded in his studies, and " *made haste slowly*," he is advised by all means to make an attempt at composition. All knowledge is in progression, and it is only by degrees that excellence can be obtained. To acquire facility in composition much practice is absolutely necessary.

Should it be said that genius and talents are requisite to make a composer, we answer certainly : to make a *great* composer these gifts are indispensable ; but they are equally so to make a great poet, painter, or architect, *&c.* But shall none compose, write poetry, paint, *&c.*, but those who are thus gifted ? No one will pretend to say, that those numerous composers who have lived from the earliest time to the present day, have *all* been, or are, in possession of those peculiar gifts ! Shall we not build houses because we have not the genius and means to construct palaces ? Is it then absolutely necessary in order to compose that we possess the genius and imagination of a Gluck, a Handel, a Mozart, or a Beethoven ? Shall none dare to write but those who can produce a grand sinfonia, serious opera, or oratorio ? May not pleasure as well as profit be derived from the composition of songs, glees, sonatas, rondos, airs with variations, *&c.* ? *Let us but make a beginning.* This, however, it must be confessed, has hitherto been the great stumbling-block. How shall I begin ? How shall I set about it ? These, it cannot be denied, are very natural and reasonable questions. If the pupil, however, has carefully studied the construction of periods and melodies, the necessity of asking such questions no longer exists ; for what beginning can be more simple, or what path more secure than that which is pointed out to him from Ex. 361. For instance : he draws an outline of his intended composition, fills it up with fundamental basses, extracts inverted basses, and constructs a counter melody ; to which he adds the rest of the parts, dissonances, passing and auxiliary notes, *&c.* All this is accomplished without difficulty, because the rules are all determined, and nothing is left to chance. During this process, no peculiar musical genius or feeling, no imagination or nicely-discriminating musical ear is

2 T

required *: moderate talents, accompanied with a little patience and reflection, are sufficient to produce that which will lead and encourage him to higher exertions †.

The student will find, as he proceeds, new matter perpetually springing up as it were spontaneously under his hands; subjects, which at the commencement appear as mere trifles, may subsequently, by a little contrivance (but still according to rule) be made most interesting.

By way of illustration of the above, and encouragement to the student to make the attempt at composition, we shall first trace the gradual progress and subsequent changes of a simple melody and harmony as it emanates from the outline, or sketch; and then show by what a simple and easy process the original materials are afterwards capable of being converted into new matter, almost endless in variety and effect.

Let us suppose, for instance, that a melody has been constructed and harmonized according to the rules commencing from Ex. 361. The inner parts of the harmony may, perhaps, only with a slight alteration, furnish melodies which may be reharmonized in a variety of ways, by merely changing each time the original fundamental bass and inversions.

2*dly*, By re-harmonizing the original melody and adding a few modified basses, the inner parts of which will again furnish new melodies.

3*dly*, By harmonizing the original melody according to the rules commencing from Ex. 180.

4*thly*, By adding modified basses to the air thus harmonized. Let it be recollected that at each change of harmony, a corresponding change of dissonances and passing notes also takes place.

Hitherto we have only considered what may be effected by a mere change of *harmony ;* but what shall we say when,

5*thly*, We likewise alter the *measure of time and rhythm* of the original subject, or any of those subjects which have arisen from it? Indeed, the change, on these

---

* A German author says: " Eine Theorie der Kunst ist Schönheit ohne Gefühle und Phantasie." The theory of an art is beauty without feeling and imagination. *How true!*

† In proof of this, it is only necessary to examine the gradual progression of the outline of the melody from Ex. 361 to 371.

occasions, is frequently so great, that the original source from which these harmonies have emanated is no longer to be recognized.

6*thly*, By letting the alto and tenor interchange places.

7*thly and lastly*, Extension of periods, and imitation between the parts.

Now, that all these endless varieties of effects do arise from a simple outline, such as has just been described, cannot be denied. Then, where is the difficulty which shall deter the student from making an attempt at composition? The process here pointed out is so simple, and, it may be added, interesting, that it only requires in us the will, and the object is accomplished. The author repeats once more, that if the student but makes the attempt, and follows the rules contained in this work with patience and perseverance, he will not only have no cause to be dissatisfied with his progress, but will discover a source of amusement and improvement, of which he can form no adequate idea without the trial.

F I N I S.

LONDON:
PRINTED BY WILLIAM CLOWES,
Stamford-street.

THE

ROYAL SERAPHINE,

A NEW MUSICAL INSTRUMENT,

BY

J. GREEN,

33, SOHO-SQUARE.

THE sound of this extraordinary Instrument is produced on a principle never before applied to musical purposes; and it is after four years of uninterrupted perseverance and incessant labour, that all its advantages have been perfected and combined as now accomplished, and which will ensure the Seraphine a distinguished and permanent station in the catalogue of musical instruments.

The deep tones of the organ are produced by *pipes* of a very large size; and it is impossible, *upon that principle*, to construct an instrument of the desired depth of tone within the dimensions convenient for domestic purposes.

The sound of the Seraphine proceeds from the vibration of metal acted upon by wind; producing, within the space of a few inches, the same tone which would require a pipe sixteen feet long; and thus comprising a *Domestic Organ*, of wonderful powers, within the following dimensions, *in the shape of a chiffonnier.*

High, from the floor, 2 ft. 10 in.

Wide, from right to left, 3 ft. 4 in.

Deep, from back to front, 1 ft. 8 in.

This convenient portability renders it capable of being readily removed into any apartment, and it may be placed in any situation, even in the centre of the room, the case being finished at the back as well as in front; but, where required, it may be made to assume any appearance, and may be ornamented to correspond with any description of furniture.

From its small dimensions also, it will be found peculiarly adapted to the ship's cabin, where it will afford to the musician, during a long voyage, a fund of enjoyment, of which he has been frequently deprived by the inconvenient bulk of the piano-forte.

The *principle* upon which this instrument is constructed is the *most simple* possible, and of such a nature as *not* to be sensibly *acted upon* by any *variation in the temperature of the atmosphere;* consequently, after being once tuned, it is *scarcely liable to any observable change,** and, being divested of all complicated movements, it is *the less liable to go out of order,* and the more readily regulated:

---

* Some pains have been taken to ascertain the most generally acknowledged concert pitch, which is found exactly to accord with the one agreed upon by Madame Billington and the most distinguished vocal and instrumental musicians of that time, and to this day preserved and enforced by Sir George Smart: it is therefore desirable that all piano-fortes should be tuned to this standard.

but if, by any unforeseen accident, it should ever be required, it is more easily tuned than any other instrument; and every purchaser removing to a distance from London will, if desired, be made capable of tuning and regulating it for himself: in town, Mr. Green offers the most effectual guarantee by undertaking to keep every Seraphine in tune without expense.

The case is not necessarily a part of the instrument, as in the piano-forte, but is a mere covering, which might be injured or even destroyed without detriment to the part which produces the sound.

Thus, independently of its novelty, it cannot fail to be valuable as an article of merchandize in the hot climates.

The compass of the keys is the same as that of the largest organ in existence, *i. e.* five octaves complete, or sixty-one keys, from F to F; indeed, in every respect, it is an *organ in miniature*, peculiarly adapted for domestic use: as such, it will be considered a valuable acquisition by all lovers of serious music, and thus will it increase the means of our social enjoyments, and the number of our fire-side pleasures.

It may be played upon at once, *without previous practice*, by any performer on the piano-forte or organ; is admirably adapted for the private study of the young organist; and, at the same time will be found useful to the piano-forte practitioner in the acquirement of the legato style.*

Its ordinary tones, resembling the rich chalumeau of the clarionet, are truly pathetic in simple melodies, and may be advantageously employed in concert pieces, to fill

---

* This remark will suggest the probability that the introduction of this new instrument may produce a beneficial change in the musical taste of this country. The very best compositions of the best writers are hidden treasures, and must continue to be so whilst our domestic instruments are incapable of producing the intended effects: the sublime blending of sounds and interweaving of heavenly harmonies to be found in the sacred writings of the great masters, cannot possibly be felt and appreciated without the aid of an instrument similar to the one for which they were composed.

up the parts of the flute, oboe, clarionet, bassoon, violoncello, &c.; for, the *quality* of the sound is capable of being modified at pleasure by the simplest possible means, so as closely to imitate the sound of the particular instrument required; offering also a desirable accompaniment to the piano-forte.

It is worthy of remark, that the sound is produced by precisely the same process as that of the human voice, with the reedy tone of which (providentially) the ear is never cloyed.

On this part of the subject the " Lady's Magazine" for Jan. 1831, makes the following observations :—

" The peculiar quality of its tone will be " found particularly applicable to this pur" pose; the human voice being of that pecu" liar texture which will not admit, without " injurious effect, of combination with sounds " more smooth or less vibratory than itself. " Those who have had the good fortune to hear " Pasta, accompanied by Willman's clarionet, " will understand why we consider the tone " of the Seraphine so admirably adapted " to accompany the voice."

When employed to accompany many voices, the full chords of this instrument produce a most extraordinary effect, the vibrations exciting, as it were, an atmosphere of harmony; its own tones not being separately distinguishable, whilst the voices are firmly sustained, and, at the same time, thrown out (if the expression may be allowed) in high relief.

Thus it is not necessarily confined to domestic purposes; it is sufficiently powerful for small churches or religious meetings, where the expense or appearance of an organ may be objected to.

It is impossible to conceive so small an instrument capable of producing such an immense volume of harmony; at the same time it is capable of the utmost possible delicacy of *diminuendo* and *crescendo*, from the soft sighing of the Æolian harp to the grandeur and majesty of the full choir, in a degree of excellence never yet claimed by any other instrument.

Besides this, it will be found to possess the power of producing many other new and beautiful effects, perfectly peculiar to itself, which it is impossible here to particularize; what has been already stated will be sufficient to make known its general character; and every possessor of the instrument will readily become more intimately acquainted with its particular capabilities.

The Seraphine *may* be adapted, as an extra stop, to an organ, supplying the place of a powerful trumpet; the space required being the width of the keys, 6 or 8 inches deep, and as much as can be spared from back to front. However, in such a case as this, it would be desirable not to throw away entirely the advantage of its present portability, but rather to prepare a Seraphine complete, so that the keys and speaking part may be readily removed into the organ when required.

All music written for the organ is suitable for the Seraphine; also all Handel's compositions and the works of the older masters; the character of the instrument being rather grave than gay, sacred music and slow airs are best adapted. These general observations will suffice to direct the choice; at the same time it is Mr. Green's intention occasionally to publish a collection of such airs as produce the most pleasing effect, marked so as to direct the judicious employment of the diminuendo and crescendo pedal, and adding such observations on any peculiarities of the instrument, as may be deemed necessary for performers on the piano-forte, who may not be acquainted with the organ.

He has also just published *a Seraphine and Organ Tutor*, explaining more at large the Touch and Style of Performance adapted to these instruments, and the fingering calculated to produce the best effect; illustrated in an extensive collection of *approved* and *original Chants*, all fingered.

Mr. Green will have pleasure in rendering any personal service where purchasers may desire it; but a few hours only are necessary to make the piano-forte performer perfectly acquainted with the instrument.

The Seraphine may be packed, exactly as it is, in a square case, and may be carried to any distance, by any kind of conveyance, without the slightest risk of injury.

It is finished in mahogany and rose-wood cases, of various degrees of elegance, the price varying accordingly from 42 to 55 guineas; being, with reference to its actual cost, the cheapest keyed instrument ever introduced. This, and the heavy expenses incurred during so long a period in bringing it to perfection, it is hoped will excuse the demand of prompt payment.

Mr. Green will feel obliged by the visits of the curious, but is under the necessity of respectfully requesting that all letters of inquiry may be post-paid.

He will be most happy at all times to afford every information desired, and hopes that, in all cases where parties may not have an opportunity of forming their own judgment, application may be made directly to himself, or through some friend whose opinion will be unbiased.

It is, at the same time, but justice to those Professors and Dealers who candidly commend the instrument, to acknowledge that it must be the result only of their liberal conviction, Mr. Green not having it in his power to conciliate their good offices in the usual way from his desire to render the price as favourable as possible to the public.

Finally it may be necessary to remark that, since the introduction of this instrument there have been many attempts at imitation, and some instruments on a similar principle have been imported from the Continent; but, without any disrespect to the ingenuity of others, it may be permitted here to apprize the public, that the instrument, which is the subject of this publication, bears upon its front board this inscription:

ROYAL SERAPHINE,

BY

J. Green,

33, SOHO-SQUARE, LONDON.

N. B. At Mr. GREEN's Warehouse may be procured, Piano-fortes of every description, Harps, Guitars, Violins, Military and other Instruments; Music, Strings, and every article appertaining to the musical business.